Social Protest in Contemporary China, 2003–2010

China's economic transformation has brought with it much social dislocation, which in turn has led to much social protest. This book presents a comprehensive analysis of the large-scale mass incidents that have taken place in the last decade. The book analyses these incidents systematically, discussing their nature, causes and outcomes. It shows the wide range of protests—tax riots, land and labor disputes, disputes within companies, including private and foreign companies, environmental protests and ethnic clashes—and shows how the nature of protests has changed over time. The book argues that the protests have been prompted by the socioeconomic transformations of the last decade, which have dislocated many individuals and groups, whilst also giving society increased autonomy and social freedom, enabling many people to become more vocal and active in their confrontations with the state. It suggests that many protests are related to corruption, that is failures by officials to adhere to the high standards that should be expected from benevolent government; it demonstrates how the Chinese state, far from being rigid, bureaucratic and authoritarian, is often sensitive and flexible in its response to protest, frequently addressing grievances and learning from its own mistakes; and it shows how the multilevel responsibility structure of the Chinese regime has enabled the central government to absorb the shock waves of social protest and continue to enjoy legitimacy.

Yanqi Tong is an Associate Professor in the Department of Political Science, University of Utah

Shaohua Lei is a postdoctoral researcher in the Department of Political Science, Tsinghua University

China Policy Series
Series Editor
Zheng Yongnian
China Policy Institute, University of Nottingham, UK

1. **China and the New International Order**
   Edited by Wang Gungwu and Zheng Yongnian

2. **China's Opening Society**
   The non-state sector and governance
   Edited by Zheng Yongnian and Joseph Fewsmith

3. **Zhao Ziyang and China's Political Future**
   Edited by Guoguang Wu and Helen Lansdowne

4. **Hainan—State, Society, and Business in a Chinese Province**
   Kjeld Erik Brodsgaard

5. **Non-Governmental Organizations in China**
   The rise of dependent autonomy
   Yiyi Lu

6. **Power and Sustainability of the Chinese State**
   Edited by Keun Lee, Joon-Han Kim and Wing Thye Woo

7. **China's Information and Communications Technology Revolution**
   Social changes and state responses
   Edited by Xiaoling Zhang and Yongnian Zheng

8. **Socialist China, Capitalist China**
   Social tension and political adaptation under economic globalisation
   Edited by Guoguang Wu and Helen Lansdowne

9. **Environmental Activism in China**
   Lei Xei

10. **China's Rise in the World ICT Industry**
    Industrial strategies and the catch-up development model
    Lutao Ning

11. **China's Local Administration**
    Traditions and changes in the sub-national hierarchy
    Edited by Jae-Ho Chung and Tao-chiu Lam

12. **The Chinese Communist Party as Organizational Emperor**
    Culture, reproduction and transformation
    Zheng Yongian

13. **China's Trade Unions**
    How autonomous are they?
    Masaharu Hishida, Kazuko Kojima, Tomoaki Ishii and Jian Qiao

14. **Legitimating the Chinese Communist Party since Tiananmen**
    A critical analysis of the stability discourse
    Peter Sandby-Thomas

15 **China and International Relations**
The Chinese view and the contribution of Wang Gungwu
Zheng Yongnian

16 **The Challenge of Labour in China**
Strikes and the changing labour regime in global factories
Chris King-chi Chan

17 **The Impact of China's 1989 Tiananmen Massacre**
Edited by Jean-Philippe Béja

18 **The Institutional Dynamics of China's Great Transformation**
Edited by Xiaoming Huang

19 **Higher Education in Contemporary China**
Beyond expansion
Edited by W. John Morgan and Bin Wu

20 **China's Crisis Management**
Edited by Jae Ho Chung

21 **China Engages Global Governance**
A new world order in the making?
Gerald Chan, Pak K. Lee and Lai-Ha Chan

22 **Political Culture and Participation in Rural China**
Yang Zhong

23 **China's Soft Power and International Relations**
Hongyi Lai and Yiyi Lu

24 **China's Climate Policy**
Chen Gang

25 **Chinese Society**
Change and transformation
Edited by Li Peilin

26 **China's Challenges to Human Security**
Foreign relations and global implications
Edited by Guoguang Wu

27 **China's Internal and International Migration**
Edited by Li Peilin and Laurence Roulleau-Berger

28 **The Rise of Think Tanks in China**
Xufeng Zhu

29 **Governing Health in Contemporary China**
Yanzhong Huang

30 **New Dynamics in Cross-Taiwan Straits Relations**
How far can the rapprochement go?
Edited by Weixing Hu

31 **China and the European Union**
Edited by Lisheng Dong, Zhengxu Wang and Henk Dekker

32 **China and the International System**
Becoming a world power
Edited by Xiaoming Huang and Robert G. Patman

33 **China's Social Development and Policy**
Into the next stage?
Litao Zhao

34 **E-Government in China**
Technology, power and local government reform
Jesper Schlæger

35 **Social Protest in Contemporary China, 2003–2010**
Transitional pains and regime legitimacy
Yanqi Tong and Shaohua Lei

Social Protest in Contemporary China, 2003–2010
Transitional pains and regime legitimacy

Yanqi Tong and Shaohua Lei

LONDON AND NEW YORK

First published 2014
by Routledge

2 Park Square, Milton Park, Abingdon, Oxfordshire OX14 4RN
711 Third Avenue, New York, NY 10017

Routledge is an imprint of the Taylor & Francis Group, an informa business

First issued in paperback 2017

Copyright © 2014 Yanqi Tong and Shaohua Lei

The right of Yanqi Tong and Shaohua Lei to be identified as authors of this work has been asserted by them in accordance with the Copyright, Designs and Patent Act 1988.

All rights reserved. No part of this book may be reprinted or reproduced or utilised in any form or by any electronic, mechanical, or other means, now known or hereafter invented, including photocopying and recording, or in any information storage or retrieval system, without permission in writing from the publishers.

Notice:
Product or corporate names may be trademarks or registered trademarks, and are used only for identification and explanation without intent to infringe.

British Library Cataloguing in Publication Data
A catalogue record for this book is available from the British Library

Library of Congress Cataloging in Publication Data
Tong, Yanqi, 1954-
  Social protest in contemporary China, 2003-2010 : transitional pains and regime legitimacy / Yanqi Tong and Shaohua Lei.
    p.. cm. – (China policy series ; 35)
  Includes bibliographical references and index.
  1. Social conflict–China. 2. Protest movements–China. I. Lei, Shaohua. II. Title.
  HN733.5.T66 2014
  303.60951–dc23
              2013009580

ISBN: 978-0-415-60569-4 (hbk)
ISBN: 978-0-8153-7478-7 (pbk)

Typeset in Times New Roman
by Taylor & Francis Books

For those we love

Contents

List of illustrations		x
Acknowledgements		xii
1	Introduction	1
2	Analyzing social protests	18
3	An overview of large-scale social protests	47
4	Subsistence expectation protests	67
5	Benevolence violation protests	98
6	Protests over developmental syndromes and identity	121
7	Creating public opinion pressure: Large-scale Internet protests	146
8	Government responses and regime resilience	174
9	Conclusion	206
Bibliography		218
Index		228

Illustrations

Figures

2.1	Structure of state-society relations before the reforms	23
2.2	Structure of state-society relations after the reforms	25
2.3	Legitimacy structure in China	28
3.1	Frequencies of large-scale social protest by year, 2003–10	49
3.2	Frequency of large-scale social protests by type, 2003–10	50
3.3	Frequency of major types of large-scale social protest by year, 2003–10	58
3.4	Map showing large-scale labor protests in state-owned enterprises, 2003–10	62
3.5	Map showing large-scale labor protests in nonstate sectors, 2003–10	63
3.6	Map showing large-scale land-related protests, 2003–10	64
3.7	Map showing large-scale mass disturbances, 2003–10	65
4.1	Selected indicators of the state-owned industrial enterprises, 2002–10	70
4.2	Frequency of large-scale labor protests in SOEs, 2003–10	70
4.3	Distributions of major causes of the labor protest	71
4.4	Frequency of major causes of labor protest by year	72
4.5	Selected indicators of private industrial enterprises, 2002–10	80
4.6	Selected indicators of foreign-invested industrial enterprises, 2002–10	80
4.7	Frequency of large-scale labor protest in private sectors, 2003–10	81
4.8	Large-scale labor protest in the nonstate sector in 2010 by month	83
4.9	Large-scale land-related protests, 2003–10	88
5.1	Frequency of large-scale disturbances by year	99
7.1	Number of Internet users by year	147
8.1	Distribution of types of social protest tolerated by the government	187
8.2	Distribution of the types of social protests where the government makes concessions	188

8.3	Distribution of the types of social protests suppressed by the government	190
8.4	Distribution of the types of social protests ended with disciplinary measures against officials	191
8.5.1	Government responses by type of protest	194
8.5.2	Government responses by type of protest	195
8.5.3	Government responses by type of protest	196
8.5.4	Government responses by type of protest	197
8.5.5	Government responses by type of protest	198
8.6	Multilevel responsibility of the administrative structure involving Wukan village	200

Tables

3.1	Large-scale social protest within the state sector by type, 2003–10	51
3.2	Land-related protests, 2003–10	54
3.3	Major types of protest in the "other" category	57
3.4	Large-scale social protest by type and year, 2003–10	58
3.5	Frequency of large-scale social protest by province, 2003–10	60
3.6	Major types of large-scale social protests by province, 2003–10	61
4.1	Ownership origins and the frequency of labor protest in the nonstate sector	84
5.1	Differences in GDP per capita	110
7.1	The age composition of Internet users	147
7.2	Education levels of Internet users	148
7.3	Internet users by profession	148
7.4	Income structure of Internet users	149
7.5	The number of large-scale Internet protests by year, 2003–10	150
8.1	Government responses to large-sale social protests	185
8.2	Government responses to social protests	186
8.3	Government responses by type of protests	193

Acknowledgements

This book originated from a series of background briefs on social protests in China by us when Yanqi Tong was a visiting senior research fellow at the East Asia Institute at the National University of Singapore in 2010. We would like to express our sincere gratitude to Dr Zheng Yongnian, director of the East Asia Institute, for his encouragement for us to develop our research on this important topic into a book.

During the long and arduous process of research and writing, we have received help from many scholars, friends and institutions. Special thanks go to Dennis Yehua Wei, Ji Feifei, Xiahong Feng, Eric Posmentier, Wenfang Tang, Harry Harding, Pan Wei, Xu Bing, Wang Weibing, Ren Yuzhong, Shen Mingming, Sun Jie, Wang Wenyan, Shang Ying, Zhang Xiaojin, Jing Yuejin, Liu Yu, Zhong Yangsheng, Zhang Yihong, Li Xuanliang, Lei Guanfeng, Qi Mingliang, Wang Wujun, Liu Bing, Guo Junwen, Huang Zankun, Zhuang Junju, Luo Feng, Wang Xiaoming, Chen Yingwu, Zhang De'an, Jiang Yong, Wang Guoxing, Yuan Yun, Liu Chunmei, Zhang Fuhai, Geng Zhimin, Wang Chao, Shen Xin, Zhao Yonggang, Gu Jinsheng, Lu Jingxian, Gao Ying, Zhou Qiuping, Jiang Huaming, Li Dongyu, Wang Zhi, as well as some who prefer to remain anonymous.

We would like to acknowledge the assistance from the News Department at China Central TV Station, the Domestic News Department at Xinhua News Agency, the Institute of Labor and Criminal Reformation of the Ministry of Justice, the Fourth Institute of the Ministry of Public Security, the Center of American Studies for the Institute of Shanghai Pudong Reform and Development, and the Center for Chinese and Global Affairs at Peking University. Many local governments have provided assistance to facilitate our field work and we would like to thank these county governments from Shaanxi, Jiangxi, Sichuan, Hebei and Hainan Provinces.

We would like to thank our editor Peter Sowden for his interest and confidence in the project, as well as Peter's assistant Helena Hurd, production editor Dominic Corti and copy editor Alison Neale, for their able and efficient work.

Sections of Chapter 2 and Chapter 7 were published in 2011 by the *Journal of Chinese Political Studies* and in 2013 by the *Journal of Contemporary China*. We are grateful to these journals for permission to adapt our previous articles.

Finally, Shaohua Lei would like to thank his wife Chenyuan, who has had to bear many sacrifices and his sleepless nights, for her unfailing support.

1 Introduction

Ever since China embarked on the course of socioeconomic transformation in the late 1970s, social protests have accompanied the process every step of the way just like inseparable shadows. The redistribution of wealth and power inevitably produces winners and losers. The further and deeper transformation proceeds, the more social protests break out. The types of social protest range from tax riots to land and labor disputes, and from environmental protests to ethnic clashes. The breadth of the social protest types reflects the extensiveness of the transformation. According to various sources and calculations, the collective protest incidents increased from 8,700 in 1994, to 90,000 in 2006, and to an unconfirmed 127,000 in 2008.[1] This number might have fluctuated between 150,000 and 200,000 since 2009.[2]

Socioeconomic transformations involve profound structural changes. The profound structural changes inevitably produce broad displacement, affecting state employees, migrant workers, farmers, ex-servicemen, teachers and ethnic minorities. We have witnessed changes from central planning to market-oriented economic operation, and from state-subsidized education, medical care and housing to the state withdrawal from these areas. Together with the collapse of the work units and rural collectives, social groups and individuals have to face the increasing and oftentimes irregular market logics that are not necessarily beneficial to those who are not familiar with them. Yet, all these changes are not occurring on a blank page. Previous frameworks (both institutional and conceptual) have their inertia. People continue to hold the state responsible for their well-being despite the official effort to institute market logics. The chaotic changes also involve rampant official corruption and perceived injustice that violate the principles of what people believe to be a good government.

To be sure, this social unrest exemplifies the pains and challenges associated with China's development. To a certain extent, they are normal symptoms for any society that experiences profound social and economic transformation, yet the prolonged and widespread social unrest may very well trigger regime transition.[3] Since social unrest is believed to be the expression of intense social discontent and a barometer for regime stability, the study of social protest in contemporary China has become a rapidly growing industry among American social scientists.[4]

2 *Introduction*

A brief review of this growing body of literature will give us some background knowledge about the development of social protest in contemporary China. The existing scholarship has primarily explored four aspects of social protests in China: the origins of social grievance; the framing of the protest movement; strategies and tactics of protests; and government reactions and the implications for the political future of China.

Careful readers may find that we have left out writings on the role of the nongovernmental organizations (NGOs). As important as the NGOs may be in changing China's public landscape, their impact on social protest is negligible in the current political climate. The NGOs may have staged some small-scale petitions over issues related to public good, such as environmental protection, yet most of the time they intentionally stay away from social protests in order to survive under the tight surveillance of the government.[5] Moreover, since our interests are in collective protest, we will not discuss protests by individuals, such as the resistance to birth control or relocation of individual households.

Origins of social grievance

The natural question for any study of social protest is why it occurs. The literature on the origins of grievance mainly details the specifics of how the market-oriented economic reforms led to the outburst of social protest. In the 1990s, as the market reforms moved into the state sector, the reform measures abolished many benefits for state employees guaranteed under the previous planned economy. With the official cancellation of the permanent employment system and the introduction of the labor contract system in 1995, state workers lost their "iron rice bowl"—a Chinese metaphor for job security. The number of laid-off workers soared. When the inefficient or bankrupt state-owned enterprises fell behind in paying minimum living allowance to their laid-off workers and pensions to their retirees in the late 1990s, labor unrest and pension protests ensued.[6] In short, a barrage of reform policies had brought about massive lay-offs and destitution for veteran workers in state sectors.[7] While Chinese workers have increasingly learned to take their labor and pension disputes to court,[8] many more have adopted collective action and taken this to the street.[9] It was estimated that more than 3.6 million workers were involved in some kind of protest in 1998.[10]

In rural areas, the introduction of a "household responsibility system" had, in the 1980s, successfully raised production efficiency in agriculture, yet small-scale agricultural production soon reached its limit. There is only so much a piece of land can produce. In the meantime, the central government has adopted a "gross domestic product (GDP)-first" strategy and used economic growth as a measuring stick for the performance of local officials. The official developmental frenzy in the post-household responsibility system era at first led to excessive taxation on farmers and later the predatory land requisition for industrial and commercial development. Both were met with furious peasant resistance.

In efforts to raise funds for developmental infrastructure or to pay the bill for an ever-enlarging grassroots bureaucracy, the financially destitute local officials in poor agricultural regions sought to increase their revenues from extra taxation on farmers.[11] The extraction of excessive taxes and fees combined with brutal collection methods caused villagers great economic distress and led to protest and violence.[12] Later, the huge profits generated by land requisition induced local governments to ally themselves with the developers and to deny the land ownership rights of the natural village. Land disputes have replaced tax protests as the primary trigger of collective action in rural China.[13]

The priority given to high economic growth often led to environmental degradation. Economic growth involves the exploitation of natural resources for expanding production of material goods and may involve the dumping of the waste of this production into the environment. Increased use of energy and insufficient facilities and technologies to treat industrial and life waste cause serious air and water pollution and other environmental degradation problems. The resulting environmental degradation increases public environmental grievance and often leads to grassroots protests over pollution.[14]

Further along the analysis of the origins of social protest, contentious politics scholars find that not only economic status, but also gender, ethnicity, generation and regional location, constitute powerful sources of conflict and spurs to resistance in the reform era.[15] For example, there is a significant correlation between Falun Gong membership and elderly and laid-off workers.[16] A young generation of migrant workers leads China in the volume of arbitrated labor dispute.[17] In the end analysis, all these correlations are closely related to the disadvantaged groups—women, minority groups, the elderly, laid-off and migrant workers—at various stages of China's long march to development and prosperity.

Framing the meaning of the protest

Social movement theories suggest that defining problems, assigning blame and giving meaning to collective actions are crucial to the success of the protest movement.[18] Students of contentious politics in China have recognized two primary tendencies in framing the purpose and meaning of social protests in the reform era. One is the emerging consciousness of individual rights, which was foreign to Chinese before the country's opening up in the 1980s. The other tendency is the adoption of traditional symbols to generate public support or the more familiar political idioms from Mao's period.

The thesis of "rightful resistance" is among the first to argue that the notion of being a citizen is seeping into popular discourse and that people should not underestimate the implications for the Chinese population. By using the laws or central government directives to challenge the abusive practice of the local government, the rural resistance activities have shown a sign of growing rights consciousness and a more contractual approach to political life.[19] The rightful resisters, according to O'Brien, are loudly proclaiming their allegiance to the core values of the regime. Instead of treating the law as inaccessible, arbitrary and alien—an approach the powerless groups tend to take[20]—Chinese farmers have learned to exploit the potent symbolic capital rooted in the notions of equality, rights and rule of law.[21] As long as a gap exists between rights promised and rights delivered, the rightful resistance scholars argue, there is always room for rightful resistance to emerge.[22] Following this line of analysis, most rural protests were framed as a confrontation between an emerging "rights-conscious peasantry" and rapacious or entrepreneurial bureaucrats.[23]

The increasing "rights talk" among the Chinese protesters is warmly embraced by many China observers as the major changes in the last two decades of the twentieth century. They believe that, conceptually, a growing sense of rights consciousness, particularly of political rights among the Chinese population at large, signals a fundamental breakthrough in the state-society relationship. Practically, this newfound claim to citizenship would pose a fundamental challenge to state authority and produce in China changes as profound as those that ended the communist regimes in other former communist countries.[24]

Amid the excitement that the Chinese have gradually adopted the universal concept of individual rights, some scholars have detected "a distinctly normative tone, inflected with an Anglo-American language of human rights."[25] This "rights talk" by the protesters is merely a new bottle for the old wine. Instead of absorbing the Western conception of individual rights, scholars of social protests in traditional China see an enduring emphasis on collective socioeconomic justice—a salient feature of peasant rebellion in the history of China—in the framing of collective protests from the past to the present.

Heaven, a symbolic term for justice in traditional China, has loomed large in contemporary urban, as well as rural, protests. For example, many rural protesters marched behind banners proclaiming "Prepare the Way for Heaven" and "The People's Anger Overwhelms Heaven," as they demanded lower taxes.[26] Heavenly justice in contemporary circumstances represents a fundamental right to subsistence. With the collapse of the paternalistic institutional arrangement for state workers, there has been a clear effort by protesters to frame their demand in a more traditional subsistence ethic. Laid-off workers have used the traditional ideas of the right to subsistence to justify their protests, such as "We Want Survival!" and "We Want Food!"[27] It is the insistent demand for socioeconomic justice, rather than the rights of being a citizen, that provides a thread that binds many of the disparate incidents together.[28]

In the meantime, the state-owned enterprise (SOE) workers have also shown a tendency to return to the rhetorical resources that had been used in the recent past—the Mao period. Slogans during Mao's era, such as "Yes to Socialism, No to Capitalism," "Factories Belong to All the Workers," "Down with the New Bureaucratic Bourgeoisie," were on display during labor protests.²⁹ The adoption of such slogans may reflect on the one hand the deep appeal of socialist principles to state workers, and on the other hand a paucity of language available for the protesters to employ.

The different framing may depend on the types of ownership and the composition of the labor force. For example, in her comparison of the labor protests in rustbelt and sunbelt areas, Lee pointed out the differences in framing. Rustbelt refers to the Northeast state-owned industries and sunbelt refers to the coastal regions where private and foreign-invested enterprises prosper. She argues that in the rustbelt there were "protests of desperation," in which workers were staking their claim on moral and legal grounds. In contrast, migrant workers in the sunbelt staged "protests against discrimination," which primarily resorted to legal activism. The common feature of all the protests was the passionate fight against official corruption as both immoral and illegal.³⁰

This dichotomy of framing the protests—the protesters either borrow from the West or the past—presents an intricate picture of a society in transition. Protesters picked the language that they perceived would be the most effective in mobilizing participants as well as acquiring government concessions. Yet, no matter from where the protesters borrowed these languages or how they combined these terms, their grievance is more derivative of a subsistence crisis than a struggle for individual rights, as most of the protests were driven by economic grievance.

Strategies and tactics

The third aspect of social protest is the strategies and tactics employed in contentious politics in China. Like contentious politics in all other societies, disruption—such as blocking traffic, burning vehicles and attacking government agencies—is the typical form of social unrest in China, and it is widely regarded as an important source of protest efficacy.³¹ In addition to the commonly used disruption, we can discern three streaks of protest strategies and tactics.

First, corresponding with the framing of protest in traditional terms, the strategies of protest also tend to invoke traditional symbols and methods. For example, people express their dissent through ironic and ambiguous doorway couplets and body cultivation practices.³² In rural areas, the beliefs and rituals surrounding local temples, churches, deities, spiritual masters, ancestral halls, and festivals often provide inspiration for collective mobilization. Social protest draws on themes and images sanctified by tradition, such as the eruption of fertility goddesses in a protest against polluted water that might affect fertility.³³

Petition—a method with long historical roots—is often the preferred way of seeking redress for grievance. Petitioners in China sometimes exert pressure on government officials via symbolic tactics, such as kneeling down, self-mutilation and self-immolation, displaying symbols of grief, singing revolutionary songs and displaying honorary symbols, such as military medals.³⁴

The second streak is to seek divisions within the state and try to make allies with the elite, which is also a common strategy in all social movements. Yet this strategy is particularly salient in China. The Chinese multilevel administrative structure provides a convenient opportunity for protesters to manipulate and achieve their goals. Organized petitions often tried to exploit the division among leaders and different levels of government. A decentralized authoritarian system enables the villagers to use the policies from the central government to put pressures on local government. For example, farmers use the central policy, which explicitly prescribes the reduction of peasant financial burdens, to challenge local authorities' tax policy.[35]

This kind of policy-based resistance[36] is also reflected in environmental protests. Organizers of environmental protest in China not only appear highly aware of the country's environmental laws, but they also know the importance of taking advantage of fissures within the government to find allies or at least sympathizers among the leadership. With the government environmental policies and the backing of environmental protection bureaux,[37] protesters in China are capable of launching well-organized and forceful protests against environmental abuses.[38]

Using the central directives to exert pressures on local government, again, is not a contemporary invention of the modern citizenry. In his research on land expropriation and rural conflict, Xiaolin Guo found that the villagers constantly differentiated the "malign" local government from the "benign" central government.[39] This distinction is not a mere protest tactic, but has its roots in the structure of Chinese rural society as perceived by Vivian Shue as "an enormous honeycomb of small, similar, connected yet more or less fully bounded cells."[40] According to Guo, the further the spatial distance, the more likely the state-villager relationship is maintained at a moral level. The central state is "by definition just."[41]

There are, however, some dissenting voices to the almost consensual theme of "justice from above," that is protesters have more trust in and receive more satisfactory redress from higher-level authorities—be it a protest tactics or a moral tradition. For example, Ethan Michelson raises a counter-thesis of "justice from below."[42] He argues that while protesters may have high expectations from the central government, local, informal solutions are the more effective means of balancing the needs of justice with the imperative to preserve local social relationships. Village leaders played a critical role in delivering satisfaction than higher-level government in resolving grievances.[43]

Revisiting the thesis of "rightful resistance," which is translated into Chinese as "resistance according to law" (依法抗争), Yu Jianrong argues that the rural protests should be characterized as "resistance by using the law" (以法抗争). The difference between the two is that the former is making appeals to the state, whereas the latter is using laws to challenge the local government directly. In the latter's case, the protesters become the masters of their contention.[44]

The third streak is the increasing use of the Internet. The rapid development of the Internet in China has become an important vehicle for organizing protests. Mobile phones, text messages and public forums in cyberspace play a vital role in mobilizing collective action. For example, Falun Gong protesters used emails and messages to call for action. The Internet and text messages were also instrumental in mobilizing student anti-Japanese protests in 2005.[45] Easier communication channels have greatly facilitated the ability of media representatives and transnational human rights organizations to circumvent Chinese state authorities.[46]

In addition to the provision of communication channels, the web has also become a new platform for lodging protests. Together with China having the largest number of Internet users, web space has become the basis for Internet activism. Chinese citizens increasingly rely on the Internet for public communication, organization and mobilization. The more radical forms of Internet activism involve the hacking of websites and the mobilization of street demonstrations. Launching online signature petitions and verbal protests are some of the moderate forms.[47]

Government reactions and future implications

The fourth aspect of the literature on social protest in China concerns government reactions and the implications of social unrest for the political future of China. As in other aspects, there are several lines of argument. Different analytical frameworks present different readings of China's situation. The spectrum of analyses ranges from the coming collapse/revolution of China at one end to the social protests serving as a component of regime stability at the other end. While most observers agree that the increasing large-scale social unrest represents a serious domestic threat to the communist regime, it is also apparent to all that despite a plethora of strikes, protest and everyday resistance, no large-scale political movements have challenged the Party rule.

The conventional view about government reactions to social protests is that nondemocratic governments tend to use force to repress social protests.[48] Following this assumption, Wright argues that in situations where there are no independent political parties, social organizations, media sources, or autonomous judicial system, there is a high likelihood of repression and the risks of protest are heightened immensely. The political opportunity structure in China is a kind of "fear of repression" structure. Effective, reform-oriented political protest is close to impossible.[49] To be sure, harsh suppression has always been one of the options in dealing with social protest.[50] For example, the arrest and imprisonment of labor activists has continued to send a powerful message concerning what the state designates as a forbidden path of resistance: organized political dissent.[51] Many have documented harassment, intimidation and arrest as the common state responses to social protests.

Some scholars of authoritarianism believe that nondemocratic governments are in a dilemma when they face social protests: Making concessions tends to trigger more resistance or even the collapse of the regime, but reliance on repression damages the regime's legitimacy and makes it less sensitive to popular demands. This dilemma pretty much dooms authoritarian regimes if they cannot break through it.[52]

There is a strong view among scholars both inside and outside China that the widespread social protests reflect the illness of China's political system. Substantial political reforms are the only way out of the quagmire of social unrest. While scholars inside China have refrained from making an outright call for democratic reform, they have strongly urged Chinese leaders to establish institutional mechanisms that can aggregate, represent and articulate various social interests as well as a genuine rule of law.[53]

However, contrary to the assertions of repression, it seems that the Chinese government has developed many strategies to deal with social protests, not just using coercion to stifle public protest. We have witnessed that instead of beating and arresting protesters as they might have some years ago, Chinese officials seem more willing to accommodate, negotiate or simply pay them off. As long as demonstrators don't make personal attacks against top leaders or demand political change, they are often free to vent their anger.[54]

Even the Chinese officials have started to recognize that the old strategy of deterring and demonizing protest movements is failing. Scholars found that there have been internal debates within the state apparatus in which many unleashed frank criticisms of the old-fashioned thinking that treated social unrest as an enemy conspiracy.[55] As a result, in fact, the government has adopted a variety of strategies, such as indentifying with the protestors, co-opting potential opposition leaders, expanding individual freedoms, promising populism and sustained growth, and appealing to nationalism in addition to strengthening coercion.[56] Some scholars also find a more dynamic and accommodating state power. Using the data from a city district in southern China, Su and He argue that labor protesters often receive resolutions in their favor. The government has become more flexible and less repressive.[57]

Taking an historical perspective, traditional social protest scholars argue that the long history of China has proven that social protest is actually one of the major components of social stability. The protests serve as checks against the abuse of power by leaders and as mechanisms to ensure the accountability of the government. In an authoritarian polity, where elections do not provide an effective check on the misbehavior of state authorities, protest can help to serve that function, thereby undergirding rather than undermining the political system.[58] Claims to a basic subsistence that stay within local confines have seldom been deemed threatening by the Chinese regime. Many point out that as long as protesters' actions are not politically oriented but self-limiting to purely economic and livelihood demands limited to a single factory, the state tends to tolerate them and make limited concessions.[59]

Still others take a structural approach to analyze the impact of social protests. As the multilevel administrative structure helped the protesters to manipulate and achieve their goals, these same structures help to protect the legitimacy of the central government and the regime. First, the decentralized power structure allows the central government to distance itself from blame-generating situations when local governments use repression. Second, given that local governments assume considerable power and autonomy, the variation in their policy implementation may reduce citizens' blame of the political system.[60] Therefore, according to Bernstein and Lu, popular resistance in China has not only helped to force the central government to strengthen the implementation of policies favoring citizens, but has also contributed to the adjustment of unpopular national policies.[61]

Finally, with regard to the political impact of the development of the Internet on social protest, there are two opposite groups of views. One group argues that the Internet empowers civil society by fostering public debate and facilitating activities of social organization.[62] The other group believes that the development of the Internet is more likely than not to consolidate China's authoritarian regime. The state is able to control and censor the ways the Internet is used by social actors.[63]

In response to the above polarized arguments, Zheng Yongnian believes that the ongoing interaction between the state and social protest has resulted in a mutual transformation of both sides. The Internet has created a new infrastructure for the state and society in their engagement with each other. The public discussion of major social events has generated tremendous pressure on the government to adjust its policies, which in turn benefits society.[64]

In search of a big picture

All this scholarship has significantly advanced our understanding of social protest in China. It also seems that some of the recent literature on social protest in China has moved from macrolevel analysis to microlevel studies. Scholars have started to focus on the details of the protests, such as their repertoire and leadership.[65] However, as most of the research works were based on case studies or small-scale opinion surveys, the existing literature has left ample space for further inquiry. We remain unable to gauge a big picture of social protest in China. For example, how widespread exactly is social protest in China? What is the proportion of each type of protest on a national scale? What are the patterns of social protest? Have there been any changes over the years with regard to content, strategies, types and participants of protests? How do we explain the paradox that the communist regime continues to be stable despite these social protests? The inability of the existing literature to present a big picture is understandable, for it is next to impossible to collect data on issues that the Chinese government deems sensitive. As a result, we are bombarded by ad hoc journalistic reports and hearsay. We have ample impressions but little knowledge.

In order to obtain the big picture that characterizes the cost of China's epochal socioeconomic transformation and to generate data that are as systematic as possible, we have adopted a compromised research strategy. Instead of collecting the information on all social protests in China, we chose to focus on large-scale mass protests only. This would greatly reduce the difficulties in collecting a more or less complete data set while at the same time not losing our sight of the big picture.

The advantage of this research strategy is that it is more manageable to collect information on large-scale social protests. They are more visible and difficult for local authorities to cover up. Eyewitness accounts would appear on major Internet forums. Moreover, issues or problems that could inspire large-scale social protest are more reflective of the acute social tensions in contemporary China and have a larger impact on the stability of the system. They are the tip of the iceberg. To be sure, this approach would omit smaller cases that could be as dramatic and revealing as the large-scale ones. The data may lose important information on social protest. This is a trade-off. Since it is impossible to collect information on 150,000 to 200,000 protests, focusing on large-scale social protests would give us a bigger picture than any study of small cases would.

Our data set includes all the large-scale social protests from 2003 to 2010. Definitions and data sources will be discussed in a later chapter. Altogether, we have recorded 548 large-scale social protests during these eight years. Some readers may be surprised by the number of only 548 large-scale social protests and expect a significantly higher number. This misperception is created by the sensational media coverage of selected cases that gives the public an impression that there were protests everywhere and all the time, hence, the conclusion that China is sitting on the mouth of a social volcano. Our data suggest that is not the case. We are confident that our list of large-scale social protest is the most exclusive so far in the field.

The big picture of social protests in China also includes putting these protests in the context of transition in China. Without a national database, even if it is limited to large-scale protests, we will not be able to gauge the rise and fall of certain types of social protest that accompany transition. Social protests are not isolated incidents. While the state has been trying to distance itself from its all-encompassing socioeconomic responsibilities inherited from its benevolent tradition and communist ideology, the collapse of the intermediate layer of work units and rural collectives has put individuals and the state in the unfamiliar territory of direct friction.

The exclusive list of large-scale social protests enables us to map the situation of contentious politics in contemporary China. With an eye on the big picture, we will primarily use the case studies to complement the statistical findings. We will undertake this study through detailed analyses of different types of social protest and, whenever possible, make comparative case studies.

An integrated structural approach

Most analyses of social protest in China take an approach of state-society dichotomy and focus on the antagonism in such a relationship. In the hope of casting different lights to the study of social protest, we would like to employ a structural approach in our study. The basic argument is that the causes, contents, patterns and results of contemporary social protests are determined by the change and continuity of social, economic and political structures.

First, we argue that most of the protests are the result of socioeconomic transformation. The structural changes have produced serious dislocations for individuals and groups and generated tremendous social pain. On the one hand, the state is trying to let the market play a bigger role in economic and social lives, yet the immature market more often than not fails in many aspects. Then the state interferes, thus creating further confusion as to in which direction the country is moving. On the other hand, society is learning the market rules. However, when people lose in the market, such as on the stock market or when housing prices go beyond ordinary people's ability to afford, they tend to blame the government for manipulating the market too much or not regulating the market enough. It would be abnormal if there were no social protests in such epochal transformation. Furthermore, we want to emphasize that these pains are transitional—that is, they are generated by structural transition and they will be over once the transition moves on. Viewing social protest in a transitional context will help us gain a better understanding of these events.

Second, the epochal socioeconomic transformation inevitably affects state-society relations. As the planned economy has been changed into a market-oriented economy and the state is bailing out of many areas for which it was previously responsible, the structure of state-society relations has changed. All these changes will determine the nature and content of social protest. Empowered by more economic autonomy and social freedom, society has changed from a weak and passive mass to a plurality of more active and vocal actors. At the same time, the buffer zone between the state and society—work units and collectives—has disappeared, which has resulted in more direct confrontations between the state and society over economic matters.

Third, we argue that the soft structure of state-society relations—regime legitimacy—is the key to understanding contemporary social protest. Soft structure refers to the informal understanding (informed by tradition and values) that underpins state-society relations. This argument is based on two premises. Despite the fact that China is ruled by a communist and authoritarian regime, we believe that the state-society relationship is not necessarily dichotomist or antagonist. There may be antagonism between the state and society from time to time, but it does not characterize the entire relationship. Also, regime legitimacy in China is not based solely on economic performance or physical coercion. We argue that it is a responsibility-based legitimacy that provides a moral bonding between the state and society. This responsibility-based legitimacy has three overlapping layers: official morality, benevolent governance and state responsibility for the well-being of the people. Soft structure, as it has accumulated over thousands of years of history, changes much more slowly than hard structure. Social protests erupt either in expectation of the state to address economic grievances of a particular group, or in frustration over the state violation of official morality and benevolent governance.

Fourth, in order to study government reactions to social protest, we also unpack the Chinese state into a multilevel responsibility structure. The multilevel administrative structure differentiates the locations of responsibility. Local governments gained more autonomy during the reform eras and emerged as distinctive layers of the state hierarchy. On the one hand, the central government can avoid the blame of social protest and continue to hold its legitimacy. On the other hand, while the local governments take the blame and responsibility for social protests, they do not suffer too much in terms of legitimacy and credibility, as they are just parts of the whole that continues to enjoy legitimacy. The central government would simply replace a couple of top local leaders and then it would be a new game.

None of these is completely new. We have borrowed heavily from other scholars. However, this is the first attempt to use a structural approach to analyze social protests in contemporary China in an integrated manner. Different approaches may result in different conclusions and provide different future scenarios. We hope that our study will cast some different light on the study of social protest in China in particular, and the field of social movement in general.

Organization of the book

In the following chapter we will lay out our analytical framework. We will put social protest into a transitional perspective and elaborate on the structural roots of contemporary social protest in China. The primary focus is on the soft structure of state-society relations—regime legitimacy. Tracing the long tradition of the "mandate of heaven" and moral economy, we argue that there is a clear pattern of responsibility-based legitimacy between the state and the population. The informal understanding of regime legitimacy will shape the calculations and expectations of the political actors involved. Our framework of legitimacy emphasizes the bond, rather than the antagonism, between the state and society as the key to understanding social protest in China. This responsibility-based legitimacy has three layers: morality of the ruling elite, benevolent governance and state responsibility for the welfare of the population. Legitimacy means that people accept the rule of the regime and expect the government to fulfill its part of the responsibilities. The social protests, therefore, can be categorized by those in which people expect the state to fulfill its responsibility for their subsistence, and those in which people protest against perceived breaches of benevolent governance. We also suggest the emergence of a multilevel responsibility structure of the government hierarchy in China. This structure divides the state responsibility and cushions challenges to the central government. As a result, despite numerous social protests, the regime has been able to preserve stability and legitimacy.

Chapter 3 gives an overview of the large-scale social protests in China from 2003 to 2010. After a brief discussion of the definitions and the data sources, we will present the types, the geographical distributions and the changing trends of these large-scale social protests. This overview will establish the contours of the forests of social protest in China. We will also provide a brief account of each major type of large-scale social protest, such as labor protests, land and relocation protests, disturbances and riots, ethnic conflicts and a variety of other protests.

Chapters 4 and 5 discuss the major components of large-scale social protest in contemporary China. Chapter 4 describes the large-scale social protests that originated from economic grievances and rose in the expectation of state responsibility for people's subsistence, such as labor protests (both in SOEs and the private sector), land-related protests and veteran protests. We will deliberate the causes and patterns of each type of protest and look at some of the typical cases. These protests exemplify the social costs and pains of socioeconomic transformation. Chapter 5 looks at the social disturbances and riots that are generated from nonmaterialistic grievances, such as moral outrage and cumulative frustration. Official corruption and police brutality are often the causes of such outbursts. These incidents are much more threatening to regime stability than the economic grievance-driven protests.

Chapter 6 presents some other types of protest, such as environmental protest, anti-Japanese nationalist demonstrations, ethnic conflict and demonstrations to defend local dialects. These protests are less frequent than those of labor- or land-related protests, but they highlight some of the social issues that accompany the processes of transformation and development, such as environmental degradation and the salience of the issue of identity. They supplement the big picture of the transitional pains in contemporary China.

Chapter 7 will discuss Internet mass protests. This is a new type of protest and the government has to develop new means to deal with it. Unlike the Arab Spring of 2011 in which the Internet was used as a mobilization tool, the Internet in China serves as a platform for people to voice their concerns and generates public opinion pressure. The regime, which is preoccupied with social stability, has been very sensitive to such public opinion pressure. As a result, the government often adjusts its policies accordingly. We will examine several cases and their characteristics, and assess their impact on the political future of China.

Chapter 8 examines the government's response to social protest. We argue that since the market reforms, China's political system has evolved into a multilevel responsibility structure. Such a structure has been able to contain the shock waves of the social protests and insulate the central government from taking the blame. The central government instead has acted as an arbitrator and claims credit in addressing the grievances that originated the protests. There are basically five types of government responses: tolerance, compensation, appeasement, repression and disciplining officials. We argue that the political system in China is capable of learning and making policy and institutional adjustment. Within the current framework of regime legitimacy, social protests do not pose a serious challenge to the regime. It is possible that some social protests will become more and more institutionalized.

We hope this book will present a big picture of social protest as transitional pain in a framework of regime legitimacy. The chapters will detail the different types of transitional pain: the dying pains of the state-owned enterprises, the growing pains of the nonstate sector and the modernization pains of urbanization. In the concluding chapter, we will deliberate on the future scenarios of social protest, the prospects of democracy in China, and implications for regime legitimacy.

Notes

1 The figure for 2008 was an "estimate" reported by Andrew Jacobs, "Dragons, Dancing Ones, Set-off a Riot in China," *The New York Times* (February 10, 2009). In another news report, an estimate of 90,000 such incidents annually for 2007, 2008 and 2009 was quoted from a Chinese insider by John Garnaut, "China Insider Sees Revolution Brewing," *Sidney Morning Herald* (March 2, 2010).
2 This is an unofficial estimate by a staff member from the Ministry of Public Security, personal interview.
3 Guillermo O'Donnell and Philippe Schmitter, *Transitions from Authoritarian Rule. Tentative Conclusions about Uncertain Democracies* (Baltimore: Johns Hopkins University Press, 1986); and Adam Przeworski *et al.*, *Democracy and Development: Political Institutions and Material Well-Being in the World, 1950–1990* (Cambridge: Cambridge University Press, 2000).
4 Elizabeth Perry, "Chinese Conceptions of 'Rights': From Mencius to Mao—and Now," *Perspective on Politics* Vol. 6, No. 1 (2008): 37.
5 Yanqi Tong, "Environmental Movements in Transitional Societies: A Comparative Study of Taiwan and China," *Comparative Politics*, Vol. 37, No. 2 (2005): 167–88; and Andrew Mertha, *China's Water Warriors: Citizen Action and Policy Change* (Cornell University Press, 2008).
6 Feng Chen, "Subsistence Crises, Managerial Corruption and Labor Protests in China," *China Journal*, No. 44 (July 2000): 41–63; and William Hurst and Kevin O'Brien, "China's Contentious Pensioners," *China Quarterly*, No. 170 (2002): 345–60.
7 Ching Kwan Lee, "Pathways of Labor Insurgency," in Elizabeth J. Perry and Mark Selden (eds) *Chinese Society: Change, Conflict and Resistance* (London: Routledge Curzon Press, 2003, 2nd edn), 71–92.
8 Mary Gallagher "Hope for Protection and Hopeless Choices," in Elizabeth Perry and Goldman Merle (eds) *Grassroots Political Reform in Contemporary China* (Mass.: Harvard University Press, 2007), 206.
9 Yongshun Cai, "The Resistance of Chinese Laid-off Workers in the Reform Period," *China Quarterly*, 170 (June 2002): 327–44; Yongshun Cai, *State and Laid-off Workers in Reform China: The Silence and Collective Action* (Routledge, 2005); and Su Yang and Xin He, "Street as Courtroom: State Accommodation of Labor Protest in South China," *Law and Society Review* Vol. 44, No. 1 (2010): 157–84.
10 Feng Chen, "Subsistence Crises, Managerial Corruption and Labor Protests in China," ibid.
11 Cao Jinqing, 黄河边上的中国 [China by the Yellow River] (Shanghai Wenyi Press, 2000).
12 Thomas Bernstein and Xiaobo Lu, "Taxation without Representation: The Central and Local States in Reform China," *China Quarterly*, No. 163 (September 2000): 742–63; and Xiaobo Lu, "The Politics of Peasant Burden in Reform China," *Journal of Peasant Studies* Vol. 25, No. 1 (October): 113–38.
13 Peter Ho, "Contesting Rural Spaces: Land Disputes, Customary Tenure and the State," in Elizabeth J. Perry and Mark Selden (eds) *Chinese Society: Change,*

Conflict and Resistance (London: Routledge Curzon Press, 2000), 101–22; Peter Ho, "Who Owns China's Land? Policies, Property Rights and Deliberate Institutional Ambiguity," *The China Quarterly* (2001): 394–421; Xiaolin Guo, "Land Expropriation and Villagers' Complaints in Northeast Yunnan," *China Quarterly* No. 166 (June 2001): 422–39; and David Zweig, "To the Courts or to the Barricades? Can New Political Institutions Manage Rural Conflict?" in Elizabeth Perry and Mark Selden (eds) *Chinese Society: Change, Conflict and Resistance* (London: Routledge Curzon Press, 2003, 2nd edn), 123–47.

14 Jun Jing, "Environmental Protests in Rural China," in Elizabeth Perry and Mark Selden (eds) *Chinese Society: Change, Conflict and Resistance* (London: Routledge Curzon Press, 2003, 2nd edn), 197–214; and Yanqi Tong, "Environmental Movements in Transitional Societies," ibid.
15 Elizabeth Perry and Mark Selden (eds), *Chinese Society: Change, Conflict and Resistance* (London: Routledge Curzon Press, 2003, 2nd edn), 12.
16 Patricia Thornton, "The New Cybersects: Popular Religion, Repression and Resistance," in Elizabeth Perry and Mark Selden (eds) *Chinese Society: Change, Conflict and Resistance* (London: Routledge Curzon Press, 2003, 2nd edn), 215–38.
17 Ching Kwan Lee, "Pathways of Labor Insurgency," ibid.
18 Doug McAdam, John D. McCarthy and Mayer N. Zald (eds) *Comparative Perspectives on Social Movements: Political Opportunities, Mobilizing Structures, and Cultural Framings* (Cambridge and New York: Cambridge University Press, 1996).
19 Kevin O'Brien and Li Lianjiang, *Rightful Resistance in Rural China* (NY: Cambridge University Press, 2006), 4.
20 James Scott, *The Moral Economy of the Peasant: Rebellion and Subsistence in Southeast Asia* (Yale University Press, 1976).
21 Kevin O'Brien and Li Lianjiang, *Rightful Resistance in Rural China*, ibid., 4.
22 Ibid., 64. It should be noted that O'Brien and Li have carefully qualified the meaning of rights in a Chinese context that is different from that of the Western conception.
23 David Zweig, "To the Courts or to the Barricades? Can New Political Institutions Manage Rural Conflict?" ibid.
24 Pei Minxin, "Rights and Resistance: The Changing Contexts of the Dissident Movement," in Elizabeth Perry and Mark Selden (eds) *Chinese Society: Change, Conflict and Resistance* (London: Routledge Curzon Press, 2003, 2nd edn), 31–56; Merle Goldman and Elizabeth Perry, *Changing Meanings of Citizenship in Modern China* (Harvard University Press, 2002); and Maria Heimer and Stig Thogersen (eds), *Doing Fieldwork in China* (Honolulu: University of Hawaii Press, 2006).
25 Elizabeth Perry "Chinese Conceptions of 'Rights'," ibid., 37.
26 Ibid., 43.
27 Ching Kwan Lee, "Pathways of Labor Insurgency," ibid., 68.
28 Elizabeth Perry, "Chinese Conceptions of 'Rights'," ibid., 44.
29 Feng Chen, "Subsistence Crises, Managerial Corruption and Labor Protests in China," *China Journal* No. 44 (July 2000): 63.
30 Ching Kwan Lee, *Against the Law: Labor Protests in China's Rustbelt and Sunbelt* (University of California Press, 2007), 159.
31 Xi Chen, "Between Defiance and Obedience: Protest Opportunism in China," in Elizabeth Perry and Merle Goldman (eds) *Grassroots Political Reform in Contemporary China* (Harvard University Press, 2007), 274.
32 Patricia Thornton, "Framing Dissent in Contemporary China: Irony, Ambiguity and Metonymy," *China Quarterly* No. 171 (September 2002), 665.
33 Jun Jing, "Environmental Protests in Rural China," ibid., 204.
34 Xi Chen, "Between Defiance and Obedience: Protest Opportunism in China," ibid., 256.
35 Thomas Bernstein, "Unrest in Rural China: A 2003 Assessment," UC Irvine: Center for the Study of Democracy, 2004, www.escholarship.org/uc/item/1318d3rx.

36 Kevin O'Brien and Li Lianjiang, *Rightful Resistance in Rural China* (NY: Cambridge University Press, 2006).
37 There are discussions on how environmental agencies reach out and use environmental protests to strengthen their institutional positions. See Carlos Wing Hung Lo and Sai Wing Leung, "Environmental Agency and Public Opinion in Guangzhou: The Limits of a Popular Approach to Environmental Governance," *China Quarterly* (September 2000): 677–704; and Barbara J. Sinkule and Leonard Ortolano, *Implementing Environmental Policy in China* (New York: Praeger Press, 1995); the environmental movement has also tried to form a partnership with the local government in its efforts to protect the environment. See Caroline Cooper, "Quietly Sowing the Seeds of Activism," *Far Eastern Economic Review*, April 10, 2003, 30.
38 Jun Jing, "Environmental Protests in Rural China," ibid.; and Yanqi Tong, "Environmental Movements in Transitional Societies," ibid.
39 Xiaolin Guo, "Land Expropriation and Rural Conflicts in China," *China Quarterly* 166 (June 2001): 435.
40 Vivienne Shue, *The Reach of the State: Sketches of the Chinese Body Politic* (Stanford, Calif.: Stanford University Press, 1988), 130.
41 Xiaolin Guo, "Land Expropriation and Rural Conflicts in China," ibid.
42 Ethan Michelson, "Justice from Above or Below? Popular Strategies for Resolving Grievances in Rural China," *The China Quarterly* No. 193 (2008): 44.
43 Ibid.
44 Yu Jianrong, 于建嵘, 中国的骚乱事件与管治危机: 2007年10月30日在美国加州大学伯克利分校的演讲 [Riot Incidents and Crisis of Control: Speech at UC Berkeley, October 10, 2007], China Elections and Governance (2007), www.chinaelections.org./NewsInfo.asp?NewsID=118361 (accessed April 30, 2010).
45 Susan Shirk, "The Echo Chamber of Nationalism: Media and the Internet," *Fragile Superpower* (Oxford University Press, 2007), 79–104.
46 Patricia Thornton, "The New Cybersects: Popular Religion, Repression and Resistance," in Elizabeth Perry and Mark Selden (eds) *Chinese Society: Change, Conflict and Resistance* (London: Routledge Curzon Press, 2003, 2nd edn), 232.
47 Zheng Yongnian and Wu Guoguang, "Information Technology, Public Space, and Collective Action in China," *Comparative Political Studies* Vol. 38, No. 5 (June 2005): 507–36; Zixue Tai, *The Internet in China: Cyberspace and Civil Society* (London: Routledge, 2006); Zheng Yongnian, *Technological Empowerment: The Internet, State, and Society in China* (Stanford University Press, 2007); Ashley Esarey and Xiao Qiang, "Political Expression in the Chinese Blogosphere: Below the Radar," *Asian Survey* Vol. 48, No. 5 (2008): 752–72; Guobin Yang, *The Power of the Internet in China: Citizen Activism Online* (New York: Columbia University Press, 2009); Zhang Xiaoling and Zheng Yongnian (eds), *China's Information and Communications Technology Revolution: Social Changes and State Responses* (London and New York: Routledge, 2009); Susan Shirk, "Changing Media, Changing China," in Susan Shirk (ed.) *Changing Media, Changing China* (Oxford University Press, 2011), 1–37; Qiang Xiao, "The Battle for the Chinese Internet," *Journal of Democracy* Vol. 22, No. 2 (April 2011): 47–61; Rebecca MacKinnon, "China's 'Networked Authoritarianism'," *Journal of Democracy* Vol. 22, No. 2 (April 2011): 32–46.
48 Kurt Schock, *Unarmed Insurrections People Power Movements in Nondemocracies* (Minneapolis: University of Minnesota Press, 2005), 8.
49 Teresa Wright, *The Perils of Protest: State Repression and Student Activism in China and Taiwan* (Honolulu: University of Hawai'i Press, 2001), 3.
50 Cai Yongshun, "Local Governments and the Suppression of Popular Resistance in China," *The China Quarterly* No. 193 (2008): 40.
51 Lee Ching Kwan "Pathways of Labor Insurgency," ibid., 58.

52 Jack Goldstone and Charles Tilly, "Threat (and Opportunity): Popular Action and State Response in the Dynamics of Contentious Action," in Ronald R. Aminzade, Jack A. Goldstone, Doug McAdam, Elizabeth Perry, William Sewell, Sidney Tarrow and Charles Tilley (eds) *Silence and Voice in the Study of Contentious Politics* (New York: Cambridge University Press, 2001), 179–94.
53 孙立平 [Sun Liping], 中国社会正在加速走向溃败 [Chinese Society is Accelerating its Decay], 2010, new.21ccom.net/plus/view.php?aid = 7550 (accessed April 30, 2010).
54 Elizabeth Perry and Mark Selden (eds), *Chinese Society: Change, Conflict and Resistance*, ibid., 24.
55 Murray Scot Tanner, "China Rethinks Unrest," *The Washington Quarterly* Vol. 27, No. 3 (Summer, 2004): 137–56; Murray Scot Tanner, "Rethinking Law Enforcement and Society: Changing Police Analysis of Social Unrest," in Neil Diamant *et al.* (eds) *Engaging the Law in China: State, Society, and Possibilities for Justice* (Stanford University Press, 2005), 193–212.
56 Susan Shirk, *Fragile Superpower*, ibid., 81.
57 Su Yang and Xin He, "Street as Courtroom: State Accommodation of Labor Protest in South China," ibid., 159.
58 Elizabeth Perry, *Challenging the Mandate of Heaven* (Armonk, NY: M.E. Sharpe, 2001); and Elizabeth Perry "Chinese Conceptions of 'Rights'," ibid.
59 Lee Ching Kwan, "Pathways of Labor Insurgency," ibid., 58.
60 Yongshun Cai, "Power Structure and Regime Resilience: Contentious Politics in China," *British Journal of Political Science* Vol. 38, No. 3 (July 2008): 430.
61 Thomas Bernstein and Lu Xiaobo, *Taxation without Representation in Contemporary Rural China* (NY: Cambridge University Press, 2003).
62 Guobin Yang, *The Power of the Internet in China*, ibid.; Eric Harwit and Duncan Clark, "Shaping the Internet in China: Evolution of Political Control over Network Infrastructure and Content," *Asian Survey* Vol. 41, No. 3 (May/June 2001): 377–408; Michael Chase and Jarnes Mulvenon, *You've Got Dissent! Chinese Dissident Use of the Internet and Beijing's Counter-Strategies* (Rand, 2002); and Larry Diamond, "Liberation Technology," *Journal of Democracy* Vol. 21, No. 3 (July 2010): 69–83.
63 Christopher Hughes and Gudrun Wacker (eds), *China and the Internet: Politics of the Digital Leap Forward* (London and New York: Routledge, 2003); Shanthi Kalathil and Taylor Boas, *Open Networks Closed Regimes: The Impact of the Internet on Authoritarian Rule* (Carnegie Endowment for International Peace, 2003).
64 Zheng Yongnian, *Technological Empowerment*.
65 Xi Chen, "Between Defiance and Obedience: Protest Opportunism in China," ibid.; and Li Liangjiang and Kevin O'Brien, "Protest Leadership in Rural China," in Peter Hays *et al.* (eds) *Chinese Politics: State, Society and the Market* (London and New York: Routledge, 2010), 85–108.

2 Analyzing social protests

The study of social protest usually revolves along two analytical approaches. One is the social movement theories and the other is state-society relations. The social movement theories primarily concern all the factors that give rise to and sustain protest movements. The framework of state-society relations is more interested in how a particular state-society structure constrains the nature and pattern of the protests and how the protests in turn affect such structure. In this chapter, we will briefly discuss these two approaches and elaborate our analytical framework.

Political opportunity, mobilization and framing

Social protest is one form of social movement. Theories of social movement therefore provide useful analytical constructs for us to examine social protest in China. Writings on social movement are too numerous, and nor is it necessary, to be reviewed here. In general, scholars have suggested that the emergence and development of social movements depend on the dynamic interaction of three broad sets of factors.[1]

First, social movements are shaped by the broader political constraints and opportunities unique to the national context in which they emerge. These constraints and opportunities involve the institutional structure and the informal power relations of a given national political system, such as the relative openness or closure of the institutionalized political system, the stability of the elite alignments that undergird the polity, the presence or absence of elite allies for a particular social movement, and the state's capacity and propensity for repression. In other words, the favorable political opportunities for the emergence of social movement include a more open and tolerant political system, a more fragmented ruling elite within which the protest movement may find an ally, and less state propensity for repression.

The second set of factors concerns the forms of organization (informal as well as formal) available to mobilize people into collective action. There must be organizational resources to resources may include the preexisting organizations, such as informal networks, voluntary associations and religious groups, as well as the movement-initiated organizations. Different types of social movements may need different organizational forms. The organizational culture of a given society may also affect the forms of social movement.

The third set of factors is the collective process of interpretation, attribution and social construction that gives meaning and value to collective action. By bringing shared meanings and definitions to their situation, people who feel aggrieved about some aspect of their lives can become more optimistic that by acting collectively, they can redress their problem. Framing would also facilitate the formation of a movement identity that connects loose individuals and networks into coalitions.[2] Without proper framing, it is highly unlikely that people will mobilize even when afforded opportunities to do so. Apparently the framing process is very much conditioned by the culture and ideology of a given society and the strategic thinking of social movement groups.

In addition to these three sets of factors, social movement scholars have also dwelt upon repertoires of contentious politics. Petition, assemble, strike and march are relatively peaceful tactics but require major costs of coordination. Because the protest groups usually are poor and disorganized, they tend to use a variety of tactics to compensate for their shortage of resources. The more violent repertoires, such as occupying premises, obstructing traffic, setting fires and attacking others with intent to do bodily harm, are the easiest kinds of collective action for small groups to initiate. By obstructing the routine activities of bystanders or authorities, protesters force them to attend to their demands.[3]

These are very rich theoretical sources from which constructive concepts can be extracted, given our subject of study. First, social protests in China tend to be short-term outbursts over subsistence crises, which require less political opportunity to take place. Historically, subsistence protests have been tolerated even during the most authoritarian periods in China. The subsistence issues are more likely to gain sympathy from within the state and ruling elite and have greater opportunity to be addressed and incite little repression. Second, unlike nongovernmental organizations (NGOs) that intend to last for a long while, instantaneous mass protests do not need sustainable mobilization structures and resources. Yet since the subject of our study is social protests with more than 500 participants, there had to be a minimum amount of coordination during the protest. Different types of protests will utilize different resources and employ different mobilization structures. Lastly, framing is important regardless of the duration of the protests. The way the protests are framed, such as the slogans and banners employed, will inform us a lot about the nature of the protests and their environment. Moreover, the formation of temporary movement identity in riots helps to explain the sudden explosion of such events. We will incorporate necessary aspects into later analysis.

Disaggregation, interaction and legitimacy

The second approach to the study of social protest is to use a state-society relations framework. Mass protests typically are instances through which social groups challenge state policies. The nature and patterns of such challenges and the state responses would be reflective of, and constrained by, the particular state-society relationship.

The conventional approach of totalitarianism or authoritarianism basically takes a "state versus society" dichotomy in analysis. Many writings employ a top-down "strong state, weak society" argument.[4] This argument treats state-society relations as characterized by state control and domination from above and societal resistance from below. Any gains by society are a loss to the state, and vice versa. Scholars who hold this approach either argue that society rises and challenges the regime, which may consequently change the balance of their relationship, or they claim that the state is in serious trouble, with some kind of "concession-repression" dilemma.[5]

In efforts to break away from this conventional approach, some scholars have adopted a perspective that is similar to that of the "state-in-society" thesis.[6] The core argument of this perspective is to "disaggregate the monolithic state," and society, for that matter. As Gries and Rosen put it, their conceptual move to "deconstruct and reconstruct" their understanding of state and society is to add an "s" to both concepts. Segments of the state and social forces may form alliances rather than being antagonistic as suggested by the simple state-society dichotomy.[7] Some have also emphasized a "relational approach" by focusing on the interaction between the state and societal forces.[8] As admirable as these efforts are, the problem with both "disaggregation" and "relational" approaches is that they fail to break away from the fundamental feature of the traditional state-society dichotomy—repressive state (plural or not) versus righteous society (plural or not). As a result, the interpretations derived from these approaches have not carried us very far. The Chinese experiences continue to defy most of the theoretical predictions.

Despite some having argued for a win-win scenario or a "strong state, strong society" thesis in the state-society relationship,[9] not very many have attempted to apply it to the study of social protests in nondemocratic systems. Zheng Yongnian's work on Internet-based civil engagement in China is one of the very few that suggests a process of mutual empowerment between the state and society in China. He argues that the Internet empowers both the state and society and has created a new infrastructure in which the state and society can engage each other.[10]

Zhao Dingxin probably is the most notable in his single-authored analysis of the Tiananmen student movement. Employing the state-society relations framework, Zhao uses legitimacy as the entry point to his analysis. According to him, moral and economic performances are the two major dimensions of regime legitimacy in China.[11] He argues that various actors' behavior during the movement was based on their perceptions of such legitimacy.

Our analysis in this book tries to incorporate the useful elements of the above approaches into an integrated structural approach. We believe that legitimacy is a conceptual vehicle that delivers meaning about social protests in a state-society framework. Yet we will put our analysis into a broader perspective of transitions and focus on structural changes. We also conceive legitimacy differently. Instead of a performance-based legitimacy, we argue that the regime legitimacy in China is multilayered and responsibility-based. This responsibility is all encompassing and rooted deeply in China's political tradition. Such conception departs completely from the traditional state-society framework, as it emphasizes the bondage, rather than antagonism, between the two. The following sections will elaborate our thesis in more detail.

An integrated structural analysis

Our analysis contains four sets of structural variables. The first is macro-structural change as a result of socioeconomic transformation. This process necessarily generates dislocation and transitional pains. The second set is the consequential change in the state-society structure that determines the pattern of social protest. The third is the legitimacy structure that defines the perceptions, expectations and frustrations that give rise and sustain social protest. The fourth set is the multilevel responsibility structure that originated from China's administrative hierarchy. This structure limits the scale of social unrest, provides flexibility to the regime and prescribes government reactions to the protests.

Transitional pains

There are plenty of scholarly works on transition. In the 1950s and 1960s, the transition literature focused on the transition processes from traditional to modern societies.[12] Since the 1990s, the attention has been on the political transition of communist and authoritarian regimes to either democracy or something else and the economic transition from a planned economy to a market economy.[13] Scholars have long observed the costs of transition. For example, Adam Przeworski pointed out in the early 1990s that there will be a "valley of transition" where the standard of living will take a significant drop.[14]

Scholars observed and studied the reform costs in the early stages of reform in China, such as inflation, unemployment and inequality.[15] However, with the rapid economic growth and China becoming the second largest economy in the world, the continued transitional pains are somewhat overlooked. Scholars tended to treat social protests as symptoms of a sickness in China's political system. While the problems of the current political system share the cause of social protests, we would like to put social protests back into the context of transition. We believe that these social protests are the products of mounting social discontent and rising tensions between citizens and the authorities during the epochal social and economic transformation of China. As a traditional Chinese medicine phrase frames the malfunction of the body, "it hurts when the flow was blocked" (不通则痛). Whereas in medicine the "flow" refers to the circulation of energy and blood, in social sciences studies such flow could mean the flow of information, communication, grievance and anger. The socioeconomic transformation has created many displacements in the existing structure, which in turn caused the blockage of such flows. The social pains thus express themselves in the form of social protest.

Continued transition continues to generate structural displacement, hence continued pain. From the data we have collected, we have detected four general types of transitional pain. The first type is the dying pains of the traditional state sector. The all-inclusive state sector is dying out. Large numbers of laid-off workers are displaced, losing income and welfare packages that they deemed their entitlement. The second type is the growing pains of the private sector, especially the foreign-invested enterprises. A new generation of workers in the private sector want to move out of the sweat-shop style of working conditions and have decent wages. The third type of pain is more conventional—the pains of urbanization, or the pains of modernization. In China's context, it is the result of urbanization amid chaotic marketization. City expansions necessarily take land away from the farmers, yet the irregular land market and rampant corruption create serious frictions in land transactions. The last type of pain is not driven by material interests as are the first three. Instead it is a psychological pain resulting from various frustrations. People are frustrated over the costs of transition, the widening wealth gap, social injustice and, most importantly, the official corruption that permeates all levels of government.

Structural change of state-society relations

Socioeconomic transformation inevitably changes state-society relations. During Mao's era, Chinese society was completely dominated by the state and there was no clear demarcation line between the state and the society. With a highly centralized and unitary power structure, the central government controlled all possible resources. Local government, from provincial level down to the township level, was a weak layer in this structure. They submerged into the unitary system and did not have a distinctive role in this particular state-society structure. The enforcers of the state power were work units in the cities and grassroots collectives in the rural areas. They served as the joints between the state and the society. Figure 2.1 is a demonstration of such a structure.

Of special importance in this structure is the function of the work units and grassroots collectives. China's huge bureaucracy links up with the Chinese citizen at the level of the work unit. For most, this refers to the place of work—factory, research institute, ministry and so forth. For students it was the school where they studied. For unemployed urbanites it was the neighborhood "residents' committee." When agriculture was collectivized, the peasant's unit was the collective, mainly the village.[16]

On the one hand, they were the agents of the state.[17] For example, rural public order was maintained by the militia of the collectives. In the cities,

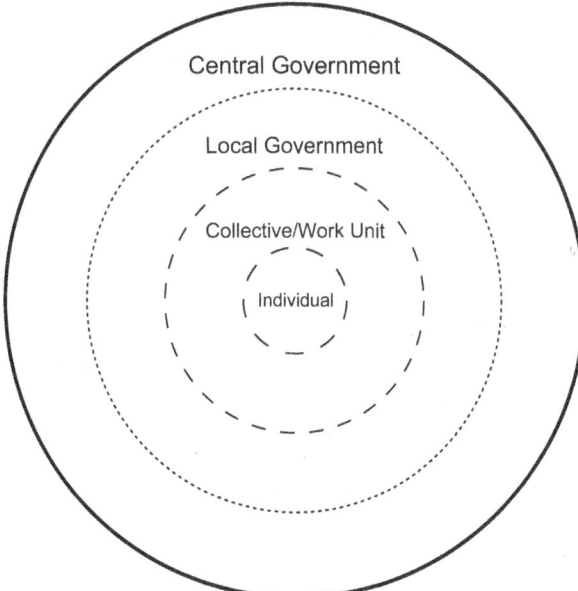

Figure 2.1 Structure of state-society relations before the reforms

each work unit had its public security unit. Public Security Bureaux and their branches mainly dealt with those who did not belong to any work unit. If someone in the work unit committed a minor offense, the work unit representatives would go to the Public Security Bureau and take them back, then adopt disciplinary measures according to the code of the work unit. Policy implementation, such as the family planning policy, was also enforced by the work units and collectives, which usually would establish a comparable position to be in charge of the policy. In such a structure, the state as the power holder and its agents had a symbiotic relationship.

On the other hand, the work units and collectives provided a sense of identity and functioned as a community. Public welfare was distributed by these agents. The welfare provisions of the work unit have become so comprehensive over the years that work units operate as self-sufficient and multifunctional social communities. Each work unit came to constitute a "small society" with little need for interunit exchanges.[18] Even though individual freedom was limited and the standard of living was low, the work units, representing the state, provided basic public welfare and security. People did not have to worry about housing, medical care, pension and education. As a result, individuals and their families had strong work unit identities. If the work units provided housing quarters, which most of them did, the employees would develop a strong sense of community as well. These work unit identities even continued well into the reform era, as the initial reforms did not touch the work unit structure. For example, during the Tiananmen protest movement, participants even held out labels of their work units, such as *"People's Daily"* and "Peking University."[19] The rural collectives had fewer welfare functions, though they provided elementary school education and some care for the elderly. Yet the village identity was established on a geographical and familial basis, which is a cohesive foundation for community.

During Mao's era, welfare distribution was more or less egalitarian. Government officials were relatively honest. As the state agents—work units and collectives—incorporated most of the individuals into their coverage, there were no clear demarcation lines, as well as confrontational attitudes, between the state and society. Except for the state-initiated mass movements, such as the Cultural Revolution, society had no capability to confront the state. Protests in China during the Maoist period were mainly "cellular protests," because of the limited contact across unit boundaries.[20] Despite several attempts to decentralize or recentralize the power structure during Mao's era between the center and the local governments, the work units and collectives that served as the linkage between the state and the individuals remained untouched.

Vivienne Shue once argued that this was a honeycomb cell structure, in which the individual social life was wrapped by the work units and collectives.[21] She believed that the work units and collectives provided some insulation for individuals from the penetration of the Party state. While this observation of the compartmentalization of the social structure is very insightful, she overlooked the dual nature of the work units and collectives. They, after all, have a symbiotic relationship with the state. The work units and collectives were not a neutral buffer zone between the state and individuals. They were more active agents that not only distributed state goodies to the individuals but also kept the potential instability in control. When people had problems, they went to their work unit for solutions.

Since the reforms of the 1980s and 1990s, there have been two extremely visible changes in state-society relations. One is the emergence of local government as a distinctive layer in the structure. Decentralization of power and responsibility has strengthened the role of local government—they are no longer a hidden layer of a bureaucratic complex. The tax reform of 1994 has also consolidated local governments' financial responsibility as a separate entity of the administration.

The other change is the disappearance of the layer of work units and collectives. In the rural areas, the household responsibility system replaced collective agriculture. Individual households, instead of the collectives, became the entities that pay taxes and deliver grain procurement to the state. In the cities, a market economy started to replace the planned economy. The state-owned enterprise (SOE) reforms have led to large-scale lay-offs. Tens of millions of workers lost their jobs as well as all the social welfare benefits that were provided by the work units. Work units no longer serve as the source of identity. Nationally issued individual identification (ID) cards have replaced

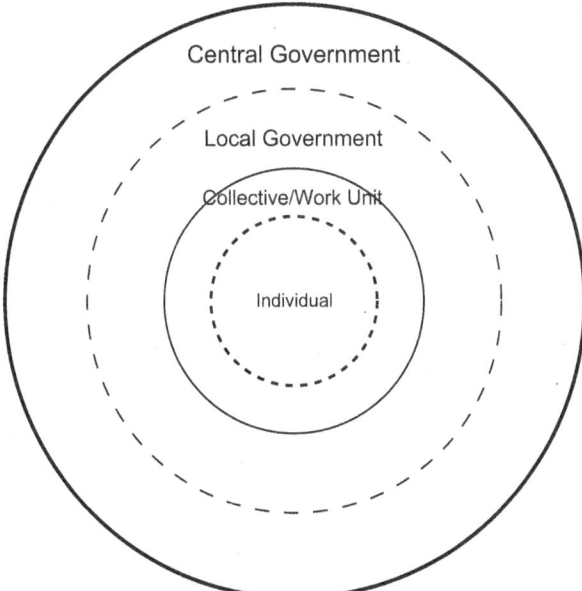

Figure 2.2 Structure of state-society relations after the reforms

the work unit ID cards as the only legitimate ID cards. The buffer zone between the state and individuals has evaporated and the division line between the state and society has hardened. The state and individuals now have to confront each other directly. Figure 2.2 is an illustration of this changing structure.

In her famous honeycomb analysis, Shue argued that when the market reforms erode the middle layers, the state may have more effective control over individuals.[22] The reality is that not only does the state have more control over individuals, but individuals also can directly confront the state. In the past, people would go to the work unit with their problems. Now, people turn to the government. Yet there are few institutional channels through which both sides can communicate, let alone solve problems. A legal channel could be a solution, but the underdeveloped court system, which is already overwhelmed by the explosion in lawsuits, has been unable to deal with grievances caused by the broad structural change. This is why the government becomes the target in many protests—economic interest-driven social protests.

Reconceiving legitimacy

Legitimacy is an important concept in the study of politics. As the recognized right to rule, it not only enables the state to control the population at much lower cost, but also captures the essence of the state-society relationship. Saturated with traditions, values and perceptions, legitimacy is the soft structure of the state-society relationship. To what extent does the population trust the state? What are society's expectations of the state? What is perceived as proper state behavior? As such, legitimacy would provide great analytical value for us to understand social protests in China. Since legitimacy is central to our analytical framework and our conceptions of legitimacy are very different from the conventional ones, we will spend the most time elaborating on the conceptualization.

Most contemporary discussion of legitimacy starts with Max Weber's typology of legitimacy. Weber has described three types of legitimate authority: traditional, charismatic and rational-legal. The traditional type of legitimacy refers to the long-accepted values, such as the "divine right of kings," which belong to the "eternal yesterday." The charismatic source of legitimacy refers to those leaders who possess the exceptional qualities that inspire a broad range of followers. This is especially true for some religious or revolutionary leaders, such as Khomeini, Castro and Mao.[23] Legality of the political institutions and elections are the typical features of the rational-legal source of legitimacy.[24] In the real world, most authorities are based on different combinations of the three.

Since none of these three categories could explain the communist regimes that had lasted for a long while, except for a couple of charismatic leaders most of whom had passed away, scholars have developed a fourth category of legitimacy: socioeconomic performance. Seymour Martin Lipset pointed out that "prolonged effectiveness over a number of generations may give legitimacy to a political system. In the modern world, such effectiveness means primarily constant economic development."[25] It is believed that the communist regimes relied on the socioeconomic performance and provision of welfare benefits to gain legitimacy from their population. This formula is suggested as a kind of "social contract" in which the population surrendered their political and civil liberties in exchange for a high level of social welfare, such as comprehensive education, health care, job security, and modest but steadily rising living standard.[26]

Those who suggest that communist regimes have relied on socioeconomic performance for their basis of legitimacy are also aware that no regime could guarantee a continuously successful performance.[27] With the inevitable economic slowdown, communist regimes would have to shift some of the burden of legitimation to political and procedural bases, such as more competitive elections and more political incorporations.[28] Consequently, some of the political openings in the late 1980s doomed the communist regimes in Eastern Europe.

While Weber's classification has remained central to most modern discussions of legitimacy, the end of the Cold War has prompted the study of legitimacy in two directions. In the first direction, the rising tide of the third wave of democratization has tilted the discussion of legitimacy toward the legal-rational type. To many, democratic election has become the only legitimate source of legitimacy in the contemporary world in most political discourses. Oftentimes, when scholars or politicians argue that a regime has no legitimacy, they primarily mean the absence of free elections. In an attempt to explain the legitimacy of the authoritarian Chinese regime, many have picked economic performance and always pointed out that it is not sustainable.

The other direction is motivated by the fact that many authoritarian regimes continue to endure, and create a puzzle for analysts. China is a good example in this regard. Scholars are searching for some viable explanation and often go back to the particular cultural conditions. Zhao has incorporated morality into his analysis of the student movement in 1989. While his analysis is insightful, the weak point of his conceptualization is the vague definition of moral performance. He loosely refers to it as the "proper behaviors and ritual that good rulers should perform."[29] As important as the concept of morality has been in Chinese political tradition and in his analytical scheme, it is disappointing that Zhao has provided a thin definition with the only reference from Durkheim (in footnote 72).

Further down the path, Vivienne Shue argues that it is the government's capacity to sustain stability and social order that is essential to regime legitimacy. According to Shue, the three key components in the logic of state legitimation are truth (knowledge of the universe), benevolence (taking responsibility for the welfare of the people and showing compassionate care for them), and glory (pride of a secure, wealthy and rising power). She specifically argues against the popular idea that regime legitimacy in China is performance based (Shue 2004). These characterizations of regime legitimacy have greatly advanced our understanding of the subject and indeed explained many phenomena in China today. For the purpose of our analysis of social protest, we will further explore the cultural, political and economic traditions of Chinese conceptions of legitimacy.

"Legitimacy" as a theoretical concept was introduced into contemporary Chinese political vocabularies in the 1980s and became popular in the 1990s. With free elections becoming the major parameter, the legitimacy of the Chinese communist regime has been repeatedly called into question by groups of intellectuals on the ground that the government is not genuinely elected. The reasons for the illegitimate regime lasting this long are believed to be the application of harsh repression and the submissiveness of the Chinese people. This is a conceptual fallacy. Any regime that can sustain its rule for a long time has legitimacy. If a regime can last for several generations without legitimacy, then this concept is meaningless. So long as the general population accepts the right of their rulers to rule, for whatever reasons, the regime enjoys legitimacy.

We argue that regime legitimacy in China is responsibility based. It is an understanding between the state and society of the responsibility of each side. Our analytical framework suggests that there are three overlapping layers of this responsibility-based regime legitimacy in China: morality of the ruling elite, benevolent governance, and state responsibility for the well-being of the

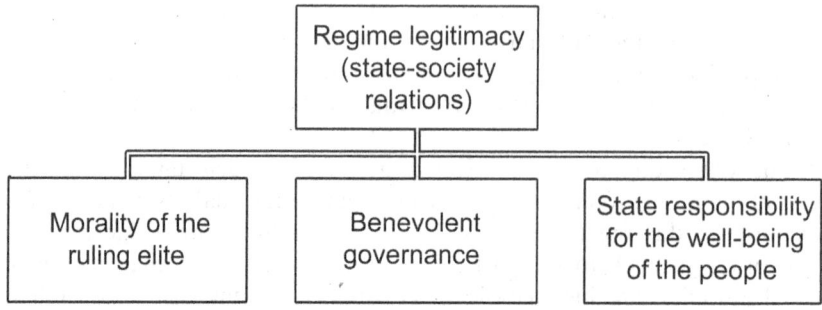

Figure 2.3 Legitimacy structure in China

people (Figure 2.3). We also argue that the interplay of the Chinese multilevel power structure and the layers of regime legitimacy have cushioned potential legitimacy crisis.

In this perspective, there are two types of social protest. One is the protest against the perceived breaches of the understanding between the state and society, such as malevolent governance and official corruption. The other is the protests in which people expect the state to fulfill its part of the responsibility—that is solve their grievances. Most of the social protests in contemporary China fall within the latter. To a certain extent, the expectation of state responsibility is an endorsement for regime legitimacy. In other words, a legitimacy crisis is not a cause for protest, but will be the result if the regime fails to address these grievances. We will elaborate on the traditional roots and contemporary implications of these layers in the following sections.

The mandate of heaven and morality

With more than a 4,000-year history of governance, the Chinese have tackled the question of legitimacy since the very early ages. In Chinese political tradition, the legitimacy of the dynasty came from the so-called "mandate of heaven." Despite the mysterious ambiguity of heaven, the idea was created to justify the rule of dynasties precisely because the Chinese people had questions concerning regime legitimacy.

For example, when the Shang Dynasty (1600–1100 BC) overthrew the Xia Dynasty (2100–1600 BC), it claimed that the Xia emperor had lost his mandate from heaven. When the West Zhou Dynasty (1100–1771 BC) replaced the Shang Dynasty, many people asked why heaven had previously given the power to Shang but now changed its mind and endorsed the power to Zhou. The Zhou rulers had to explain that "heaven does not favor anybody; only morality makes heaven trust you." In this way, the mandate of heaven was related to morality. According to Zhou rulers, if the prince can behave morally, protecting the people, the people will voluntarily obey him and the heaven will forever trust him with the power to govern.[30]

All these teachings reveal a couple of key points for our understanding of legitimacy. First, as early as the Shang Dynasty, legitimacy was a big concern for the rulers. Second, legitimacy comes from the mandate of heaven, and the mandate of heaven comes from the morality of the rulers. In order to maintain the mandate of heaven, the rulers have to maintain their morality. This is a crucial connection between the right to rule and the morality of the rulers. As the highest ruler, the emperor was expected to be the top moral example for all his subjects. Moreover, all his officials have to be morally upright as well. While the Chinese invented the merit-based civil service examination system to select government officials, moral standards have always been the top criterion for recruitment.[31]

Confucius was not the one who first created the concept of "the mandate of heaven" or morality as the basis for it, but he, and Mencius, are the ones who developed these ideas into systematic teachings. He elaborated that the concept of a good government was fundamentally a matter of morality. He did not question the hereditary right of the emperors to rule, but he insisted that their first duty was to set a proper example of sound moral conduct. In the Confucian scheme the ruler was to be a role model for moral behavior, displaying benevolence, filial piety, faithfulness, courtesy, integrity and frugality. If an emperor does not behave himself, he cannot expect his people to behave themselves, because it is like pursuing a straight shadow with a curled body.[32] In a time when might was right, Fairbank and Reischauer commented, it is remarkable that Confucius argued that the ruler's virtue and the contentment of the people, rather than power, should be the true measures of political success.[33]

With morality becoming the justification of political power, the political and moral orders are inevitably intertwined. The state—the political authority—has also become the undisputed moral authority. Politics is moralized. As a result, any political criticism inevitably became moral criticism.[34] The personal morality of the politicians becomes a public matter. Politics is filled with charges and counter-charges of corruption—a typical characteristic of immorality.[35]

If a ruler was considered to have lost his virtue, then he also lost the mandate to rule, and a revolutionary moment would come. The perceived lack of morality would be vital to the regime survival. John Fairbank once characterized Chinese history as a series of dynastic cycles, with new dynasties replacing the old ones every several hundred years.[36] Most of these replacements were accomplished through large-scale peasant rebellions. In all these occurrences, the doomed emperors were accused of being ruthless, fatuous, rotten and ultimately lacking in virtue. The concept of the mandate of heaven was employed to justify not only the "right to rule" but also the "right to rebel."[37] The rise and fall of the dynasties has illustrated how the illegitimate regimes were removed and replaced.

Once the emperorship fell vacant, it was open to whoever won out among the competing forces. The old Chinese saying the "royal family does not have hereditary bloodlines"[38] demonstrates on the one hand that the Chinese do not necessarily respect royal bloodlines and believe everybody has a chance to be the emperor. On the other hand, it also reflects a cultural tradition that people do not care where their rulers come from and how they come to power. Whether they are in power because of election or conspiracy, it is their capability or fortune. However, once you are in this position, you have to bear the responsibility to the people and rule by virtue. Legitimacy does not come from the way a leader obtains power, but lies instead in the way he exercises it.

It should be noted that there are other philosophies in Chinese political tradition. Not all of them advocate the same moral arguments. Legalism and Daoism are among the most influential. Legalism does not believe in moral education and argues for strict and harsh punishment for criminal behavior.[39] Yet the debate between the two schools has become a non-issue when Confucianism becomes the official ideology. Instead, there was a process of Confucianization of the legal system.[40] Daoism is in large part a philosophy of retreat and withdrawal. Thinkers who were appalled by perpetual warfare, instability and death turned away from the struggle for power, status and wealth.[41] The passivity of Daoism complements, rather than posing much of a challenge to, the Confucian order.

The acceptance of Confucianism as the official ideology during the reign of Han Wu, emperor of Western Han Dynasty (156–87 BC), injected a heavy dose of moral obligation into the state. As Lucian Pye pointed out, "Chinese morality and government blended, means and ends became indistinguishable, and ethical conduct was not only the guide for government, but government was there to improve the ethical conduct of all."[42] The mandate of heaven is the source of legitimacy not only for the emperor, but also for the governments of various levels. Adherence to moral principles, thus, became the top obligation of the government and its officials.

Punishing immoral officials is one of such moral obligations of the state. "Wise rulers discipline the officials not the masses [明主治吏不治民]" was an important principle of Chinese political tradition. In Chinese history, the punishment for corrupt officials was cruel. For example, the first emperor of Ming, Zhu Yuanzhang, wrote the legal code *Great Warnings*, which empowered commoners to perform citizens' arrest and brought local corrupt officials to the central authorities for prosecution. Crowds of commoners locking up corrupt officials in the capital became a common scene during Zhu Yuanzhang's reign. The punishment went to the extreme during the Ming Dynasty. Not only were their personal properties confiscated and the officials tortured to death, but their relatives and friends would also be given the death penalty. It was estimated that several tens of thousands of officials were executed in Zhu's time.

While the *Great Warnings* ceased to be used, due to its extreme cruelty, after Zhu Yuanzhang passed away, the severe punishment has become a political tradition exemplified by the popular phrase "No public anger could be assuaged without the death penalty [不杀不足以平民愤]." If the government does not prosecute immoral officials, then the government is immoral. This tradition has led to a Chinese society with a strong mentality of revenge and a high endorsement of the death penalty. The current Chinese legislature has attempted several times to remove the death penalty for malfeasance and economic crimes from criminal law, but has failed each time because of strong public resistance.[43] China is now one of the few countries that maintains the death penalty for malfeasance and economic crimes. Moral consideration has always received priority over legal consideration.

Benevolent governance

A crucial part of the ruler's virtue is to protect his people and rule by benevolence. The ancient Chinese philosopher Mencius pointed out that:

> it is not by sealing up the borders to hold the people in; it does not rely on dangerous mountains and difficult rivers to defend a state; it does not rely on sharp weapons to rule the world. One who finds the right way of ruling enjoys abundant support, while the other who loses the right way of ruling finds less support. The former can end up by enjoying loyalty from all the people, while the latter may make his own relatives betray him after all.[44]

This right way of ruling features benevolent governance. Confucius summarizes the central theme of benevolence as "showing compassionate care for the people."[45] He further lamented that "rule by virtue is just like the North Star, once placed in the correct position, all the other stars will align."[46] Officials should behave like parents, with a duty to plan and worry ahead of the people and enjoy the fruits after the people.[47] Once the government officials were morally upright, they could rule by moral persuasion not by cruel punishment.

More specifically, benevolent governance includes socializing moral values, encouraging agricultural production, recruiting the best and most capable to the government, exercising fairness in legal punishment and allocating duty to the state equally.[48] Mencius has clearly stated the connection between a benevolent government and legitimacy: "If we exercise benevolent government in the country, the people will be very happy with it, and ruling the country will become very easy."[49]

With the entire political system revolving around the idea of morality, the state has to take responsibility for socializing moral values among the masses. The early development and dominance of Confucianism has left little room for the emergence of influential religions.[50] As a result, the state institutions are responsible for preaching moral principles. This Chinese style of fusion of the state and "religion" (that is, morality) is a much tighter combination than the Western style of the alliance between the state and the church. No matter how close the alliance, the state and the church are two separate entities. In contrast, Confucianism does not have its own institution and has to attach to the state. In this sense, the Chinese state is the "church."

Aside from the state role as the moral preacher for society and to select officials who are capable of administration (both in terms of ability and morality), the more important part of benevolence for the masses is that the government rules in a generous and just manner. The traditional Chinese state does not interfere much in economic activities. Encouraging agricultural production means that the state should encourage people to produce more and, hence, have a comfortable living. The common measure was to adjust taxes in favor of the farmers. Exercising fairness in legal punishment and allocating duty to the state equally are the basic prerequisites for a benevolent government. The former requires the officials to be cautious in handing out sentences. Rather let the guilty free than kill the innocent. The latter particularly emphasizes that the government should not put a heavy duty burden on the poor, and not overwork those who are not smart and let the slackers get their way.[51] As a Confucian saying goes, "if one person bemoans, the entire right way of ruling collapses."[52] These prescriptions indicate an ideal state of government. While this is not the normal state of government, any serious violation of these ideals would undermine the principle of benevolence and, hence, the regime legitimacy.

When the benevolent government was at its best, such as periods during the Tang and Ming dynasties, the economy was prosperous and social life was safe and moral. People would return what they picked up on the street and would not lock their doors during the night (路不拾遗，夜不闭户). The concept of benevolent governance also reinforces the culture of pursuing substantive justice. In essence, the emphasis on substantive justice demands moral considerations to override legal codes and procedures. This went along with the state role as a moral preacher. Only a benevolent government will put moral considerations over legal deliberations. It inevitably leads to a negligence of legal procedures and results in the practice of "rule by man," because legal codes do not take moral exceptions on a case-by-case basis.

It is interesting to note that all these prescriptions for benevolent governance did not touch on the equal distribution of wealth. The extent to which people "care not about poverty but inequality" is a debatable subject. Based on the egalitarian appeals in peasant uprisings in Chinese tradition, many believe that the widening income gap in China would trigger widespread social protests. However, income inequality alone rarely instigates collective protest, because this is an individualized and diffused matter. Common parameters are needed to mobilize people to the street—they have to suffer from a common cause. It is much easier to organize protest if there is a late payment of wages or pensions, or people lose their jobs from the same place at the same time. In fact, historically, even though the peasants framed their uprising demands in egalitarian terms, the ultimate cause of the uprising was not inequality but subsistence crisis.

In his research on perceptions of inequality in contemporary China, Martin Whyte argued that people usually are not dissatisfied with the wealth gap, per se. They would accept that there are rich people, but are unhappy about the procedural injustice (Whyte 2009). While we agree with his conclusion that China was not sitting on the mouth of a volcano, public anger toward the wealthy and inequality has led to some eruptions of social riots. These sporadic and isolated eruptions do not qualify for a volcano-like situation; however, the idea that the Chinese people now start to care about procedural justice is somewhat misleading. Even if people frame their complaints in the name of procedural fairness, their sense of fairness was rarely about procedures, but about moral justice. The concern about the income gap is not about the idea that everybody should receive the same, but the hatred for the rich who are perceived to have obtained their wealth by corruption.

Moral economy and state responsibility

The crucial component of regime legitimacy is the state responsibility for the subsistence of the people. This is not written in any document or teachings, but an unwritten understanding between the state and society. The concept of the government being responsible for the subsistence of the people has a deep root in the traditional agricultural economy. In the 1970s, James Scott introduced the concept of a "moral economy," based on his research on peasant rebellion in Southeast Asia.[53] This concept challenged the fundamental tenets of classical economics that emphasized that economic behavior was based on the rational pursuit of profit maximization. Scott argued that there are subsistence ethics in a traditional agricultural society. The vulnerability of traditional agriculture to unpredictable weather makes the peasants heavily dependent on their community and government, and leads them to develop the concept of a "right to subsistence." For peasants, it is more important to minimize disaster than to maximize profit return, if the two imply different strategies.

While Scott's work is mainly derived from the study of Southeast Asia, the theory of "moral economy" has a broader application, especially the idea of a "right to subsistence." With a long history of traditional agriculture, Chinese society has included subsistence ethics as part of a broader pattern of moral politics in China's political order. While the expectation of communal assistance during disastrous seasons is common in most agricultural societies, the expectation of government assistance may be a particular Chinese characteristic. As Scott indicated, colonial governments in Southeast Asian countries could rarely be counted on in such instances. To the contrary, the colonial government in Southeast Asia tended to create more rigid tax schemes and the taxes were more forcefully collected than the precolonial governments.[54] In China, under the concept of "right to subsistence," the government is expected to reduce or abolish tax when there is a natural disaster, and to provide disaster relief when the disaster is devastating.

The principle of reciprocity implies that if the peasants have to count on government assistance in disasters, they support the government in return. This relationship represents how the peasants view a decent social relationship. Rich people have to do charity work, otherwise they would lose respect and moral standing. "There is some pattern of reciprocity, some pattern of rights, which peasants claim as the duty of those who control scarce resources."[55] The emperor bears the responsibility to guarantee that his subjects do not starve to death, and this responsibility in turn becomes the right of his subjects. It can be argued that the concept of right in a traditional agricultural society has been subsistence in nature and not about civil or political liberties.

To illustrate the implication of moral economy in the Chinese context, let's look at the history of government disaster relief efforts. Throughout the thousands of years of history, China experienced uncountable natural disasters. Being "the land of famine," no single year passed without some kind of natural disasters. According to one estimate, from 1766 BC to 1937, there were 5,258 recorded natural disasters, such as flooding, drought, insect damage, earthquakes and epidemics, averaging one every six months.[56] From 1949 to 1988, China had eight droughts and six floods on an annual basis. Damage by insects and pests also broke out frequently.[57]

As a traditional agricultural society, the frequent natural disasters made the peasants extremely vulnerable. In addition, the Chinese state inevitably bears the burden of disaster relief, which became the most important administrative function for any dynasty. The administration of famine prevention and relief efforts were so critical that it was termed "famine governance" (荒政). For example, the Ming and Qing dynasties developed a set of well-defined procedures for famine governance. The procedures included several steps: report, inspection, relief confirmation and the final relief distribution. Once there was a disaster, local officials and victims needed to file a report. Then the upper-level governments would send out officials to inspect and classify the degree of the disaster on a 1–10 scale. Next, the upper-level governments determined the amount of relief assistance. The final step was to release the assistance.

The most common famine relief measure was the opening of grain storage. In the Ming Dynasty each disaster victim household would receive about 95 kg of grain. In the Qing Dynasty each adult would receive 0.75 kg (children half the amount) of grain per day for a month. Usually the large amount of grain needed in disaster relief had to be transported from other areas, which required central government coordination. The state would also give gratuitous relief money to those who could not afford coffins and consolation money to the general victims. The state would even pay to help the family who sold their children in desperate circumstance to get them back. For example, during the earthquake of 1678, those who could not afford to repair their collapsed houses received 2–4 taels of silver each. Those who could not afford coffins received 2 taels of silver.[58] Since the number of victims was often in the hundreds of thousands with each disaster, all this grain and silver was no small burden on the state.

The state also played a crucial role in post-disaster reconstruction. First, the government would reduce or eliminate taxes for the disaster victims, depending on the seriousness of the disaster. Second, the government would pay for the transportation of the displaced population to return to their deserted land. Then the government would provide crop seeds and other funds for the peasants to resume production. Disaster prevention, especially flood control and irrigation maintenance, falls squarely on the shoulders of the government, due to the enormous scale of the project. The first emperor of the Xia Dynasty (twenty-first century BC–sixteenth century BC), Da Yu (大禹), became a legend for his achievements in flood control. Every Chinese knows from childhood that Da Yu was so devoted to his work in flood control that he passed his home three times but never went in. It illustrates the role the government should play—being responsible for the well-being of society.

The Chinese state probably is the only government that has devoted so much resource and effort into disaster relief throughout thousands of years of history. As R. Bing Wong's study of state making in China and Europe indicates, "located mainly in county seats and small market towns, [a system of state] granaries represented official commitments to material welfare beyond anything imaginable, let alone achieved, in Europe."[59]

Because of the large amount of resources being poured into disaster relief, there were all kinds of problems in management. The most serious one was corruption. There were many instances where officials used their power to embezzle disaster relief money or sell the relief grain for private gain. These corruptive behaviors often reduced the efficiency of the relief efforts. If discovered, the penalty was extremely severe for those who misreported a disaster and was guilty of corruption.

This subsistence ethics became a moral bind between the rulers and the ruled for thousands of years. If the peasants believed that the government did not fulfill its responsibility, then the government would lose the mandate of heaven, and peasant rebellions would break out. This usually occurred when the central government was in financial crisis and the emperor and his bureaucracy were incompetent, and also when natural disasters hit one after another or simultaneously. There have been several hundreds of peasant rebellions of various sizes in Chinese history. Among them were 40–50 large-scale peasant rebellions, starting with the Chen Sheng and Wu Guang rebellion in the late Qin Dynasty and with the Taiping Rebellion from 1850 to 1864 as the latest. Some of them resulted in a change of dynasty.

This responsibility of the state for the welfare of its citizens naturally bears certain paternalistic overtones. The traditional idea of so-called "parental officials" is the typical reflection of this state-society relationship.[60] Since the enlightenment movement of the early 1980s, there has been continuous criticism of this usage, which does not fit the model of a modern citizenship. However, as this concept is persistently creeping back into people's day-to-day vocabulary, it shows that it enjoys much greater cultural endurance than some critics would like it to have. The fact is, not only do government officials consider themselves to be "parental officials," but ordinary people also think the same way. Lucian Pye has pointed out that "Chinese people crave leaders who can solve all their problems."[61] As long as the government continues to take responsibility for the people's livelihood, the concept of "parental officials" will remain in the societal subconscious.

Legitimacy in contemporary times

So far we have elaborated three interrelated layers of regime legitimacy in Chinese political tradition. All together, these layers create a moral bondage between the state and society. It can be argued that this is a morality-based legitimacy, as it requires the morality of the officials and governance. It can also be called a responsibility-based legitimacy, as it specifies the government responsibility for the welfare of the people as the core principle of morality. We adopt the responsibility-based legitimacy in this book because responsibility is central to the analysis of social protests. The government will enjoy legitimacy as far as society expects it to fulfill its end of the deal. None of these is the unconditional acceptance of the ruler's right to rule. Just as a Chinese saying describes, "the water that carries the boat can also overturn it." The three layers of legitimacy could turn out to be the constraints on the regime behavior.

How do the layers of legitimacy manifest in contemporary China? The cultural traditions precipitate in the subconscious of society and continue to condition current political transformation. The Chinese political system has incorporated modern political products, such as the party system, rule of law and elections. Yet, as Zheng Yongnian has argued, the purpose of incorporation is not to transform China's political system into democracy and political pluralism of Western types, but to reproduce and sustain the existing system. This existing system, according to Zheng, is featured by an organizational emperorship, a continuation of the traditional politics.[62] Consequently, the traditional framework of regime legitimacy continues as well.

After the Communist Party came to power in 1949, it tried hard to maintain a clean and corruption-free image for its official corps. Under Mao, the Communist Party was fairly honest and obtained popular support and trust. Yet, corruption has become widespread during the reform era. Whereas the morality of the government officials remains important, the theme of anticorruption has always been the most powerful appeal to mobilize mass protests and an effective instrument in power politics. For example, the causes of the 1989 protest movement have been studied extensively. Many scholars (including one of the authors) believed that it was because the ordinary people were frustrated by the negative consequences of the economic reform, such as inflation, inequality and corruption that they decided to support the students,[63] whereas in fact, it was the slogan of opposing official corruption that appealed to the hearts of the people. The widespread corruption in today's China badly undermines the moral foundation of the state legitimacy.

Moreover, many high-ranking government officials have fallen in the power struggle under the accusation of corruption, such as Chen Xitong of Beijing and Chen Liangyu of Shanghai.

Having the commanding height on moral issues legitimizes the state power. The Chinese government has been hypersensitive to open criticism. What in other societies would be considered normal criticism is therefore regarded as regime threatening in China. To maintain such legitimacy, the state has to be the sole moral authority and has, therefore, tried hard to reduce the moral authority of other political actors. This is one of the reasons why the Chinese government has been so nervous about the underground church or other religious organizations, for they possess not just organizational resources but also a moral appeal.

The communist regime under Mao could hardly be characterized as benevolent. Instead it featured an emphasis on class struggle and constant political campaigns that could be labeled anything but benevolent. The principle of the dictatorship of the proletariat is just the opposite of benevolence. However, the lack of benevolence was not devastating to regime legitimacy because the Party was able to create its own brand of justice and was successful in indoctrinating the majority of the population to accept its logic of governance. People actively participated in political campaigns that purged "enemies." During the reform era, when the regime gave up on the principle of dictatorship, the ideal of benevolence was raised again. Benevolence in contemporary terms is not qualitatively different from that in ancient times. Scholars, such as Kong Xiaoguang specifically, call for a "benevolent government."[64] Others have emphasized a principle of "minben [民本]"—people as the start and end points of governance. It starts with compassionate care for the people and proceeds with fairness in administration (legal punishment and taxation). While the communist regime today has not openly embraced the term of benevolence, social protests have reflected exactly what society wants of its government: benevolence. Contemporary large-scale peasant protests targeted the unfair and excessive levies imposed on the poor farmers by the local officials. Police brutality and city management corps rudeness are often the triggers of social riots.

With regard to state responsibility for the welfare of the people, the communist regime went even further by creating a huge state sector that provided most urbanites cradle-to-grave welfare coverage. This probably lent the most solid legitimacy to the regime. During the reform, the government tried to extract itself from the all-inclusive responsibility that had created serious social grievances. Even though the Chinese economy today has industrialized and agriculture represents only a small portion of gross domestic product (GDP), the culture of the state moral responsibility continues to be part of social expectations. Many Western analysts were surprised that all the popular polls in China had demonstrated high government support rates. They suspect that there was a fear factor in such polls. In fact, in China, this is not about people supporting the regime but about people having high expectations of the regime in providing for their livelihood. When people lost money on the stock market, they expected the state to help them out. When the owner of a foreign venture deserted the factory because of financial troubles, the workers expected the government to pick up the back wages. As Elizabeth Perry has summarized, "the idea that good governance rests upon guaranteeing the livelihood of ordinary people has been a hallmark of Chinese political philosophy and practice from Mencius to Mao—and beyond."[65]

During his fieldwork in a southern Chinese village, Hok Bun Ku noticed that the villagers repeatedly make references to the government *"zeren"* (responsibility). In the Chinese context, if a person owes any kind of responsibility to someone, then the two have a relationship. If people have a relationship, this implies that they must fulfill a responsibility to one another. Ku found that villagers often have extended and applied the principle of responsibility to define their relationship with the state. Villagers are willing to fulfill their responsibility if, and only if, the government does so too.[66]

It is apparent that this government responsibility for the well-being of the people is not based on competitive democratic elections. The point is, even though government officials are not elected by the people, they regard themselves as bearing responsibilities to the people. Similarly, *even though the people do not elect government officials, they believe that the government should be responsible to them.* This is the critical part in the hidden social contract, which is rooted in thousands of years of Chinese political tradition.

It should be noted that the contents and meaning of subsistence has changed over the long historical process. In an agricultural society, having enough to eat is the first and foremost concern. With the rapid economic growth since the 1980s, the meaning of subsistence has started to change. As a World Bank report indicated, China has successfully lifted 517 million of the population out of poverty.[67] As Cao Jinqing discovered in his fieldwork along the Yellow River, food is no longer a problem even in the least developed agricultural areas.[68] In today's China, subsistence has variously been conceived as affordable housing in the cities, education, health care and elderly support. As the idea of the moral economy is in a process of shifting to that of a moral society, the state responsibility remains the same.

Some people may ask what the difference is between state responsibility for the well-being of the society and performance-based legitimacy. Isn't the state responsibility for an economic welfare kind of state performance? If the state fails to take its responsibility, then it fails to deliver performance. To be sure, there are many overlaps between a performance-based legitimacy and a responsibility-based legitimacy. Yet, there are fundamental differences between the two in practical implications and philosophical roots.

Many believe that the legitimacy of the communist regime in China, especially after 1989, has been based on economic performance. The Chinese government receives popular support because of the welfare brought by rapid economic growth. This argument also leaves a strong implication that once the performance declines the legitimacy will disappear and the regime will be in trouble.⁶⁹ The thesis that the Chinese communist regime is desperate to sustain high economic growth to maintain legitimacy has been widely accepted as an analytical logic in the studies of Internet control or the energy scramble in Africa.

The responsibility-based legitimacy suggests that, contrary to such predictions, an economic crisis that produces rising unemployment, falling stock markets, or soaring prices will not lead to revolution or rebellion or any activities to overthrow the government. At the moment of crisis, people will depend even more on the state, and will expect the government to lead them out of the economic recession, control prices and intervene in the stock market to reverse the downturn. If the government collapsed, then the people would lose everything. If a country like the United States, which has been an adamant proponent of a free market economy, had to resort to government intervention in its 2008 economic crisis, it would be even more so in China, which has a long tradition of government dependency.

As long as the people have expectations of the government, the government will continue to enjoy legitimacy. While performance is part of how the responsibility can be evaluated, it is not the only indicator. As the famine governance indicated, the more severe the disaster, the bigger role the government is expected to play in dealing with it. Historical precedent suggests that only when the government repeatedly fails to address economic disasters, will rebellion break out.⁷⁰

From a philosophical perspective, responsibility indicates a moral commitment, whereas performance-based legitimacy is based on rational calculation. These are different conceptual categories. Moral commitment implies a bonding relationship and rational calculation implies partnership on the grounds of pure interest. We would rather incorporate performance—sometimes it could be a measure of responsibility—into moral commitment, than stretch performance to incorporate morality.

Multilevel responsibility structure

China has a unique administrative structure that entertains scholarly interests. On the one hand, China is a unitary system with the central government holding the utmost power over all the segments of the government. On the other hand, local governments enjoy a substantial amount of autonomy and control over their own economic development and resources. Some scholars view China's power structure as fragmented, segmented and stratified, which necessitates a policy process of negotiation, bargaining and seeking consensus among affected bureaucracies.⁷¹ Others see in China a decentralized authoritarianism in its vertical power structure.⁷² Some analyses even argue that China is "de facto federalism."⁷³

Cross-national indicators suggest that China is one of the most decentralized countries in the world, measured by the subnational share of total government revenue.⁷⁴ With power decentralization a part of the reform strategy,⁷⁵ local governments have gained more autonomy as well as more responsibility. They are responsible for the economic development and social stability of their localities. As a part of the "state," local governments act as part of the administrative apparatus, but they are distinct entities apart from the central state and society, with their own agendas, and increasingly with their own resources.[76]

While a multilevel power structure is a commonly used term to describe China's political structure, we would like to propose a different perspective—multilevel responsibility structure—to analyze the state responses to social protest. The difference is "responsibility" instead of "power." After all, China remains an authoritarian system. No matter how much financial autonomy the local governments have obtained, they have never gained crucial control over personnel appointment, which is retained by the center. Therefore the concept of a "divided power structure" or "multilevel power structure" is too vague to reflect the nature of the local autonomy. We need to analyze China's political institutional arrangement through the lens of responsibility, not power.

This multilevel responsibility structure has effectively enhanced the flexibility of the regime. The central government has shifted the responsibility to maintain social stability and minimize social protest to local governments. The local government therefore takes all the blame for policy mistakes and misconduct of the officials. The corruption or misbehavior of the local government officials is much more visible to the local people and government failure to guarantee the subsistence of the people has a direct impact on the local population. The legitimacy of local government is constantly on the line. Yet, even if local government lost legitimacy in the eyes of the population, few would extend that to the central government. The central government does not lose much legitimacy since the breaches of the hidden social contract only manifest at local levels. This structure also breaks through the dilemma that authoritarian regimes often face when dealing with social protests: concession would encourage more protests and repression would alienate the population. Repression, if any, will be carried out by the local government. As a result, the multilevel responsibility structure creates space for the central government to distance itself from local contentious politics.

We have observed a distinctive pattern in which people have the highest trust of the central government. Their trust of the government at local levels progressively comes down with each administrative level.[77] The old Chinese saying "the masses only oppose the corrupt officials but never the emperor [只反贪官，不反皇帝]" best exemplifies the state legitimacy in the multilevel power structure. In his household interviews in the villages, Xiaolin Guo found that villagers often distinguish between the "benign" central state and the "malign" local state. This bifurcated state in the eyes of the villagers is a result of the spatial distances between the villagers and local government, and between villagers and the central government. In this structural setting, Guo argues, the interaction between the villagers and the central state is symbolic and maintained at a moral level, whereas their relationship with the local government is social and economic.[78]

It should be noted that no matter how much autonomy the local government possesses, the Chinese political structure remains a cohesive system. The center has been able to hold all the autonomous parts from breaking loose.[79] The center's legitimacy would also compensate for local erosions. However, there is a chance that continuous erosions at the local level would eventually undercut the center. If the organizational atrophy outruns the Party's adaptive capacity,[80] the entire system may break down.

Interpreting social protest within the structure of responsibility-based legitimacy

Our analysis of the large-scale social protests in China will proceed within the state-society relations characterized by a responsibility-based legitimacy. As discussed earlier, this responsibility-based legitimacy has three layers: morality of the ruling elite, benevolent governance, and state responsibility for the welfare of the population. Legitimacy means that people accept the rule of the regime and expect the government to fulfill its part of the responsibilities. This structure shapes the nature and pattern of social protest in China.

The transitional pains we have observed are the symptoms of the structural displacement caused by socioeconomic transformation. Workers in SOEs are desperate when losing their jobs and welfare benefits during market reform. Workers in the newly developed nonstate sector, especially foreign-invested enterprises (FIEs), are fighting the private capital to improve their working conditions and wages. Farmers battle to maximize the value of their land in an irregular land market. All the social protests that arose from the transitional pains were shaped by the framework of regime legitimacy. The majority and foremost demands were asking the state to fulfill its responsibility for people's livelihood. This is why most of the protests, regardless of their target (be it private company or foreign business owner or just another village) were staged or ended up in front of the local government. This is because protesters view, and rightly so, the government as the ultimate solution. We would call those social protests that are driven by economic grievances "subsistence expectation protests." The political opportunity, mobilizational structure and framing of these protests are also consistent with this line of reasoning on both the state and society sides.

The transition from a planned economy to a market economy has bred widespread corruption. Corruption may not directly hurt any individual interest, but it is the most abhorred official behavior throughout history in China. Official corruption obviously violated the morality of the political officials as well as the ideal of a benevolent government. The accusations of official corruption always accompany the framing of various types of protests. The frustration over corruption may not trigger protest, but has been accumulating. When there is a minor incident, such as police or city management brutality, which apparently violates the idea of the benevolent government, accumulated frustration breaks out and often turns into a riot. Unlike the economic grievance-driven protests that demand government help, protests precipitated by social frustrations erupt to protest the immoral and corrupt government. We term this type of social protest "benevolence violation protest" for analytical consistency.

Anticorruption is not only the major framing in benevolence violation protests, but is also widely adopted in the framing of subsistence expectation protests. It serves as the major appeal to mobilize the participants of any type of social protest in China. As a side note, on the one hand people protest against the corrupt officials breaking the hidden contract that rulers have to set the moral example for the people, while on the other hand many people also believe that if the officials do not follow the moral standard, they do not have to behave morally either. This is the reason why we have observed a profound decline in public morality since the reforms began.

To be sure, there are plenty of overlaps of economic and social grievances. Sometimes corruption and misbehavior of the local government are the causes of economic grievances. Economic grievances may also play a role in social protest generated by social contempt. When we argue that inequality among social groups rarely instigates large-scale social protest, we do not mean that people are not frustrated. Inequality, especially when it is closely related to corruption, goes against people's sense of justice and morality. Cumulative frustration usually plays a role in benevolence violation protests.

Internet protests are a different type of contentious politics. Modern technology has provided a new platform for people to voice their concerns. As the participants are so diffused geographically, the appeals of protest have to be general enough to mobilize sympathy and passion. In the majority of cases, injustice and corruption are the most appealing themes to mobilize Internet protests. Such protests are often ignited by individual cases that involve official injustice or corruption. The Internet protest can generate great public opinion pressure on the government to adjust its policies or discipline the officials involved. The fact that the Chinese government has been so sensitive to public opinion pressure, much more so than any other government, also reflects the responsibility-based legitimacy relations.

As the official response to Internet protests has indicated, the government response to social protest is constrained by the legitimacy framework. Legitimacy is a two-way street. The Chinese political system is undemocratic but it does not mean that the regime would repress social protests most of the time. Contrary to common perception, the communist regime tolerated most protests. If the issues are "subsistence" related, the government accommodates—that is, makes necessary compensation. If the protests are triggered by official corruption or misbehavior, the government removes or disciplines the officials. Only when the protests start to get violent and target property and human lives does the government use forceful means to maintain social stability. The multilevel administrative structure has also helped the central government to diffuse the challenge to regime legitimacy.

In the following analysis of this book, we will discuss those protests that are driven by economic grievance and with the expectation that the state will respond to their demands. Then we will discuss the protests driven by frustrations that were triggered by minor incidents and later turned into riots or disturbances. This type of protest can usually be explained by the violation of benevolence on the part of local government. We will also discuss the Internet-based protests that are morally motivated and target government behavior and corruption. Finally, we will discuss the government response to social protests, which is also shaped by the multilevel responsibility structure and the particular legitimacy framework.

Notes

1 Doug McAdam, John McCarthy and Mayer Zald (eds), *Comparative Perspectives on Social Movements: Political Opportunities, Mobilizing Structure, and Cultural Framings* (Cambridge: Cambridge University Press, 1996); and Sidney Tarrow, *Power in Movement* (Cambridge: Cambridge University Press, 1998, 2nd edn).
2 Charles Tilly and Sidney Tarrow, *Contentious Politics* (Paradigm Publishers, 2006), chapter 3.
3 Tarrow, *Power in Movement*, ibid., chapter 6.
4 Gries and Rosen (2004) had a good review of such approach. See Peter Gries and Stanley Rosen (eds), *State and Society in 21st-Century China* (RoutledgeCurzon, 2004), 1–23.
5 Jack Goldstone and Charles Tilly, "Threat (and Opportunity): Popular Action and State Response in the Dynamics of Contentious Action," in Ronald R. Aminzade et al. (eds) *Silence and Voice in the Study of Contentious Politics* (New York: Cambridge University Press, 2001), 179–94.
6 Joel Migdal, Atul Kohli and Vivienne Shue, *State Power and Social Forces: Domination and Transformation in the Third World* (New York: Cambridge University Press, 1994).
7 There is a long list of scholarly works on the different alliances between different actors in the state and society, which produce different political outcomes (e.g. O'Donnell and Schmitter 1986; and Przeworski 1991).
8 e.g. Theda Skocpol, *States and Social Revolutions: A Comparative Analysis of France, Russia and China* (Cambridge University Press, 1979); Yanqi Tong, *Transition from State Socialism: Economic and Political Change in Hungary and China* (Rowman & Littlefield, 1997); and Gries and Rosen, *State and Society in 21st-Century China*, ibid.
9 e.g. Robert Putnam, *Making Democracy Work* (New Jersey: Princeton University Press, 1993).
10 Zheng Yongnian, *Technological Empowerment: The Internet, State, and Society in China* (Stanford: Stanford University Press, 2008).
11 Zhao also listed territorial defense as the third dimension but argued that without a pending threat from other countries, the economic performance and moral conduct therefore become the most important dimensions of legitimacy. See Dingxin Zhao, *The Power of Tiananmen: State-society Relations and the 1989 Beijing Student Movement* (Chicago: University of Chicago Press, 2000), chapter 7.
12 For example, Daniel Lerner, *The Passing of Traditional Society* (New York: The Free Press, 1958).
13 For example, Guillermo O'Donnell and Philoppe C. Schmitter, *Transitions from Authoritarian Rule* (Baltimore: Johns Hopkins University Press, 1986); Stephan Hagaad and Robert Kaufman, *The Political Economy of Democratic Transition*

(Princeton, NJ: Princeton University Press, 1995); and S. Levitsky and L. Way, "The Rise of Competitive Authoritarianism," *Journal of Democracy* Vol. 13, No. 2 (April 2002): 51–65.
14 Adam Przeworski, *Democracy and the Market* (Cambridge, 1991).
15 For example, Yanqi Tong, *Transitions from State Socialism*, ibid.; Jan Prybyla, "China's Economic Experiment: Back from the Market?" *Problems of Communism* No. 38 (January–February 1989); and Barry Naughton, *Growing Out of the Plan: Chinese Economic Reform, 1978–1993* (New York: Cambridge University Press, 1995).
16 Kenneth Lieberthal, *Governing China: From Revolution Through Reform* (NY: W.W. Norton & Company, Inc, 1995), 167–68.
17 Jan-Erik Lane, *Comparative Politics: The Principal-agent Perspective* (London: Routledge, 2008), 23.
18 Xiaobo Lu and Elizabeth Perry, *Danwei: The Changing Chinese Workplace in Historical and Comparative Perspective* (NY: M.E. Sharpe, 1997), 9.
19 David Strand, "Protest in Beijing: Civil Society and Public Sphere in China," *Problems of Communism* (1990): 1–19.
20 Xiaobo Lu and Elizabeth Perry, *Danwei: The Changing Chinese Workplace in Historical and Comparative Perspective*, ibid., 8.
21 Vivienne Shue, *The Reach of the State: Sketches of the Chinese Body Politic* (Stanford, Calif.: Stanford University Press, 1988), 127.
22 Shue, *The Reach of the State*, ibid.
23 See, for example, Carol Ann Drogus and Stephen Orvis, *Introducing Comparative Politics* (CQ Press, 2012), 42. Mao is often cited as such a charismatic figure, though in fact his personal charisma was hardly felt by the public in China.
24 Max Weber, "Legitimacy, Politics and the State," in William Connolly (eds) *Legitimacy and the State* (Oxford: Basil Blackwell, 1984).
25 Seymour Martin Lipset, *Political Man: The Social Bases of Politics* (Johns Hopkins University Press, 1981), 70.
26 Stephen White, "Economic Performance and Communist Legitimacy," *World Politics* (1986): 462–82.
27 Richard Lowenthal, "The Ruling Party in a Mature Society," in Mark Field (ed.) *Social Consequences of Modernization in Communist Societies* (The Johns Hopkins University Press, 1976), 81–118.
28 Stephen White, "Economic Performance and Communist Legitimacy," ibid.
29 Dingxin Zhao, *The Power of Tiananmen*, ibid., 23.
30 Chuxuan Zheng, *A Comparison between Western and Chinese Political Ideas: The Difference and Complementarity of the Liberal-Democratic and Moral-Despotic Traditions* (Mellen University Press, 1995), 338–40.
31 Ho Ping-ti, *The Ladder of Success in Imperial China: Aspects of Social Mobility, 1368–1911* (Columbia University Press, 1962).
32 今君身不能自治，而望治百姓，是犹曲表而求直影也（《周书》卷二十三，《列传》第十五）
33 John Fairbank and Edwin Reischauer (eds), *China: Tradition and Transformation* (George Allen & Unwin, 1979), 44.
34 梁治平 [Liang Zhiping], 法辨：中国法的过去，现在与未来 [Explicating Law: The Past, Present, and Future of Law in China] (贵州人民出版社, 1992), 116.
35 Lucian Pye, *Asian Power and Politics: The Cultural Dimensions of Authority* (Boston: Harvard University Press, 1985), 23.
36 John Fairbank, *The United States and China* (Harvard University Press, 1983, 4th edn), 100–5.
37 Ibid., 57.
38 The original Chinese quote is "王侯将相宁有种乎." It was a quote from Chen Sheng, the leader of the peasant rebellion that initiated the downfall of the Qin Dynasty in 209 BC.

39 For example, see 陈鼓应 [Chen Guying], *韩非子今注今释*, 中华书局, 1984.
40 瞿同祖 [Qu Tongzu], *中国法律与中国社会* [Chinese Law and Chinese Society] (中华书局 [Chinese Book Bureau], 1981). First of all, no Confucian scholars deny the importance of a legal order. In fact, all the Confucian officials had to be expert in the legal codes of their times, as they served as judges in Chinese courts. Moreover, important Confucian moral prescriptions, such as filial piety, had been incorporated into legal codes.
41 Fairbank and Reischauer, *China: Tradition and Transformation*, ibid., 46–47.
42 Pye, *Asian Power and Politics*, ibid., 63–64.
43 游伟[You Wei], "刑法修改需要更多民意参与," [Revision of Criminal Law Needs More Popular Participation] 人民法院报, , *People's Court News*, November 30, 2010.
44 Chuxuan Zheng, *A Comparison between Western and Chinese Political Ideas*, ibid., 348.
45 古之为政，爱民为大。（《礼记·哀公问政》）
46 为政以德，譬如北辰，居其所而众星拱之。（《论语·为政》）
47 Xuezhi Guo, *The Ideal Chinese Political Leader: A Historical and Cultural Perspective* (Praeger, 2002).
48 The Chinese originals are "敦教化," "从地利," "擢贤良," "恤狱讼," "均徭役."（《周书》卷二十三，《列传》第十五）
49 Chuxuan Zheng, *A Comparison between Western and Chinese Political Ideas*, ibid., 349.
50 李泽厚 [Li Zehou], *中国古代思想史论* [Essays on Classical Chinese Philosophy] (北京：人民出版社, 1986).
51 夫平均者，不舍豪强而征贫弱，不纵奸巧而困愚拙。（《周书》卷二十三，《列传》第十五）
52 一夫呼嗟，王道为之倾覆。（同上）
53 James Scott, *The Moral Economy of the Peasant: Rebellion and Subsistence in Southeast Asia* (Yale University Press, 1976).
54 Ibid., 92–94.
55 Ibid., 181.
56 邓云特 [Deng Yunte], *中国救荒史* [History of Disaster Relief in China] (北京出版社, [Beijing: Beijing Press, 1998]).
57 National Bureau of Statistics and Ministry of Civil Affairs, *Report of the Damage Caused by Disaster in China 1949–1995* (China Statistics Press, 1995).
58 According to one calculation based on purchasing power parity, 1 tael of silver in the Qing Dynasty equals to ¥200, ks.cn.yahoo.com/question/1307021311733.html (accessed November 11, 2009).
59 R. Bin Wong, *China Transformed: Historical Change and Limits of European Experience* (Ithaca: Cornel University Press, 1997), 98.
60 The term "parental officials" (父母官) referred to government officials, the usage of which goes back to as early as the Han Dynasty. This term was replaced by "people's servant" during Mao's era and quietly resurfaced after 1978.
61 Pye, *Asian Power and Politics*, ibid., 66.
62 Zheng Yongnian, *The Chinese Communist Party as Organizational Emperor: Culture, Reproduction and Transformation* (Routledge, 2010).
63 e.g. Yanqi Tong, *Transition from State Socialism*, ibid.
64 康晓光 [Kang Xiaoguang], *仁政：中国政治发展的第三条道路* [Benevolence: The Third Way of Chinese Political Development] (Singapore: Bafang Wenhua Press, 2008).
65 Elizabeth Perry, "Chinese Conceptions of 'Rights': From Mencius to Mao-and Now," *Perspective on Politics* Vol. 6, No. 1 (2008): 39.
66 Hok Bun Ku, *Moral Politics in a South Chinese Village: Responsibility, Reciprocity, and Resistance* (Roman & Littlefield, 2003).

67 世界银行东亚及太平洋地区扶贫与经济管理局 [World Bank Bureau of East Asian and Pacific Region Poverty Relief and Economic Management], 《从贫困地区到贫困人群：中国扶贫议程的演进—中国贫困和不平等问题评估》 [From Poor Areas to Poor Population: The Evolution of China's Poverty Relief Agenda—An Assessment of Poverty and Inequality in China] (2009 年3 月，第iii页 [March 2009, iii]).
68 Cao Jinqing, 黄河边上的中国 [China by the Yellow River] (Shanghai Wenyi Press, 2000).
69 Gordon Chang, *The Coming Collapse of China* (Random House, 2001); and Joe Studwell, *The China Dream: The Quest for the Last Great Untapped Market on Earth* (Grove Press, 2003).
70 顾诚 [Gu Cheng], 《明末农民战争史》 [History of Peasant Wars in the End of Ming Dynasty], 光明日报出版社, *Guangming Daily Press*, 2012.
71 Kenneth Lieberthal and David Lampton (eds), *Bureaucracy, Politics, and Decision Making in Post-Mao China* (Berkeley: University of California Press, 1992).
72 Elizabeth Perry, "Crime, Corruption, and Contention," in Merle Goldman and Roderick MacFarquhar (eds) *The Paradox of China's Post-Mao Reforms* (Cambridge: Harvard University Press, 1999); Jorge Martinez-Vazquez, "China's Long March to Decentralization," in Paul Smoke *et al.* (eds) *Decentralization in Asia and Latin America* (UK: Edward Elgar, 2006), 88–135; and Pierre Landry, *Decentralized Authoritarianism in China: The Communist Party's Control of Local Elites in the Post-Mao Era* (Cambridge University Press, 2008).
73 Gabriella Montinola, Yingyi Qian and Barry Weingast, "Federalism, Chinese Style: The Political Basis for Economic Success," *World Politics* Vol. 48, No. 1 (1996): 50–81; and Zheng Yongnian, *De Facto Federalism in China: Reforms and Dynamics of Central-Local Relations* (Singapore and London: World Scientific Publishing, 2007).
74 Pierre Landry, *Decentralized Authoritarianism in China*, ibid., 3.
75 Susan Shirk, *The Political Logic of Economic Reform in China* (Berkeley: University of California Press, 1993).
76 Jean Oi, *Rural China Takes Off: Institutional Foundations of Economic Reform* (Berkeley: University of California Press, 1999), 9.
77 Pierre Landry, "Does the Communist Party Help Strengthen China's Legal Reforms?" *The China Review* Vol. 9, No. 1 (Spring, 2009): 45–72; and Wenfang Tang, "Life Dissatisfaction and Regime Change in China," paper presented at the American Political Science Association Annual Meeting, Toronto, Canada, September 3–6, 2009.
78 Xiaolin Guo, "Land Expropriation and Rural Conflicts in China," *China Quarterly* No. 166 (June 2001): 422–39; and Kevin O'Brien and Li Lianjiang, *Rightful Resistance in Rural China* (NY: Cambridge University Press, 2006), 109.
79 Pierre Landry, *Decentralized Authoritarianism in China*, ibid., 202.
80 David Shambaugh (ed.), *Is China Unstable?: Assessing the Factors* (NY: M.E. Sharpe, 2008).

3 An overview of large-scale social protests

This chapter provides an overview of the large-scale social protests in China from 2003 through 2010. Specifically, we will present the general patterns, such as the frequency, nature and geographical distribution, of the social protests. Moreover, we will also discuss the causes, features and implications of different types of these events and the changing trend of social protests over time. It is our hope that the presentation will depict the contour of the forests of social protests in China.

Definition and data

The Chinese government has created the term "mass incident" for social protests. This term is adopted in all relevant documents and records. While the term "mass incident" first appeared in official documents in the 1990s, there has not been a complete official definition of the term. Summarizing several similar definitions provided by scholars, we hold in this book that a mass incident, that is social protest, generally refers to any of the following activities that involve more than 10 participants: 1 collective petition visit to upper-level government offices and sit-ins; 2 illegal assemblies, parades and demonstrations; 3 strikes (labor, merchant, student, teacher and so on); 4 traffic blocking; 5 disturbances; 6 surrounding or attacking Party/government buildings; 7 smashing, looting and burning; and 8 obstructing the performance of government administration. In many cases, mass incident and social protest are interchangeable terms. Mass incident may have a broader connotation. For example, it would include soccer fans rioting and clan feuds, since they are considered a disruption of public order, which would hardly be counted as social protest.

The sources of our data come from the following channels: media reports (both Chinese and international); personal blogs from activists; internet public discussion forums; reports from various nongovernmental organizations (NGOs) (for example, China Labor bulletin, a Hong Kong-based NGO); and personal field work. We have also collaborated and confirmed our list of large-scale social protests with the Institute of Labor and Criminal Reformation of the Ministry of Justice, the Fourth Institute of the Ministry of

48 *An overview of large-scale social protests*

Public Security, and the Center for Chinese and Global Affairs at Peking University.

Descriptions of protests are from our personal fieldwork, personal interviews with reporters covering the incidents, and Internet sources. We are well aware of the reliability issue of the Internet sources. In general, we tried to avoid web sources with obvious biases, such as those from Falun Gong. As for Internet personal accounts of the incident, we would look at as many accounts as possible to dissect common facts. It is impossible to verify the authenticity of these personal accounts. However, we believe our accounts of the individual incidents are close to what happened in reality.

For the convenience of analysis, we count the recurring social protests over a single issue in one location as one incident, such as the land dispute in Dongzhou Village of Shanwei County, Guangdong Province, even though it had several outbursts. We will also count the social protests triggered by a single issue but spread simultaneously across multiple counties as one incident, such as the taxation protest incidents in Henan and Anhui Provinces.

As discussed earlier, in Chapter 1, a large-scale social protest refers to the gathering of more than 500 participants in a protesting event. We adopt this demarcation line according to the official criteria set by the Ministry of Public Security.[1] The determination of the number of the participants is difficult. Sometimes it is hard to distinguish onlookers from participants. However, this is particularly true only in disturbances when onlookers easily turn into rioters once they identify with the other protesters during the process. On other occasions when specific economic demands are raised, random onlookers are less likely to participate. As a rule of thumb, we would only count those events that have confirmed numbers above five hundred and exclude vague accounts such as "a couple of hundred" or "several hundred."

All together we have recorded 548 large-scale social protests from 2003 to 2010. Given the secrecy of these kinds of data from official sources, we do not claim this is a complete list of large-scale social protest during this period. However, we are confident that this is the most inclusive list so far. The following sections present the general patterns we have observed from these cases.

Frequency

Figure 3.1 presents the frequencies of the 548 cases of large-scale social protest over the years. In general, the numbers are steadily on the rise. We can observe that from 2003 to 2005, the number of large-scale social protests was relatively limited. Then there was a considerable upsurge of large-scale social protests in the years 2007 and 2008, jumping from 39 cases in 2005 to 55 in 2006, 101 in 2007 and to 97 in 2008. After a slight downturn in 2009, large-scale social protests reached a new height in 2010, when 117 occurrences were recorded.

The statistical analysis also supports the visual observation. It shows that the number of cases increases significantly with time ($r^2 = 0.83$; $p = 0.0017$),

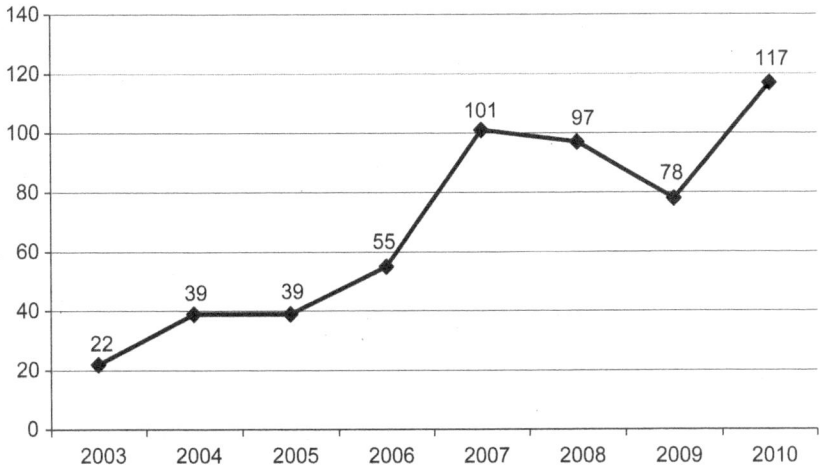

Figure 3.1 Frequencies of large-scale social protest by year, 2003–10

at a rate of, on average, 12.9 events per year nationwide. How do we interpret the rising trend of large-scale social protest in China in recent years? Surging social protests mirror two interrelated processes in China. First, this is an index of transitional pains. These protests reflect mounting social discontent and rising tensions between citizens and the authorities during the epochal social and economic transformation of China.

Second, this is a process during which both the societal forces and the regime are searching to strike a balance. The increasing numbers of large-scale social protest do not necessarily mean that Chinese society is experiencing increasing pain. It could mean that people are more willing to and capable of launching protests to pursue their interests. On the one hand protest organizers have learned not to challenge the bottom line of the authorities to provoke repression. Moreover, successful protest in one factory would encourage similar activities in neighboring factories, as occurred in the factory clusters of the Pearl River Delta areas. On the other hand the governments have learned to live with these social protests. They have tolerated most of the social protests and in some cases addressed the grievances. The less the state inclination to repress, the more political opportunities there are for social groups to launch protests. This is a process in which social protests are becoming an institutionalized fixture between the state and society.

Types

A better understanding of the trend of the large-scale social protest cannot be reached without identifying specific types of such incidents. To identify the specific social grievances and tension, we break down the social protests by

50 *An overview of large-scale social protests*

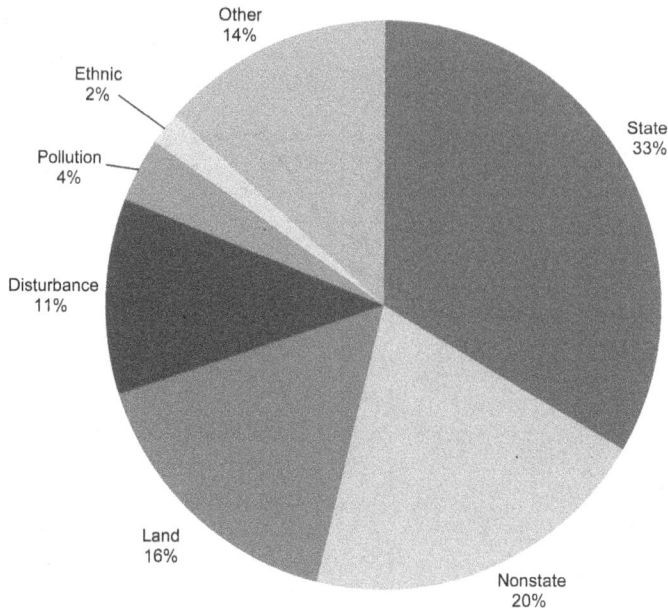

Figure 3.2 Frequency of large-scale social protests by type, 2003–10

their type. We categorize social protests primarily according to the nature of the conflict and their claims, such as labor and land disputes. Among various types of social protest, we have identified four major types that have the most frequent occurrence as well as some less frequent ones. The four most frequent types of social protests are labor protests in the state sector, labor protests in the nonstate sector, land-related protests, and disturbances. Figure 3.2 is a distribution chart of the types of large-scale social protest from 2003 to 2010.

As Figure 3.2 indicated, protests originating in the state sector are the most frequent, accounting for 33 percent of the total cases. Labor protests in the nonstate sector take about 20 percent. Land-related protests and disturbances represent 16 and 11 percent of the total incidents, respectively. Altogether, the four major types of large-scale social protest constitute 80 percent of the total. Antipollution protests represent the largest group outside of the four major types of social protest, with 4 percent. The number of ethnic conflicts is relatively small at only 2 percent. However, these conflicts tend to be the most violent of all and recorded the largest number of casualties. We will briefly discuss each type of social protest in the ensuing sections.

Labor protests in the state sector

The structural changes of the state sector generated the most displacement and most pain. The majority of the protests were caused by the privatization

Table 3.1 Large-scale social protest within the state sector by type, 2003–10

	2003	2004	2005	2006	2007	2008	2009	2010	Total
SOE	13	16	9	9	25	13	14	18	117
Taxi	2	4	2	5	3	12	3	3	34
Veteran	1	0	1	0	2	1	1	1	7
Teacher	1	0	0	1	3	5	5	6	21
Bank	0	0	0	0	1	1	1	1	4
Total	17	20	12	15	34	32	24	29	183

schemes for the state-owned enterprises (SOEs). Such pain could be observed all over the state sector, resulting in labor protests that constitute 33 percent of the total large-scale social protests (183 out of 548). Table 3.1 gives a further classification of this type of protest. Among the 183 incidents, 117 were from the state-owned enterprises, 34 were protests by taxi drivers, seven were veteran protests, 21 were teachers' protests and four were bank employees' protests.

The main cause of labor protests in SOEs (here we mainly refer to the enterprises in the manufacturing sector) was the privatization schemes that led to disputes over unemployment compensation and lost pensions. SOE workers tend to have a strong sense of entitlement and the deprivation of such entitlement generated a furious reaction. Moreover, the high concentration of SOE workers facilitates the mobilization of protests.

The reason that we treated taxi drivers' protests as a separate group is that while taxi companies are all state owned, taxi drivers sign a contract with the company as individuals. Unlike workers in the manufacturing sector, taxi drivers work on an individual basis. They are subject to market competition as individuals and have to bear the consequences individually. Their major complaints are very different from those in the SOEs, but somewhat similar to those in nonstate sectors. They protested against the lack of regulations in the taxi market and the unfair competition by the unlicensed private taxis.

Demobilized ex-military officers once were a privileged social group who would be assigned to important positions in government institutions or SOEs during the Mao and early Deng eras. With the effort to downsize the military personnel since the mid-1980s, a large amount of the ex-servicemen, especially those with lower levels of education, were transferred to civilian work. However, in the meantime, the ongoing market reforms give enterprises no incentive to offer valuable positions to these unskilled personnel. Even if some enterprises agreed to take them, they were not treated well. Frustrated by the lack of respect and lack of decent jobs and decent pay, veteran groups organized several protests.

The teachers' protests originated in a different problem. During the Cultural Revolution, the teaching profession was not well respected or desired. In order to fill the need for teachers, schools hired a large amount of uncertified teachers who are not on the official payroll. As perceptions of teaching gradually changed during the reform era, teaching again become a desirable profession. More and more graduates from normal colleges are competing for jobs with those who were recruited during the low days. Apparently, the more educated win out in this battle. Even though some of those without a certificate manage to retain their jobs, they get minimum salary rises. These teachers have a legitimate complaint that they have worked hard for so many years, yet were dumped quickly once they were no longer needed.

The bank employees' protests are an interesting case. All the banks are state owned. In order to streamline the banking institutions, the Industrial and Commercial Bank of China (ICBC), the largest bank in China, bought off the employment of some of their employees. In the beginning, those employees agreed to the terms of buying them off, which were relatively good at the time. However, with the continued economic boom, ICBC (and all the banks for that matter) has become the richest employer in China, and its employees have received ludicrous bonus and welfare payments. Those who were bought off felt cheated and demanded more compensation. Each year they would gather in front of the ICBC headquarters in Beijing and protest.

From various kinds of protests within the state sector, we can see that the old-fashioned state sector that carried huge welfare burdens is dying out. The dying pains have caused frequent large-scale social protests, which exemplified the struggle of the losers in the SOE reforms to defend their interests. As the SOE reforms have been nearly completed in recent years, the number of protests seems to have leveled off. It is likely that the number of protests will decline rather than increase in the future.

Labor protests in nonstate sectors

This category refers to the protests that occurred in foreign or private ventures, which are primarily caused by capital-labor disputes. While the targets of the protests are the management or the owner of the enterprise, local governments tend to be involved either as mediator or enforcer. In general, no final conclusion would be reached without the intervention of the government. We have recorded 112 large-scale protests from 2003 to 2010.

Labor disputes that occurred in the nonstate sector are different in nature from those in the state sector. The SOEs are the legacy of the era of the planned economy, while private or foreign ventures are the new entities in the reform era. While SOEs have been facing the transformation from old forms to new ones, the nonstate sector has experienced the processes of consolidation, expansion and regulation. The social pains generated by the nonstate sector are growing pains, in comparison with the dying pains that are associated with SOE reforms. With loose government regulations and the absence of genuine labor unions, workers in private enterprises usually enjoy few benefits and suffer worse working conditions than SOE employees. In most disputes, workers are requesting better working conditions or wage payment for extra shifts. Large-scale social protests in this category started to surge in 2007 and 2008, but dropped dramatically from 26 in 2008 to 10 in 2009, and then recorded a dramatic increase in 2010 to 44.

Discussing labor unrest in the nonstate sector, we need to take a look at the labor composition. The sources of the labor force in the nonstate sector are mainly from rural areas. There are two types of migrant workers. One type is what we call peasant-migrant workers (农民工). They are the first generation of the surplus rural laborers who sought job opportunities in industry. These are workers on a temporary basis with labor contractors. They undertake the dirtiest and heaviest jobs in the cities. We do not observe any large-scale protest from this group, except for some activities to demand back wages.

The lack of protest from this group may be attributed to several factors. First, only those who have a job are qualified to be categorized as migrant workers. By definition, they do not have an unemployment problem, which is the primary cause for labor protest in SOEs. Those who lost their job would go back to the farm field. Second, coming from rural villages that never had social welfare programs, peasant-migrant workers do not have a strong sense of welfare entitlement and would not protest to demand such entitlement. Third, peasant-migrant workers usually work on a temporary contractual basis and lack organizational resources. Therefore, we do not observe many large-scale social protests organized by peasant-migrant workers, but this does not mean that they would be more tolerant of labor abuses. According to some research, migrant workers are more willing to take their disputes to court than other social groups.[2]

The other type is those who work in foreign/private enterprises in coastal areas. They are the second generation of a rural labor force. They are better educated than the first generation and do not know how to do farm work. They have signed labor contracts with regular jobs. With the easy access to electronic media and digital networks, they are fully aware of their legal rights and have the means to organize protests. They do not have a strong sense of entitlement, but a better sense of contractual rights. Their claims are less morally based than contractually based.

Land-related protests

In this group we have included all the protests that are related to land disputes. High economic growth has led to rapid expansion of land requisition for industrial or commercial uses. In suburban areas, protests tend to occur over compensation for land requisition. In urban areas, fights often break out over the relocation of original residents. Sometimes, when the industrial project is huge, such as dam building or mining, large-scale peasant relocation is also involved. The disputed issues were mostly about compensation for requisitioned land and relocation, which was often considered unfair by the affected population. As Table 3.2 indicates, land protests have been on the rise over the years.

Table 3.2 Land-related protests, 2003–10

	2003	2004	2005	2006	2007	2008	2009	2010	Total
Land	2	3	6	10	18	7	5	13	64
Relocation	0	1	1	0	1	2	1	9	15
Corruption	0	0	0	3	1	0	0	0	4
Business	0	0	0	2	1	0	2	0	5
Total	2	4	7	15	21	9	8	22	88

Despite the impression generated by the media that large-scale social protests over land disputes were widespread, such incidents occurred much less frequently than labor protests. This is because land requisition is necessary only in rapidly developing areas or places where there are mining discoveries. Furthermore, as the peasants are usually not well organized due to their mode of production, they are unable to organize effective protests even if they are deprived. However, protests over land disputes, if organized, could be fierce.

If the land requisition is for the purpose of large state infrastructure projects, such as a highway, dam, or high-speed rail, it is usually nonnegotiable. If it is related to local industrial or commercial projects, then the farmers are more likely to fight to maximize their economic gains. With the hike in land prices due to increased demand, any price tag would look ridiculously low in a couple of years' time. In some cases the peasants accepted the land price, but later found that the value had gone up and demanded recompense.

There are two types of land dispute. One is between farmers and the local government that purchased the land use right for local projects (for example, an office building). Sometimes there are accusations of corruption for official embezzlement of the compensation. The other is between farmers and local business companies that use the land. Within this latter category, there are usually two scenarios. In the first scenario, the companies involved in the land use had strong government backing, because the related industrial projects oftentimes are part of the official development plan. In order to push for their development plan, local governments were inclined to use force on behalf of the companies. As a result, land disputes often turned into confrontations between the peasants and the government.

The other scenario has less government involvement. It is completely between peasants and private business. For example, a private mining company agreed to pay peasants a certain amount of dividend as a form of compensation for the land taken, but later refused to pay the promised amount. Such disputes usually need government involvement to settle.

Relocation in urban areas has triggered many disputes. There have been many cases of the so-called "nail households" that refuse to move out. In an extreme case, a woman set herself on fire in protest against the forced relocation.[3]

However, since those who refuse to be relocated are mostly individual households, the conflicts tend to be isolated, small-scale events, and hardly generate large-scale collective action.

Disturbances and riots

A disturbance refers to social protests in which the majority of participants do not have a particular demand or direct interest, but simply want to disturb the public order. A riot is the more radical form of disturbance in which gathering crowds commit acts of violence. These incidents are triggered either by police (or city management) brutality during the policy enforcement process, or perceived injustice over an unnatural death, or brutal enforcement of the family planning policy. We did not include in this category some of the violent land protests or relocation disputes for analytical purposes. First, we want to avoid double listing, and second, violent land disputes are still land disputes. The same reasoning applies to some of the ethnic conflicts listed below. We also exclude all the soccer fan riots and clan feuds from this group. Strictly speaking, soccer fan riots, as the label implies, qualify as disturbance. However, they do not have the political implications of other disturbances. We include them in the "other" category.

During the period 2003–10, we counted 61 large-scale mass disturbances. Although occurrences of this kind of incident are not in large numbers, disturbances/riots have steadily grown over the years and became one of the most frequent type of large-scale social protest in 2009, with 17 cases. The number of disturbances dropped to 8 in 2010. These disturbances were often triggered by minor incidents, but rapidly became confrontational between citizens and government.

Compared to social protests triggered by specific economic grievances, the eruption of social disturbances and riots that are not economic interest oriented is alarming. They reflect profound social grievances and distrust of government. Yu Jianrong, a well-known China-based scholar of social protest whose work on the subject has been widely circulated on the Internet in China, issued a warning early in 2010. Yu describes the emergence of a new type of social unrest in recent years, which he calls "venting incidents": brief, unorganized outbursts of public rage against the authorities or the wealthy.[4] Sociologist Sun Liping also highlighted the danger of "social decay," one feature of which is the loss of identity and social cohesiveness.[5] A deeply decadent society easily generates disturbance and riot. One of the major triggers of disturbance is the poor quality of local governance. Government incompetence, official corruption and brutality in regulation enforcement are the common causes of large-scale disturbances.

In 2009, the outbreak of disturbances reached 17. The government has worked very hard to prevent disturbances from breaking out. Strict responsibility systems were established for holding government officials accountable for any such occurrence. The central government also holds regular workshops for local officials on how to respond to unexpected emergencies. As a result, the number of disturbances fell to 8 in 2010.

Antipollution protest

Antipollution protest is a category that has the largest number outside of the four major types of social protest, with 20 incidents during the period of 2003–10. Pollution is an unavoidable side effect of industrialization and awareness of environmental harm is on the rise in China. People rarely take collective action over ecological issues such as global warming or the protection of extinct species, but they are firm on the perceived harm to their health.

Most of the labor or land protests were launched by disadvantaged social groups, such as laid-off workers and peasants. They were fighting for their right to subsistence. Yet the antipollution protests were mainly participated in by the new middle class in the cities. These protests reflect certain postmodern values of citizens. Environmental awareness usually emerges when a society has reached a high stage of economic development.[6] The new middle class are the beneficiaries of the economic boom in China. Therefore, their concerns are primarily about the quality of life. Unlike the protests against pollution that directly threatened the survival of an affected population, the protests in Shanghai and Xiamen are against the potential future threat, reflecting the educational and knowledge level of the urban middle class. These types of protests are rare, but have demonstrated different features of social protests in China: thousands of people were mainly mobilized by cell phone or Internet messages and the protests were peaceful in style.

Ethnic conflict

The last specific type of large-scale social protest we will discuss are the protests with a distinctive ethnic nature or the conflicts among different ethnic groups. Strictly speaking, ethnic conflicts are a specific kind of disturbance. They involve a large crowd of people venting out their resentment in a violent manner, most of the time against other ethnic groups, and sometimes against the government. There were only 10 large-scale ethnic conflicts during this period (2003–10). However, once erupted, six of these seven ethnic conflicts were characterized by violence, expanding quickly to fierce fighting among huge crowds. There is no indication of increase or decrease of such conflicts. They seem to be a constant feature of Chinese multiethnic society.

There are mainly two types of ethnic conflict. One is a random type, which is often ignited by a minor incident that turned into a large-scale disturbance. Because of the rigidity of ethnic identity lines, it is easier to generate the "us" versus "them" sentiment among different ethnic groups. It is similar to a disturbance of public venting but along ethnic lines.

The other type of ethnic conflict is much more comprehensive, organized and involves political agendas. The incidents in Lhasa in March 2008 and in

Urumqi in July 2009 belong to this category. Both had an international background and explicit or implicit separatist agendas. The government employed armed forces to suppress these two ethnic riots.

Ethnic conflicts are usually not caused by economic grievances, as economic grievances cut across ethnic lines. Ethnic differences are the most difficult to reconcile and are, therefore, the most persistent cause of social friction and the most effective means of political mobilization. Achieving and managing harmonious ethnic relations in China will be a tough challenge for the communist regime in the years to come.

Other conflicts

Finally, we lump the rest of the large-scale mass protests into the "other" category. Heavy tax burdens used to be a serious problem in the rural areas and we have recorded several taxation protests. However, such protests disappeared following the abolition of agricultural taxes in 2006. Then there were nationalist demonstrations against Japan. While the majority of the participants are students, we distinguished these nationalist demonstrations from other student protests that primarily were against school administration (disputes over diploma, dorm conditions and so on). Some of the incidents may not qualify as social protests, such as soccer fans rioting after their team lost a game or a feud between clans. We included these incidents in our record because these events disrupted public order on a large scale and the Public Security Agencies define them as mass incidents. Table 3.3 gives a detailed classification of these other protests.

Trend over time

Our data set of 2003–10 allows us to observe change over eight years. Table 3.4 and Figure 3.3 give more detailed information about how the frequency of all types of protest (including some other minor types of large-scale social

Table 3.3 Major types of protest in the "other" category

	2004	2005	2006	2007	2008	2009	2010	Total
Anti-pollution	0	3	1	4	5	5	2	20
Ethnic	1	0	0	1	2	3	3	10
Student	0	1	4	8	2	2	0	17
Anti-taxation	4	0	0	0	0	0	0	4
Anti-corruption	1	1	0	0	0	1	0	3
Anti-Japanese	0	1	0	0	0	0	2	3
Anti-illegal fundraising	0	1	0	2	3	0	1	7
Soccer fan disturbance	0	1	1	0	1	2	3	8
Other	2	2	7	9	4	5	3	32
Total	8	10	13	24	17	18	14	104

Table 3.4 Large-scale social protest by type and year, 2003–10

	2003	2004	2005	2006	2007	2008	2009	2010	Total
State	17	20	12	15	34	32	24	29	183
Nonstate	2	6	7	5	12	26	10	44	112
Land-related	2	4	7	15	21	9	8	22	88
Disturbance	1	1	2	7	11	14	17	8	61
Pollution	0	0	3	1	4	5	5	2	20
Ethnic	0	1	0	0	1	2	3	3	10
Student	0	0	1	4	8	2	2	0	17
Anti-taxation	0	4	0	0	0	0	0	0	4
Other	0	1	4	7	6	5	5	8	36
Total	19	37	33	51	69	88	58	108	548

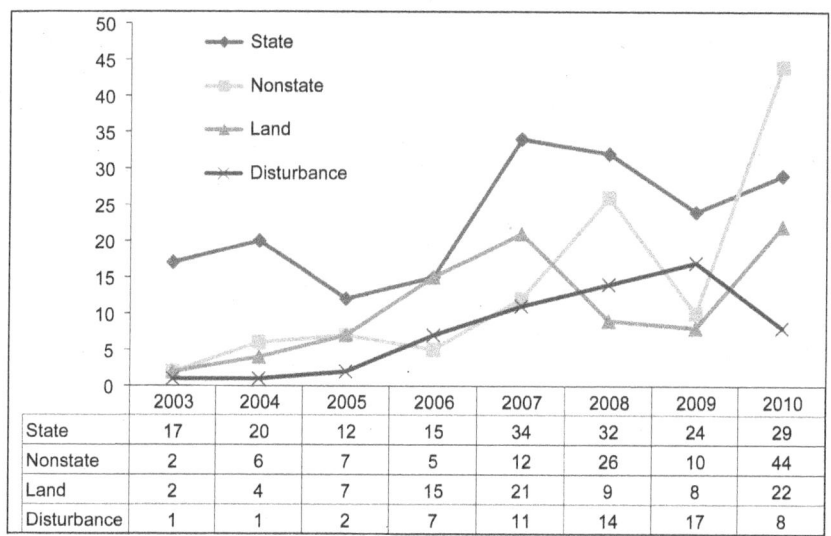

Figure 3.3 Frequency of major types of large-scale social protest by year, 2003–10

protest) has changed over the years. Labor protests in the state sector reached 34 in 2007 and somewhat plateaued in subsequent years. Labor protests in the nonstate sector surged from 2 in 2003 to 12 in 2007, and 26 in 2008. The number dropped to 10 in 2009, and dramatically increased to 44 in 2010. Land-related protests also reached a new high in 2010 with 22 cases. Disturbance is the only major type of protests that registered a decline in 2010, after years of increasing.

All four major types of social protest showed statistically significant increases, although the significance is marginal in some categories. The protests in the state sector increased at a rate of 2.1 cases per year ($r^2 = 0.46$; $p = 0.063$). Labor protests in nonstate sectors increased at a rate of 4.5 cases per year ($r^2 = 0.61$; $p = 0.022$). Land-related protests registered an increase of 2.0 cases per year ($r^2 = 0.44$; $p = 0.071$), and disturbances recorded an increase of 2.0 cases per year ($r^2 = 0.65$; $p = 0.015$).

Apparently, labor protests contributed a major share of the increase of large-scale social protests in 2007 and 2008. Subsequently, their drop in 2009 accounted for the reduction in the total number of incidents. It seems that the drop in the frequency of large-scale social protests in 2009 represents a short-term trend. Since our data are the first to reveal the decline in the number of large-scale social protests in 2009, there are no systematic analyses on the causes of such a drop. It is possible that the decline was mainly caused by tighter government control in preparation for the 60th anniversary of the People's Republic of China (PRC). Celebrating the 60th anniversary of the PRC in 2009 was the first and foremost priority of the regime and it was determined to put down any potential sources of social instability.

What accounts for the sudden surge of labor protest in 2010 in the nonstate sector? One major suspect is the world financial crisis, which started in 2008. The logic behind the suspicion is that the world economic crisis would reduce the demand for China's exports. The shrinking demand would then create financial difficulties for enterprises in the export sector, which would in turn generate labor protests in the export sector—that is, foreign ventures in the coastal regions.

If we take the bankruptcy of Lehman Brothers in September 2008 as the starting signal of the global financial tsunami, then the brunt of the world economic slowdown would hit China's export sector after September 2008 and all the way through to the entire year 2009. From September to December 2008, there were only seven cases of large-scale labor protest resulting from factory closures. However, the overall figure for large-scale labor unrest registered a huge further decrease in 2009. Altogether there were only six large-scale labor protests in the nonstate sector (where most export industries reside), with three of them related to factory closures in Guangdong. There was a sharp increase of labor protests in 2010. However, it is not very clear if they could be attributed to the financial difficulties. The content of the protests was less about back wages (a typical problem in the financial crisis), and more about low wages. The unrest seemed to be more related to the increase in labor costs. New generations of workers are going to demand better working conditions and higher pay.

Geographical distribution

The geographical distribution of the large-scale social protest does not seem to suggest much of a pattern. Table 3.5 presents the distribution of large-scale social protests by province (including four centrally administrated cities: Beijing, Shanghai, Tianjin and Chongqing).

Guangdong clearly stands out. It has the most incidents at 135, more than three times that of the next provinces in line, Sichuan and Jiangsu, which have 42 and 27 cases, respectively. In contrast, Ningxia has one taxi drivers' protest

60 An overview of large-scale social protests

Table 3.5 Frequency of large-scale social protest by province, 2003–10

Province	Frequency
Anhui	18
Beijing	13
Chongqing	21
Fujian	6
Gansu	10
Guangdong	135
Guangxi	19
Guizhou	5
Hainan	10
Hebei	10
Heilongjiang	10
Henan	23
Hubei	26
Hunan	19
Jiangsu	27
Jiangxi	14
Jilin	6
Liaoning	11
Neimenggu	5
Ningxia	1
Qinghai	3
Shaanxi	19
Shandong	25
Shanghai	8
Shanxi	10
Sichuan	42
Tianjin	4
Tibet	3
Xinjiang	7
Yunnan	17
Zhejiang	21

during all these years. Tibet has three large-scale protests, two of them ethnic conflicts.

Table 3.6 gives more detailed information on the types of social protest by province. Guangdong has the most large-scale social protests in two of the four major types. It has 70 in the nonstate sector (more than all the other provinces combined) and 24 land disputes. It is slightly after Sichuan in the categories of labor protest in the state sector (17 to 20) and disturbances (seven to eight). By comparison, Jiangsu Province, which is at a comparable level of socioeconomic development, has five in the state sector, 11 in the nonstate sector and four land disputes.

For the sake of clarity we have put the 548 cases on separate maps for the four major types of social protests, rather than all on one map. We have also only mapped the labor protests in the SOEs (hence, excluding the protests by

Table 3.6 Major types of large-scale social protests by province, 2003–10

	State	Nonstate	Land	Riot	Pollution	Ethnic	Anti-Japanese	Taxation	Other	Total
Anhui	10	1	0	3	0	0	0	0	4	18
Beijing	5	1	0	0	0	0	1	0	6	13
Chongqing	10	0	3	4	1	0	1	0	2	21
Fujian	0	2	1	0	3	0	0	0	0	6
Gansu	4	0	1	4	0	1	0	0	0	10
Guangdong	17	70	24	7	8	1	0	0	12	135
Guangxi	4	2	5	3	2	0	0	0	3	19
Guizhou	1	0	1	3	0	0	0	0	0	5
Hainan	1	2	3	3	0	0	0	0	1	10
Hebei	8	0	2	0	0	0	0	0	0	10
Heilongjiang	7	0	3	0	0	0	0	0	0	10
Henan	13	2	1	2	0	1	0	1	3	23
Hubei	16	1	5	2	0	0	0	0	2	26
Hunan	9	1	2	4	1	0	0	0	2	19
Jiangsu	5	11	4	3	1	0	0	0	3	27
Jiangxi	2	1	1	2	0	0	0	3	5	14
Jilin	5	1	0	0	0	0	0	0	0	6
Liaoning	5	3	1	0	0	0	0	0	2	11
Neimenggu	2	1	2	0	0	0	0	0	0	5
Ningxia	1	0	0	0	0	0	0	0	0	1
Qinghai	1	0	0	1	0	1	0	0	0	3
Shaanxi	11	2	1	2	0	0	1	0	2	19
Shandong	13	1	5	1	1	1	0	0	3	25
Shanghai	0	5	1	0	1	0	0	0	1	8
Shanxi	6	0	3	1	0	0	0	0	0	10
Sichuan	20	1	6	8	1	1	0	0	5	41
Tianjin	0	1	1	0	0	0	0	0	2	4
Tibet	0	0	0	0	0	2	0	0	1	3
Xinjiang	2	0	0	1	0	2	0	0	0	5
Yunnan	2	1	7	3	1	0	0	0	3	17
Zhejiang	3	2	5	4	4	0	0	0	3	21
Total	183	112	88	61	20	10	3	4	67	548

taxi drivers, veterans, teachers and bank employees), to highlight the issues associated with SOE reform.

There is no doubt that certain types of protest occur in the regions where there is a concentration of certain types of enterprises. Labor protests in SOEs tended to take place in the central region and upper Yangzi River region, where there are many former SOEs (Figure 3.4). One exception is the Northeast region, where there is a high concentration of SOEs of heavy industry (the so-called rust-belt region), which did not see many large-scale labor protests during this period. Our research indicated that when the SOE reforms started in the 1990s, the Northeast industrial clusters were hit hard and resulted in large-scale labor protests. There are many significant scholarly research works on those protests. During the period of our survey (2003–10), the peak of the protests in Northeast China had passed and we only recorded a couple of cases there.

62 *An overview of large-scale social protests*

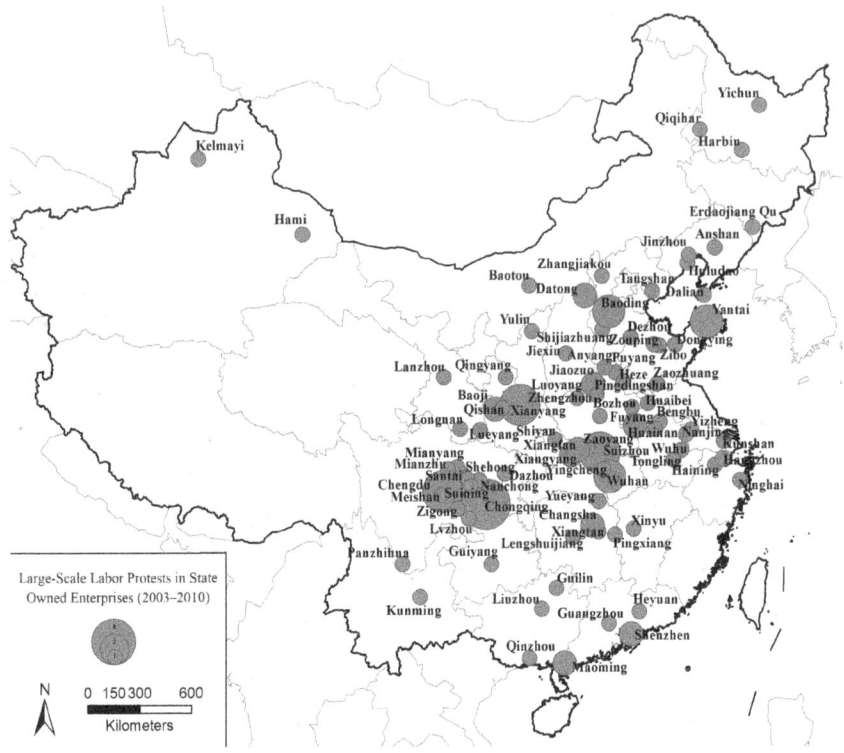

Figure 3.4 Map showing large-scale labor protests in state-owned enterprises, 2003–10

We see two big clusters of labor protests in nonstate sectors (Figure 3.5). One is the Pearl River Delta (PRD) area in Guangdong and the other is the Yangzi River Delta (YRD) area around Shanghai. There is also a small cluster at the tip of the Liaodong peninsula. Obviously all three locations are where foreign-invested enterprises (FIEs) are concentrated. We could point to the fact that with its physical proximity to Hong Kong, Guangdong has the largest number of FIEs (including those from Hong Kong, Macao and Taiwan) in the country, and therefore it has the highest number of labor disputes in the nonstate sector.

As FIEs cluster in a small area, such as designated industrial parks, labor protests in FIEs erupt in clusters. The protests have a strong demonstration effect, especially if protests have proven successful. For example, very few middle-sized cities in our data had more than two large-scale labor protests during this period (2003–10). Shenzhen City in Guangdong Province alone had 24 large-scale labor protests in the nonstate sector, with some protests separated only by a couple of days and a couple of blocks.

Yet this reasoning does not seem to stand in the same comparative framework. Jiangsu also has a large number of FIEs, about 70 percent of that of

An overview of large-scale social protests 63

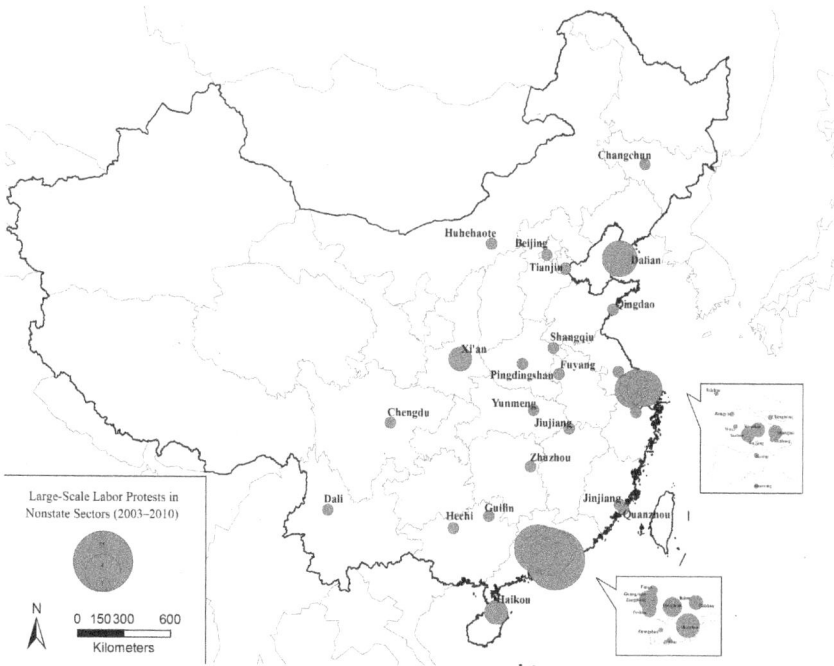

Figure 3.5 Map showing large-scale labor protests in nonstate sectors, 2003–10

Guangdong.[7] Yet instead of producing 70 percent of Guangdong's number of labor protests in the nonstate sector, Jiangsu had only 11 compared to Guangdong's 70. One possible explanation is that the export-oriented industries in Guangdong are low-end products and the local government management of these enterprises tends to be looser and lacks regulation.[8]

There is a possible political explanation. The government in Guangdong tends to be the most liberal among all the provincial governments in China. Physically, it is far away from the central government in Beijing, and closer to Hong Kong where the capitalist economic system prospers. Liberal-leaning government allows more political opportunities for social protest.[9] Organizers and participants of protests have to calculate the cost and benefit of launching a protest. The cost usually comes from potential repression and the benefit comes from the chance of success. Only when the chance of success outweighs the chance of repression would people launch a protest. Obviously in Guangdong, the likelihood of success outweighs the likelihood of repression. Guangdong also has the most liberal media in China—the Nanfang Media Group—which tends to be more sympathetic toward protesters. Altogether these present a favorable political opportunity for social protest in Guangdong.

64 *An overview of large-scale social protests*

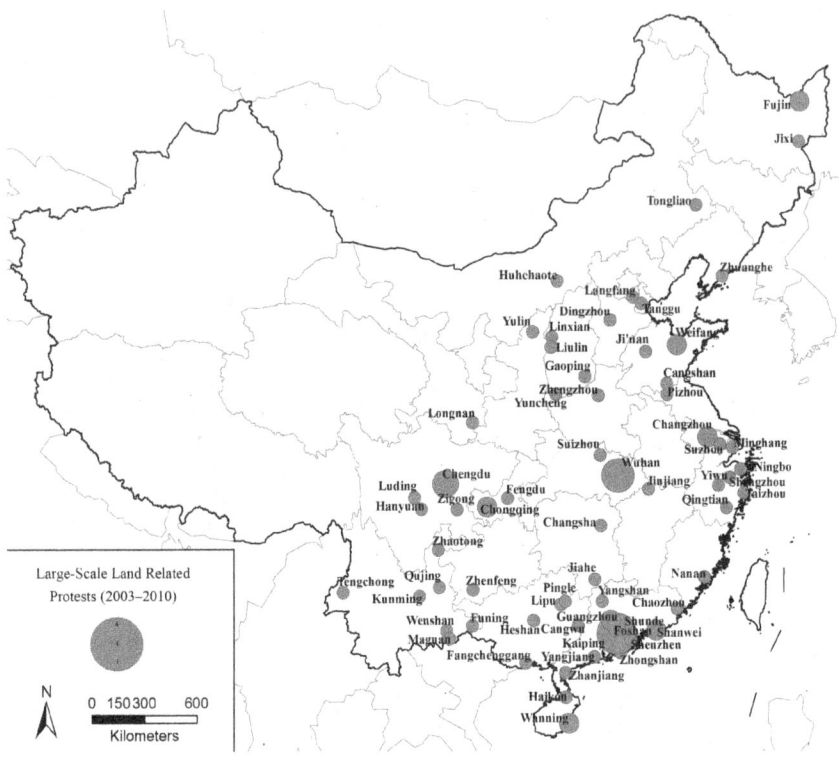

Figure 3.6 Map showing large-scale land-related protests, 2003–10

A few brief observations from the geographical distribution are interesting. If we want to identify a province as the most unstable place in China, Guangdong would hardly be on the shortlist, yet Guangdong has the most frequent large-scale social protests in China. Tibet has only three incidents in all these years, but no one has the confidence to claim that Tibet is one of the most stable regions in China. This might indicate that the occurrence of social protest does not necessarily correlate with social instability. This observation also supports the argument by the Qinghua University research group on social development that social protests are not the major threat to social stability.[10] Ningxia is an odd case. It has a large Hui population and is a Hui Autonomous Region, yet we have not observed a large amount of ethnic conflict. It also has a large number of state enterprises but no visible protests.

Conclusion

From the presentation of this chapter, we can summarize several features of the big picture of social protest in contemporary China. First, there were 548

An overview of large-scale social protests 65

Figure 3.7 Map showing large-scale mass disturbances, 2003–10

large-scale social protests nationwide over the period of 2003–10. People may find the number surprisingly low compared to their impressions. It is time to adjust those impressions. The number does not come from randomly selected cases, but from systematically collected cases confirmed by official sources. If we take the estimated number of "mass incidents" at 150,000 to 200,000 annually, then our findings mean that an overwhelming number of social protests are small-scale with fewer than 500 participants.

Second, there are four major types of social protest. The most frequent type is labor protest in the state sector, especially in SOEs, which accounts for 33 percent of the total. The second most frequent type is labor protest in the nonstate sector, with a share of 20 percent. The other two are land-related protests and mass disturbances, which take up 16 percent and 11 percent, respectively. From the dying pains of the state sector to the growing pains of the nonstate sector, from peasants trying to hold onto the value of their land to the mass venting of their accumulated frustrations, all these 548 large-scale social protests portrayed a comprehensive picture of a society in transition with social costs and their resultant pains. Various types of protest pinpointed the places where structural displacements occur. Labor protests in the state sector exemplify the social resistance to privatization, while large-scale social disturbances point to the public frustration over bad local governance.

The third feature is the geography of social protests. Guangdong Province alone takes about a quarter of the protests. This finding raises several questions that need to be further studied. First, what is the relationship between social protest and social stability, as Guangdong does not seem to be the most unstable place in China? Second, if the rising number of social protests does not affect social stability, does it mean that a process of institutionalization of social protest has begun? Third, how do we explain the phenomenon that Guangdong has the most social protests? We have suggested two possible explanations—the nature of the industry and government management style, and the better political opportunity provided by a liberal-leaning local government and media in Guangdong—yet these explanations need to be tested.

Lastly, our data also show the changing trend of social protest over time. Transitional pains are changing. The rise and fall of certain types of protest depicted the process of transition. Antitaxation protests disappeared after the abolishment of agricultural tax. Student political protests that were common in the 1980s turned into confrontation with school authorities over dorms, food and diplomas. Occasional anti-Japanese nationalistic demonstrations erupted in the 2000s. The steady increase of labor protests in the nonstate sector indicated that the labor cost is on the rise and China probably will no longer be the manufacturing paradise for FIEs.

Notes

1 陈晋胜 [Chen Jinsheng], 《群体性事件研究报告（内部发行版）》 [Report on Mass Incidents] (internal edition, 北京：群众出版社，2004年，第32页。[Beijing: Mass Press, 2004, 32]).
2 Wenfang Tang and Qing Yang, "The Chinese Urban Caste System in Transition," *China Quarterly* No. 196 (December 2008): 759–79.
3 This happened in Chengdu City in November 2009. In 2007, the city construction needed to relocate a house owned by a private entrepreneur. The negotiation for the relocation compensation failed. The government declared that the building had no proper documents and was therefore illegal. The wife of the entrepreneur set herself on fire during the process of forced demolition and died a few days later. county.aweb.com.cn/2009/12/3/480200912031340990.html.
4 "Minor Explosions: The Simmering Anger of Urban China," *The Economist* (March 31, 2010).
5 孙立平 [Sun Liping], 中国社会正在加速走向溃败 [Chinese Society Speeds Up its Decay], www.21ccom.net/newsinfo.asp?id=7550& cid = 10342300 (accessed April 14, 2010).
6 Ronald Inglehart and Christian Welzel, *Modernization, Cultural Change, and Democracy* (Cambridge University Press, 2005).
7 In 2010 Guangdong ranked first with 18,941 industrial FIEs and Jiangsu was second with 13,626: *China Statistical Yearbook, 2011*.
8 Personal interview.
9 See Sidney Tarrow, *Power in Movement* (Cambridge: Cambridge University Press, 1998, 2nd edn).
10 Referenced by Wu Zhong, "Beijing Hears Dissenting Voices on Unrest," *Asian Times Online*, April 28, 2010, www.atimes.com/atimes/China/LD28Ad01.html.

4 Subsistence expectation protests

In this chapter we will discuss the large-scale social protests that are driven by economic interests, which we define as "subsistence expectation protest." By subsistence, it does not mean that the protesters are in dire poverty (not all the protests in China are carried out by very poor people), but refers to the premises of the protests that are based on the subsistence responsibility of the government. Subsistence, therefore, is more of a symbolic concept. By expectation, it emphasizes the legitimacy framework in which these protests are primarily expecting the government to take the responsibility of the well-being of the population. Specifically, we will discuss the labor protests in state and nonstate sectors and land-related protests.

The grievances that triggered these protests typically correspond with the major structural shift in the processes of China's economic and social transformation. The labor protests in state-owned enterprises reflect the pain generated by the reform efforts to downsize the clumsy state-owned enterprises (SOEs) and make them more efficient in a market-oriented economy. Protests in private and foreign-invested enterprises typically mirror the lack of regulations, the need to upgrade the low-end manufacturing industries, and the fact that the labor cost is growing. The days of abundant supply of inexpensive labor are waning. Land-related protests have replaced tax protests as the most popular cause of rural contention as China is moving along the path of urbanization. This kind of land protest will likely continue as the process of urbanization deepens.

Political opportunity, mobilization and framing

The political opportunity for subsistence expectation protest is relatively large for two reasons. Culturally, Chinese authoritarian political tradition has always tolerated subsistence protests. As Mencius emphasized, the responsibility of the government is the provision of people's welfare. Such political culture encourages and empowers protesters to rise up from the bottom of society to challenge government leaders. Elizabeth Perry has long argued that social protest in China is one of the major components of social stability. They serve as checks against the abuse of power by the leaders and as mechanisms to ensure the accountability of the government. In an authoritarian polity where elections do not provide an effective check on the misbehavior of state authorities, Perry argues, protests can help to serve that function, thereby undergirding rather than undermining the political system.[1] As the state has assumed the responsibility of the subsistence living of the people, people, therefore, have the right to demand the state to fulfill its responsibility. This has constituted the political opportunity for protests with subsistence in nature. Even though some of the protests are not exactly about subsistence, in general, protests with material demands are tolerated and some kinds of redress are offered by the regime.

Structurally, Chinese multilevel administrative hierarchy not only limits protests to specific localities, but also provides the central government ample room for maneuverability. Specific material demands usually have a specific target, be it an enterprise or a local government. Claims to a basic subsistence that stay within local confines have seldom been deemed threatening by the Chinese regime. Narrow economic interest would hardly generate broad participation beyond those affected. In the meantime, the central government can use the protest to gauge the performance of the local government, or step in to show sympathy toward protesters.

Specific material grievances usually affect a group of people who either work together (sometimes also live together in the same or adjacent residence complexes), such as the workers who live together like the villagers. These tight relationships have made the protest mobilization much easier. As far as there are people willing to take the lead, it is easy to mobilize people who share the same grievance. In contrast, urban demolition/relocation cases rarely develop into large-scale mass incidents because few people share the grievance. To be sure, relocation affects a large area of residents, but those who put up fierce resistance usually are few. While there are instances of resistance to demolition nationwide, each incident is isolated and sporadic in its area and hardly forms collective action. In subsistence expectation protests, back wages, unpaid pensions and lay-offs affect a large collective of people. Since these workers used to work in groups and shifts together, the organizational networks in production serve as the same mobilization vehicle. Land requisition also affects the village as a whole, because it is the village that collectively owns the land. The kinship relations and natural village bonds play a role in mobilizing the villagers to protest against the perceived unfair land requisition.

Since these protests are demanding material benefit, the slogans of the protest are usually framed in subsistence terms and sentiments. As Perry points out, economic interests are often framed in terms of moral injustice and state responsibility.[2] The purposes of the protests are typically framed as "return our subsistence money" or in general moral terms such as "heaven forbidden." Sometimes, one can also see slogans from the Maoist era ideology, such as "down with the capitalist." This kind of slogan usually comes from SOE labor protests, as SOE workers benefited the most from the centrally planned economy.

Analyzing the collective contentions of the SOE workers, William Hurst argues that there are different kinds of framings depending on the different political economies of regions.[3] In Northeast China workers tend to use the Maoist moral economy, blaming the reforms for destroying a basically healthy socialist order. In contrast, in Central Coast regions, workers blamed the individual mismanagement and corruption for problems in particular firms. This framing corresponds with the "market hegemony" thesis raised by Mark Blecher, which argues that workers accept the concept of the market economy and its consequences.[4] In general, because of the more tolerant political opportunity for subsistence protest and the availability of the production organization networks for mobilization purposes, these are the most common protests we observe in China. As for the framing, it varies according to specific demands, but the demands tend to be framed in moral terms.

Labor protests in SOEs

The SOE reforms started in the 1990s and generated waves of labor protests that were documented by various scholars.[5] It is estimated that more than 30 million workers had lost their jobs from the state sector by 2002.[6] In the 2000s, the SOE reforms continued to the second stage—the State Assets Management Reform. The structural reform schemes include introducing private shareholders into the SOEs, selling SOEs to private companies and buying out the position of unnecessary employees.[7] As Figure 4.1 shows, the number of SOEs dropped from 41,000 to 20,000 from 2002 to 2010, losing about 20,000. More importantly, the number of state employees dropped from 24 million to 18 million. This was a further drop of 6 million workers from 2002 to 2010 in the same period. The decline was not as steep as it was during the late 1990s and early 2000s,[8] but it was severe enough for individual families.

The changes in the state of labor in China are among the most important of the extensive social and economic changes wrought by reform, as Mary Gallagher has argued.[9] As a result, the SOEs have greatly improved their efficiency, changing from a low-productivity, money-losing sector into a profit-generating sector. For example, the total industrial output value increased from 4.5 trillion RMB (ren min bi) to 18.6 trillion RMB from 2002 to 2010 (see Figure 4.1). However, the streamlining of a system that previously guaranteed full employment and job security would inevitably create losers. The 6 million who lost their employment were the losers in this process. Many were bought out at a low price and lost medical care and pension. Some were even unable to collect the buy-out money in full.

During this process, the state has attempted to instill an ideology of market reform and individualism into the population so that the losers should not hold the state responsible for their misfortune.[10] However, as Frazier has found out, when the state seeks to withdraw from its customary role as the provider of social welfare by way of comprehensive policy reforms, the result

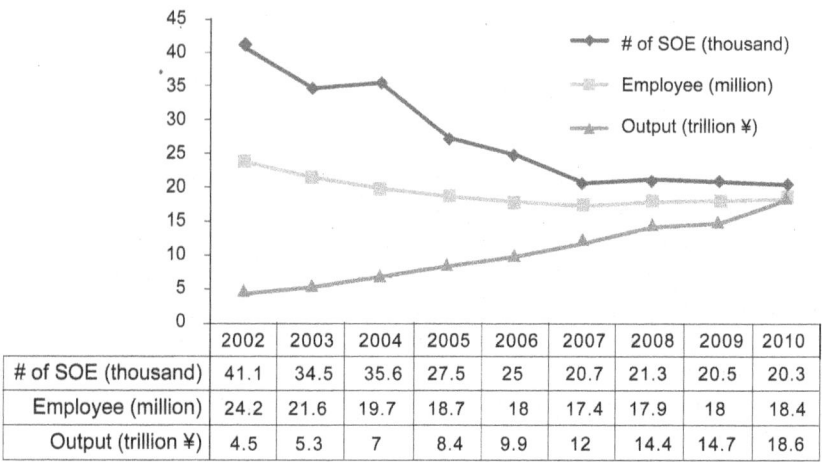

Figure 4.1 Selected indicators of the state-owned industrial enterprises, 2002–10
Source: China Statistical Yearbook, 2011

is often no policy at all when turned over to local officials for implementation.[11] This is where the structural displacements occur. Some of the losers from the structural change accepted the misfortune, some refused and, therefore, mounted protests, demanding their due benefits. Our account shows that there were 117 large-scale labor protests in SOEs from 2003 to 2010. Because of the scale of the SOEs, the number of protesters is often in the thousands. This type of labor protest peaked in 2007 and plateaued thereafter (see Figure 4.2).

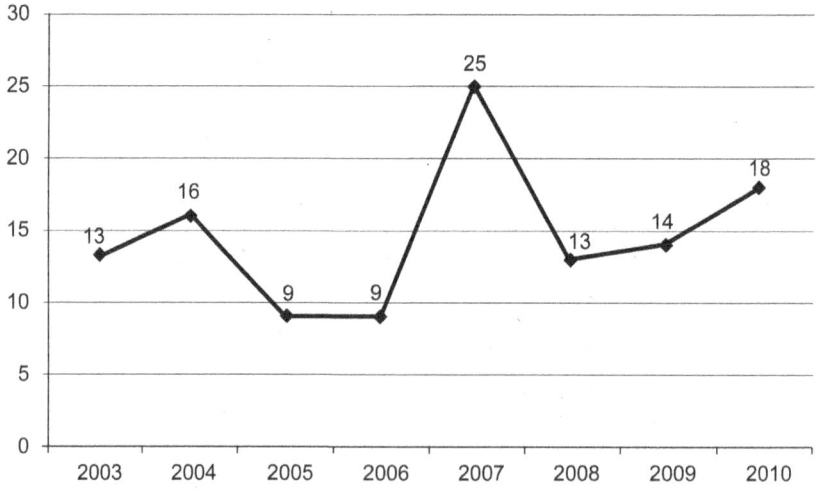

Figure 4.2 Frequency of large-scale labor protests in SOEs, 2003–10
Source: Authors own database

Subsistence expectation protests 71

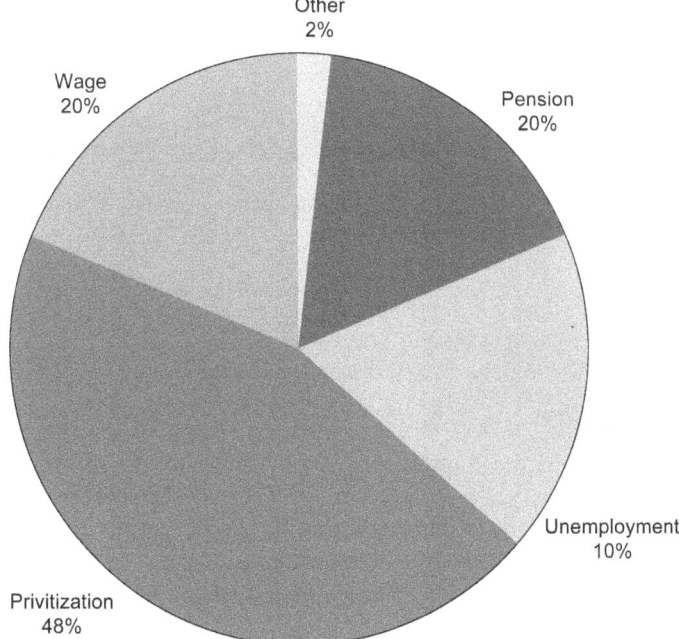

Figure 4.3 Distributions of major causes of the labor protest

Large-scale labor protests in SOEs usually had multiple, overlapping demands. A protest might simultaneously ask for jobs, pensions and other welfare packages. It is hard to pinpoint a single issue in such a protest. Still, we have attempted to identify the major demand of a given incident to gauge a full picture of the labor protest in SOEs. According to our classification, Figure 4.3 shows the distribution of major demands of labor protest in SOEs.

There are some technical issues in defining which enterprises are SOEs. This is especially true during the process of privatizing SOEs. Some labor protests occurred during or after the privatization. Are they private or state-owned enterprises? We decide to categorize the ownership type depending on the nature and demand of the protest. For example, if the protest was over privatization-related issues, such as laying off workers or lost benefits, then we determined it was an SOE. If the protest occurred several years after the privatization and the targets were about working environment and wages under the private management, we classified it as a private enterprise.

The majority of the protests were against privatization schemes: almost half of the labor protests are over privatization. Pension and wage protests rank second, with both taking 20 percent. Then came unemployment. Again, some of the unemployment and pension issues (even some of the wage issues) were side effects of privatization. For comparison, Hurst and O'Brien found from a

72 *Subsistence expectation protests*

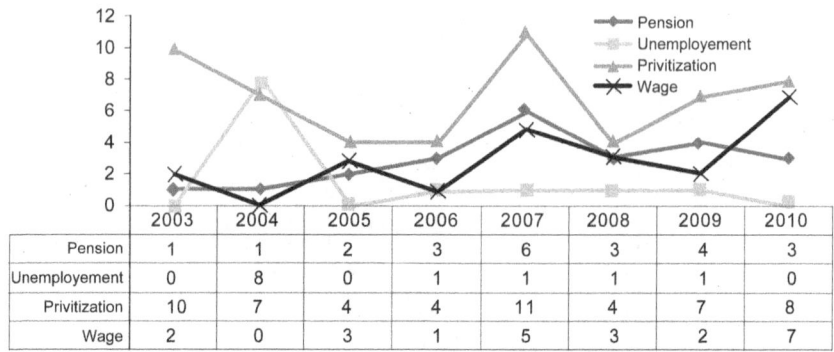

Figure 4.4 Frequency of major causes of labor protest by year

survey of news media (both international and domestic sources), from 1996 to 2001, of 62 labor protests 29 percent were about the benefits for laid-off workers, 34 percent concerned wages and 42 percent were about pensions.[12] Obviously privatization was not in full swing in the period 1996 to 2001. The major concern was pensions. Figure 4.4 gives us the frequency of these major protest demands by year.

As Figure 4.1 indicates, the SOE employees dropped from 24 million in 2002 to 22 million in 2003 to 20 million in 2004 and 19 million in 2005, then basically leveled off around 18 million. It explains the protests over unemployment reaching their height in 2004 and then ceasing to be a big issue since 2005. In a similar fashion, Figure 4.1 shows that the number of SOEs decreased dramatically from 41,000 in 2002 to 21,000 in 2008, a 50 percent reduction. These two major reductions reflected the structural reforms, especially the efforts of privatization. Consequently, privatization had consistently been the major target of labor protests. Pension disputes persisted over all these years, yet it was no longer the major cause of protest. Wage issues had gained some momentum in the latter half of this period. When people did not have to worry about their job security, they started to demand better payment. Since the structural reforms, SOEs have made strides in their general profit level as well as the betterment of their employees. The latest protests over low wages tend to occur in peripheries (such as in Gansu).

Privatization

Privatization is one of the major measures of SOE reform. It is a means to revive or sell off some of the dying and inefficient SOEs. However, it also generated a lot of friction between the workers and new management. The decision to privatize was made by the local governments (more specifically the local State Assets Commissions), as they are the state agents that exercise the ownership of these SOEs. While the remaining SOEs may have improved their efficiency rating in production, there are several problems associated with the privatization measures.

The first problem is the disappearance of state assets. Some private companies purchased SOEs at a very low price and then declared bankruptcy. This wouldn't necessarily lead to protests, as nobody was the actual owner of the state assets; however, many workers believed that the reason why the SOEs were sold cheap was because certain government officials received kickbacks from the private company. Once workers are unhappy about the consequences of the privatization, corruption accusations emerge. The second problem is the laying-off of a large number of workers with unsatisfactory benefit packages. The incoming private company would cut the excessive workforce to pursue efficiency. While the outgoing SOE management would negotiate packages for its existing workers, such packages were usually unsatisfactory for the workers. Third, there is friction between workers and the new management of the private companies over the issues, such as forced or unpaid extra shifts. Being used to the lax discipline of the SOEs, workers are frustrated with the harsh management of the profit-driven "capitalist." The following are some typical cases.

Tieshu incident (2003)

Tieshu Corporation in Suizhou (随州), Hubei Province, used to be a profit-bearing SOE that produced brand named cotton and textiles. In 2002, during the wave of structural reforms of the SOEs, it was sold to private owners. Within several months, the huge assets disappeared and the company applied for bankruptcy. A large number of workers was laid off and lost their health care and reimbursement of medical costs. Those who had retired before the privatization lost their guaranteed pension. The retirees took their case to court and received favorable rulings on their behalf, but the company refused to follow the court order and threatened: "feel free to lodge complaints to upper-level government, wherever you want."

The local government handled the protest poorly. Since the company had declared bankruptcy, the workers confronted the government over their grievance. On January 2, 2003, the deputy mayor of Suizhou held a dialogue with the workers. He claimed that the enterprise had no money and was unable to pay the workers welfare. He also dared the workers to block the railway. Right after his speech, the workers blocked railway traffic for two hours during the Chinese New Year holiday in an attempt to get the attention of central government.[13] The workers carried slogans stating "recover the subsistence money!" (讨回活命钱！) and "defending our rights according to law!" (依法维权！).

According to Han Dongfang, the founder of the *China Labor Newsletter*, the company stopped issuing various subsidies to the retired workers after declaring bankruptcy. These subsidies included price subsidy, housing and heating subsidies, and the one-child subsidy, altogether about 127 RMB, which constituted a third of the monthly income. The workers also claimed that there was about 400 million RMB of state assets that had disappeared into private pockets. Then the local government declared that these were Falun Gong practitioners and sent in the police to drive workers away.

Within a few weeks, the company announced that workers who had purchased the company shares could get some compensation, 270 RMB for 1,000 RMB. The workers had purchased about a total of 20 million RMB of the company stock shares, which now became worth only 5.4 million RMB. In the meantime, all the workers including retirees would not receive any stipend from the company. The workers protested immediately, and blocked the railroad.[14]

Tianwang incident (2004)

Tianwang Group was previously the Seventh Northwest State Textile Factory, located in Shaanxi Province. It had about 6,000 workers and 5,000 retirees, very cumbersome on the efficiency of any company. The provincial government promoted the selling of this SOE to a Hong Kong company. In 2004, the Hong Kong company Huarun Group finalized the deal to purchase 80 percent of the company shares and became the owner of Tianwang. According to the negotiation, Huarun would take on 5,549 of the previous 6,300 employees. The remainder were left to Tianwang, which had 20 percent of the shares. Tianwang also had to shoulder all the burden of the retirees and benefits owed to laid-off workers. Those who were assigned to Huarun had to go through a competitive process to become formal employees.

On September 13, 2004, the new labor contract was handed out to the workers. Workers found the provisions in the contract were not as favorable to the senior workers as they had been informed earlier. The length of the contract was much shorter and with a long probationary period. Workers started to go to the management building and asked for answers. On September 14, 6,000 workers held a strike. At its peak, there were about 10,000 participants. The police tried several times to break up the crowd but failed because of the enthusiastic societal support for the workers. The next day, workers gathered at the gate and the crowd snowballed to several thousand and traffic was paralyzed. On September 16, the management declared that the provisions in question in the labor contract were removed. However, the workers started to question other moves in Huarun's purchase of Tianwang. Why were the assets worth about 400 million RMB sold for 100 million RMB? What was the status of Huarun? Sometimes it was said to be a Hong Kong company and enjoyed certain special policy treatment, but at other times it was said to be an SOE registered in Hong Kong, therefore they did not pay "conversion money" that all the foreign ventures had to pay.

The workers had invited a lawyer to represent them in court, but the lawyer was forced by the government to give up the case. In desperation, the workers decided to block the railway in order to stir up the attention of the central government. Some 5,000 workers gathered on the railway lines that linked Xi'an and Shanghai and blocked the railway.[15]

Tonggang incident (2009)

One of the most tragic cases of labor protest occurred at Tonghua Iron and Steel Company (Tonggang 通钢) in Jilin Province in 2009. Tonggang was a state-owned enterprise. In 2005, the provincial government decided to sell 36 percent of the shares to a private company named Jianlong Group. Within three years, Tonggang had gone into the red and workers' monthly wages had dropped from 1,300 RMB to 300 RMB. In March 2009, Jianlong Group withdrew from Tonggang.

Yet right after the Jianlong withdrawal, the iron and steel market started to recover and iron and steel production seemed to be profitable again. In July 2009, the Provincial State Asset Commission agreed to let Jianlong Group return to Tonggang and become the majority shareholder with 65 percent of the shares. When the news broke among workers on July 24, rumors circulated that there would be an overhaul of the current management staff and large-scale lay-offs. The workers had had an unpleasant experience with Jianlong Group in the previous venture and preferred to maintain the SOE status of the enterprise. In an effort to fight against the measures of privatization, the workers started to riot, with close to 10,000 participants. The angry workers held up slogans like "Jianlong get out of Tonggang!" and closed down the furnaces. According to an on-site witness account, protesting workers simply turned into mobs, dragged out the newly appointed general manager from the Jianlong Group, Cheng Guojun, and started beating him. The armed police made several unsuccessful attempts to get into Tonggang, but the workers were throwing bricks and steel blocks, and overturned police vehicles.

Later in the afternoon, the government was forced to cancel the deal with the Jianlong Group. The official document stated that "since many workers, staff members, and retirees do not understand and disagree with the scheme, the government has decided to terminate the scheme, and there would never be any deal with Jianlong in the future." The message was broadcast repeatedly throughout the night. Police forces finally forced their way into Tonggang and got Chen Guojun out, but he had already been beaten to death by the workers on the first day of his appointment. Tonggang resumed production the next day.[16]

Unemployment

In addition to schemes of privatization, there are also other measures to streamline the state sector, such as laying-off or buying out the employment of an excessive labor force. As we quoted earlier, in 2003–10, 6 million SOE workers lost their jobs. This is a small number compared to the 30 million laid-off workers in the late 1990s. It was nonetheless painful to the families affected. Some of them were able to find other jobs in nonstate sectors, but some of them were not. The basic appeal of the protests was for the right to work, the right to enjoy social security and the right to subsistence.

The protests against unemployment were most prominent in 2004, with seven large-scale incidents that each involved more than 10,000 participants. In September 2004, Baoding and Tangshan Cities in Hebei Province had witnessed large demonstrations by the laid-off workers, with about 50,000 laid-off and unemployed workers taking part. Their slogans were "anti-unemployment, anti-laying-off, anti-bureaucratization, anticorruption and anti-special privileges!" The demonstrations caused traffic stoppage in Baoding City. The crowds laid siege to police vehicles and argued with officials. In Tangshan City, the crowds surrounded the city government building and burned several vehicles. In the same month, altogether 100,000 people in the Huainan Coal Mining Company of Anhui Province participated in strikes and demonstrations, protesting lay-offs, forced extra shifts and extra production quotas, and abuse of power. Protesters also demanded the improvement of working and living conditions. In the end, the government accepted some of their demands.[17]

October 2004 was also a very busy month for worker protests. About 30,000 laid-off workers demonstrated in Qiqihar City, Heilongjiang Province, asking for a back stipend. A couple of days later, nearly 10,000 laid-off workers in Baotou City Neimenggu Autonomous Region held demonstrations. In two days, several thousand laid-off workers from Panzhihua City of Sichuan Province protested.[18]

After 2005, unemployment protests dramatically declined, averaging about one a year. The primary dispute was the buyout money. The workers complained that either the money was too little or the workers were unable to collect it from the enterprises, and workers were unable to maintain a subsistence level of living standard.

Pension

Another point of contention in SOE labor protests are pensions. More than 40 years of a planned economy had produced a large number of retirees for the SOEs to take on. During the first wave of SOE reforms in the 1990s, as there were no effective programs to relieve troubled SOEs of their pension obligations, many firms began to delay or stop pension payments, either owing to a lack of funds or in an attempt to coerce the government into assuming more responsibility for retirees.[19] The pension received by state-sector retirees seems increasingly inadequate to keep up with the overall improvement of the standard of living. Back payments and an inadequate amount are the two major complaints of the pension protests.

Hurst and O'Brien found that the workers' view of pensions as the ultimate entitlement and pension gripes are perceived to be more legitimate and are felt more intensely than many other grievances. Moral indignation and survival needs are thus two reasons why pension arrears have so often sparked popular complaints. Protests launched by the pensioners used to be the most frequent type of protest in the state sector.[20] During our survey period, pension protests gradually declined and became the third most frequent protest. Here are some example cases:[21]

- In January 2004, about 3,000 retired workers from the China Petro Co. at Maoming City demonstrated in front of the company's main building. They protested that their pension was way lower than the amount prescribed by the central government.
- Anhui Bengbu Textile Company had about 10,000 retirees. In October 2004, several thousand retirees took to the street, asking for a rise in their pension, which was considered very low compared with rising consumer prices.
- On December 4, 2004, about 3,000 retired staff members and workers from Hangzhou Steel Group and Banshan Industrial Park lodged a petition with the city government of Hangzhou. Their main complaints were that their pensions were low and had no guarantee, and the burden of health care was too heavy.
- In 2007, about 20,000 retired oil workers in Xinjiang, angry about the enterprise using their pension insurance for other purposes and the low remaining pension fund that could not match inflation, blocked the city center and the roads, demanding a serious response from the company. They also blocked the hotel where one of the officials from the Petroleum Bureau was staying.

From these examples we can see that the SOEs have accumulated a large number of retirees and pensions have become a serious issue for them. Pension protests are about subsistence. The main complaint was that the amount of the pension could not match rising consumer prices. Since 2005, the State Council has raised the pension for former SOE retirees in six consecutive years. In December 2010, the rise was 10 percent. In general, the amount of pension has doubled,[22] which is why the number of pension protests has declined.

Geographical implications

William Hurst has made a very interesting study of the regional variation of the labor protests. He argues that different political economic structures of the regions in China have significant impact on the grievances, frames and tactics of the labor protests. The Northeast (Heilongjiang, Jilin and Liaoning provinces) is the "Stalinist Rust Belt" where the socialist heavy industry was most prominent. The Central Coast (Tianjin, Coastal Shandong, Jiangsu and Shanghai, plus the city of Dalian), which is characterized by the "booming market," is the most developed. The North-Central (Shanxi, Shaanxi, Inland Shandong and Henan provinces plus the cities of Lanzhou and Baotou) and the Upper Changjiang regions (Hubei, Hunan, Chongqing and Sichuan) belong to the tentative transition political economies. He argues that labor grievances in the Northeastern Stalinist rust belt tend to be moral and subsistence-related. In the booming market of the Central Coast, workers' claims are nearly always contractual and legalistic. In the tentative transition political economies of the North-Central and Upper Changjiang regions, corruption grievances and claims, along with gripes over regulatory assaults on laid-off workers' livelihoods, predominate.[23]

Hurst's regional division was somewhat vague. For example, Shandong Province belonged to two regions. Therefore, it is hard to duplicate his study. In general, Northeast China is no longer the region in which SOE labor protests are concentrated. The SOE labor protests there in this period were sporadic. Instead, the places where we observed frequent SOE labor protests from 2003 to 2010 are Shaanxi, Hubei and Sichuan provinces, all of which belong to his category of "tentative transition political economy." A quick look at some of the protests shows that they more or less confirm Hurst's characterization. The Tonggang incident in Jilin is a typical case of Maoist moral resistance to privatization. The workers protested even before anything actually happened. The Tieshu and Tianwang incidents in Hubei and Shaanxi had various demands: corruption and subsistence issues were the most prominent.

Summary

While we separate these protests into different demand categories, in reality there is a lot of overlap. Some of the protests are about all three areas (job, pension and wages). This is what we characterize as the dying pains. The collective system that guarantees a decent living from cradle to grave is fading. This is not to say that China no longer has state-owned enterprises. It still does, and the government has declared that SOEs are the first and main pillar of the Chinese market economy.[24] The point is that the SOEs have become leaner and more efficient at the cost of ridding themselves of inefficient parts and workers. The SOEs that provided the largest employment and the most comprehensive welfare coverage were disappearing; the old, familiar institution to which the people were accustomed was dying.

When workers protested, the framing usually went beyond mere material demands. There were strong accusations of corruption and serious concerns about the disappearance of state assets. This could be a strategy to obtain broad moral support or the persistence of the old-fashioned belief that workers were the masters of the factory, or a little of both.

All these labor protests reflected the conflict between state ownership and private ownership in such a transitional era. Usually where these protests occurred there were several issues involved. First, the drain of the state assets during the privatization was serious. Second, the management of the state enterprises had serious corruption problems. Third, the privatization scheme ignored the interests of the workers, and the employee representative assembly was not functioning. Lastly, the incompetence of the local government officials made the situation much worse.

At a deeper level, these protests indicated that workers are holding onto state ownership, while the government is pushing for private ownership. This is an interesting twist. Workers preferred the state welfare benefits and the government preferred the efficiency brought by private ownership. Hurst and O'Brien found that with the exception of some managers and officials, virtually all their working-class interviewees expressed open hostility toward market reforms, claiming that they and the country had been better off before reform began, and expressing varying degrees of desire to restore large parts of the Maoist social order. There was a strong Maoist moral economy nostalgia and a strong sense of entitlement.[25] Hurst and O'Brien also detected a look back to a brighter past. As members of a generation that came of age during the heyday of state socialism, today's contentious pensioners are motivated in part by a sense of longing for the security and perceived freedom of their youth, a decent living from cradle to grave.[26] These observations are once more confirmed by our data.

Labor protests in private sectors

One of the major measures of Chinese economic reforms since the late 1970s has been the encouragement of private and foreign-invested enterprises (FIEs). China was labeled the largest manufacturing workshop of the world primarily because of the flourishing export sector, which is anchored by foreign investment. China's comparative advantage that attracted foreign investors was the abundant supply of cheap, educated labor. The growth of the private sector and its contribution to job opportunities and gross domestic product (GDP) have been phenomenal. Figures 4.5 and 4.6 demonstrate the growth of private and foreign-invested industrial enterprises.

However, together with this phenomenal growth came the increasing labor disputes over salaries, treatment and working conditions. During the period of 2003 and 2010, we recorded 113 large-scale labor protests in the private sector (Figure 4.7). Among them, about 94 (83 percent) occurred in the FIEs.

Growing numbers of labor protest

The most visible feature of large-scale labor protests in the nonstate sector is their growing number (see Figure 4.7). It topped all the other types and became the most frequent type of social protest in 2010. This trend goes along with the growing number of private and foreign-invested enterprises and their employees. It is indicative of the growing pains of a market economy and the inevitable upgrading of low-end industry. The main cause of the

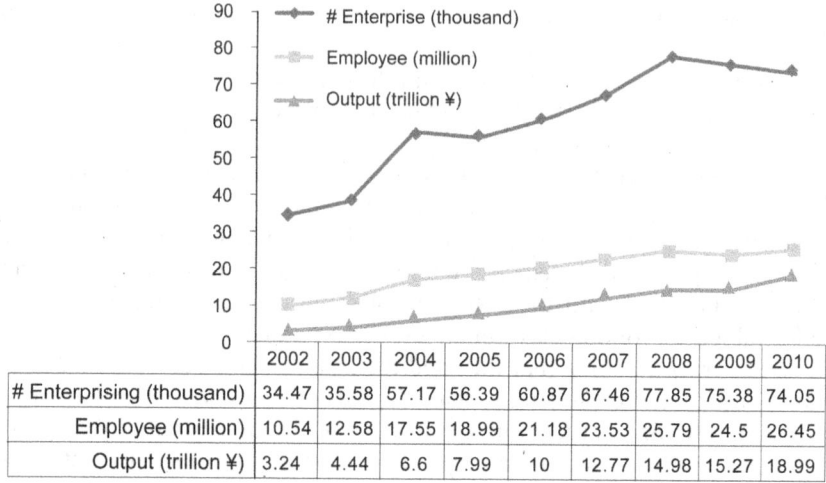

Figure 4.5 Selected indicators of private industrial enterprises, 2002–10
Source: China Statisticl Year Book, 2011

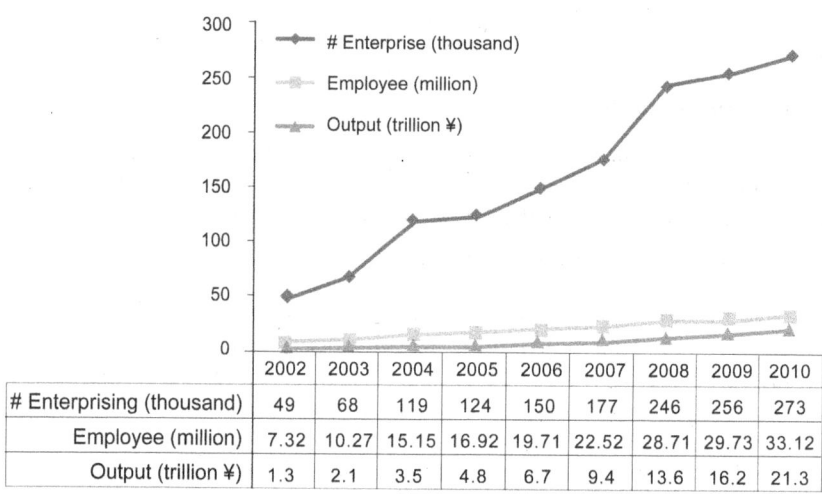

Figure 4.6 Selected indicators of foreign-invested industrial enterprises, 2002–10
Source: China Statistical Year Book, 2011

conflict is the fact that the abundant labor supply has been shrinking during the growth of the nonstate sector.[27] Consequently, labor costs will not remain cheap for long. The previously submissive workforce is going to demand improved working conditions and better pay.

There are a couple of factors that contributed to the diminishing supply of cheap labor. First, it is the result of the one-child population policy enforced since the late 1970s. Even though there were policy enforcement problems and

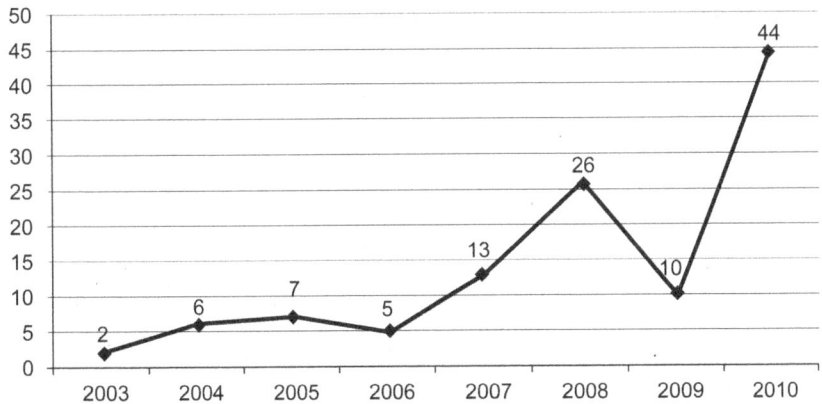

Figure 4.7 Frequency of large-scale labor protest in private sectors, 2003–10
Source: Authors' dataset

many evasions occurred, population growth has significantly slowed and has resulted in the shrinkage of labor supply. Second, the creation of entrepreneurship opportunities back in the hometowns of migrant workers also contributed to the increasing number of returned migrant workers.[28] Once there is a limit to labor supply, bargaining power is going to shift from the company to the workers, said Arthur Koreber, managing director of the research institute GaveKal-Drgonomics.[29]

Many labor scholars noted the emergence of a new or second generation of migrant workers—those born in the 1980s and after, which now constitutes 58.4 percent of all migrant workers in China.[30] It is a sociological rather than a biological category that describes the young, more educated workers—those with an urban outlook and higher aspirations. In contrast to the previous generation of migrant workers whose biggest dream was to save enough money to build a house in their home village, the new generation want to be urbanites with all the consumer goodies the city youth have. As a *New York Times* report described, "in the past, China's migrant workers were just thankful not to go hungry; today they are savvy and secure enough to start being choosy. Higher salaries, basic benefits, better working conditions and less physically taxing jobs are only the beginning of their demands."[31] As a result, the new generation tends to care more about pay, benefits and working conditions. More importantly, young workers are better informed because of the access to cell phones and the Internet. They took the opportunity of the shifting bargaining power, to fight to improve their working conditions and payment.

The nature of the labor protests in the private sector is different from that in the SOEs.[32] First, the enterprises are owned by private or foreign investors. Unlike the SOEs, there are no moral obligations for the welfare of the workers on the owners' part. The entire capital-labor relations are contractually based. Workers do not have the sense of benefits entitlement that the state employees have. Second, the composition of workers is different. Workers in the private sector are the new labor force created by the market economy and mainly came from rural areas. The mobility of this labor force is very high. Unlike the SOE workers who develop a strong sense of belonging to the enterprise, migrant workers move around different companies in pursuit of better jobs and better pay. Therefore their protests are out of a different kind of grievance: it is not about unemployment or a pension, as these are never promised. As the owner or management is not part of the state, the dispute can hardly be framed as a state moral responsibility. It is more about the working class versus the capitalist. Only if the capitalists do not respond to workers' demands do workers then take the issue to the government.

Almost all the labor protests were against the low-salary and underpaid extra working hours. Sometimes there were also protests over the working environment. For example, in October 2007, 2,000 workers from a China-Japan joint venture in Kunshan City, Jiangsu Province, held a strike in protest against suspected work-related health damage. It was suspected that the workers were starting to get cancer as a result of assembling electronic products. Workers claimed that hospitals in Shanghai had confirmed their illness, and demanded medical compensation.[33]

Demonstration effect

One notable feature of labor protest in the nonstate sector in our data is the geographic clusters of these protests. As the map in Figure 3.4 in Chapter 3 demonstrated, the Pearl River Delta (PRD) and Yangzi River Delta (YRD) are the two largest clusters of such labor protests. The next relatively smaller cluster is the Liaodong peninsula. These clusters are symptomatic of the concentration of FIEs. They also provide an ideal field for demonstration effects, as the factories are just next to one another.

Migrant workers tend to come in flocks as relatives, friends and acquaintances from the same villages or towns. Kin and ethnic networks have facilitated migration flows, which in turn become a convenient mobilization vehicle for collective action. The provision of dormitories to accommodate large numbers of migrant workers is essential for production. As a result, as Chan and Ngai argue, dormitories become the strategic sites of mobilizing labor protests.[34]

Migrant workers who come from the same place may not get into the same factory and find jobs in other factories. However, they maintain their hometown networks and pass on strike information accordingly. The geographic closeness of the factory locations and the networking among workers in different factories tends to lead to consecutive strikes in different factories. However, during the process of these strikes, Chan and Ngai have observed an emerging working-class identity has started to transcend the traditional boundaries of gender, ethnic and home origins.[35]

Here is an example of the demonstration effect. On January 8, 2008, workers of an FIE in Dongguan City Tangxia Township, dissatisfied with the calculation of compensation for extra working hours, held strikes. After negotiation with the management, the enterprise paid some compensation to the workers. Immediately after this event, workers from another FIE, only half a mile away, launched another large-scale strike and received compensation as well. There is no doubt that the second strike was informed by the first.[36]

The year 2010 witnessed the most large-scale labor protests in the nonstate sector and an apparent demonstration effect. In May 2010, reports about consecutive suicides of workers from Foxconn, a Taiwanese electronics factory in Shenzhen that assembles parts for the Apple iPhone and iPad, started to reach the public. Many speculated that it was the regimented style of management that drove the young workers to jump from the building. Because of the sensationalist media coverage of the tragic events, the Taiwanese owner had to almost double the salaries to pacify the public. No matter what the exact causes of the suicides, the concessions made after the incidents have shown the vulnerability of the capitalist. While the Foxconn incident does not qualify as a large-scale social protest, it indirectly triggered a series of strikes in other FIEs in the following month.

Workers in a Japanese-owned Honda transmission factory in Foshan City of Guangdong Province launched a strike on May 17, 2010, demanding a salary rise. According to a well-known scholar of the labor movement, the Honda workers were "well organized, strategic and assertive, demanding sizeable wage increases, proposing a pay scale and a career ladder, electing

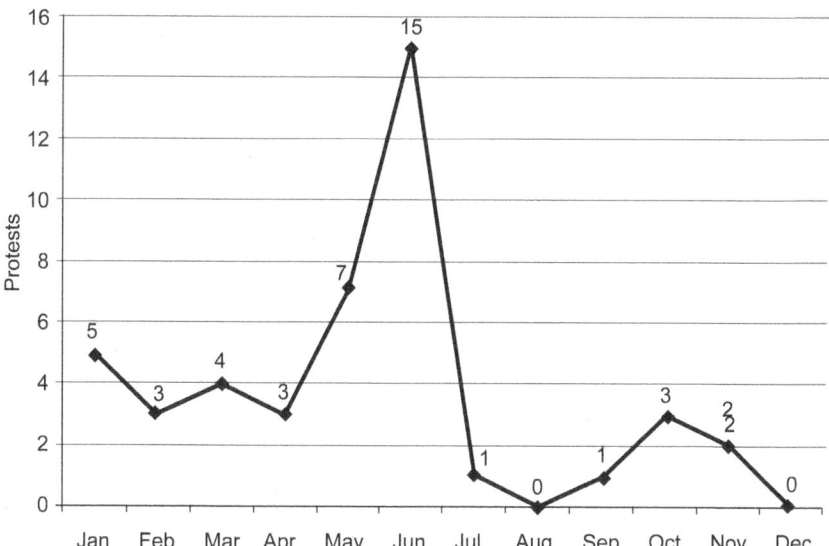

Figure 4.8 Large-scale labor protest in the nonstate sector in 2010 by month
Source: Authors database

their own representatives, and demonstrating solidarity and a determination to win."[37] The management yielded, and workers received a 24 percent pay hike. Two other Honda plants followed suit in July, all with degrees of success.

Encouraged by the success of the Honda plant, the month of June saw a series of labor strikes not only in PRD but also in YRD. For example, a similar strike occurred in the Taiwanese-owned KOK International plant in Kunshan, a suburb of Shanghai. The unanimous concerns were the unbearable working conditions, enforced unpaid overtime, and low pay.[38] Figure 4.8 shows how the Honda strike in May led to the peak of the labor protest in the following month.

Ownership origins

Scholars have suggested that the ownership of the enterprise makes a difference in labor protest. In general, Taiwanese, Hong Kong and South Korean ownership tended to be harsher to workers than the enterprises from Europe and America and, therefore, produced more disputes and protests.[39] According to Chan's observation, the Taiwanese, Hong Kong and South Korean businesses, developed in an authoritarian environment, are used to an antilabor tradition. The European and American enterprises, in contrast, have a tradition of awareness of labor rights and presumably have fewer labor issues. There are, however, exceptions to this generalization. The study by Chan and Ngai shows that the management of European investors (in their case, a German company) were by no means lenient, which caused labor protest in 2007.[40] Based on our data of labor protest, we created a table of ownership origins and frequency of large-scale labor protests in the nonstate sector (Table 4.1).

Hong Kong-invested enterprises seemed to have the most frequent labor protests, while Japanese businesses came second. Japanese business has the most regimented style of management, with strict shop floor hierarchies. A

Table 4.1 Ownership origins and the frequency of labor protest in the nonstate sector

Origin of investment	Frequency
China	19
Japan	25
Hong Kong	33
Taiwan	19
United States	5
South Korea	4
Germany	3
Italy	2
Singapore	1
Belgium	1
Netherlands	1

Source: (Authors' database)

harsh management style may or may not be the cause for labor protest, however. Korean and Taiwanese enterprises basically followed the Japanese model, yet Korean-owned enterprises had far less labor protest. Businesses from Hong Kong were a different story. They were not developed in an authoritarian environment, but they did not seem to have acquired the British model of management either. American- and European-invested enterprises clearly are not immune to labor protests. The above numbers may be deceptive because Taiwan-, Hong Kong- and Japan-invested enterprises may have much larger base numbers than the other countries, so proportionally it may not be out of the ordinary. The ownership argument is not conclusive and requires further research.

Maturation of the protest

In the early stages of labor protest until 2008, workers tended to have fierce confrontations with management. The common strategy was to block public transportation in order to attract public and media attention. Later, especially in 2010, we have noticed the rise of astute labor organizers. The protests were much more organized and disciplined. Most of the time, the organizers would only confront the capitalist and constrict the protest to the factory. The workers would not destroy property or act in a unconstrained manner.

For example, in July 2010, workers at an Omron FIE factory in Shenzhen held a strike asking for a salary rise. Following the instructions of their organizers, the workers would clock into the factory every morning but refuse to work. Then they would clock out when the shift was supposed to be over. They would clean up all the garbage and leave the chairs tidy. The process was peaceful and orderly, which was praised by public opinion and the government. With the coordination of the government, the workers had most of their demands met.[41] They also set a successful model for other protests to follow.

One of the common features in these protests was the use of information and communication technologies, such as phone messages and video uploads on the Internet. The new generation of migrant workers has middle-school education and is tech-savvy. While they restricted the strikes within the factory walls, they would inform the public via the Internet to garner public support.

The role of the government

The government, previously self-claimed to be the representatives of the working class, is now turning into a developmental state. Its policies are tilted toward the investors/capitalists. These FIEs are the big contributors to local GDP, which is a primary measurement of government achievement as well as the tax revenue that the local government is entitled to keep. The local governments have tried everything to lure the foreign investors to their localities, and would not want them to be scared away by labor unrest. The government needs to provide a favorable environment for investors, including an absence of a labor movement, which would increase the labor cost and disrupt production.

Yet, the government cannot simply ignore the interests of the workers. It continues to have a moral responsibility for the welfare of the workers in the private sector. Therefore, the government is in an awkward situation between a pro-capital stand and a moral responsibility. One of the thorny issues is the role of the trade unions. In SOEs, trade unions are government institutions, but the role of the trade unions in private enterprises or FIEs is ambivalent. Should they serve the interests of the workers or the interests of the capitalists? The government does not want an independent trade union to serve the interests of the workers and later develop into something like Solidarity in Poland. On the other hand, the government does not want the trade unions to serve the interests of the capitalist, such as was the case in pre-revolution China when the trade unions were bought off by the capitalists.

The advantage that the government has is that it is not the target of the labor protests. The government, therefore, could mediate as a third party and take credit for any progress made during the incident. It seems that the government, while taking a pro-capital position in its development strategy, is more inclined to press the owners to make concessions to workers' demands.[42] Many of the concessions made by the enterprises were due to pressure from the government.

Sometimes, the government has to use its own money to appease the workers. Here is an interesting case of two toy factories in Zhangmutou Township of Dongguan County, Guangdong Province. The two factories declared closure in October 2008. Workers had not received wages for about two months and the managers were nowhere to be found at the time of closure. All together, the two factories owed workers' wages to the total of 24 million RMB. In desperation, 7,000 employees protested in front of the township government. The township government, originally hoping to mediate the dispute, failed to find the general manager. In the end the government paid the workers out of its own pocket.[43] There are four such cases in our database and similar cases elsewhere.[44]

It could be argued that this is out of concern for stability. However, the government responsibility for the welfare of the people should not be overlooked. Shenzhen City government raised the minimum wage level significantly in 2006 and 2007. This is partially due to the strike waves in 2004 and 2005.

Summary

The number of labor protests in the nonstate sector is on the rise. Overall, we can see that the labor protests in nonstate sectors occur primarily in Guangdong Province, the so-called Pearl River Delta area, where the FIEs are crowded.[45] The next most frequent labor protest location is in the Yangzi River Delta area, where the second highest number of FIEs are located. The concentration of FIEs has facilitated the demonstration effect of labor protests. The hometown networks of the migrant workers also reinforced such effects.

The major goals of the protests were significantly different from those of the SOEs. Workers wanted better wages and protested against extra work shifts. Sometimes the complaints were also about back wages. The shift from a social contract to a legal contract has altered the way in which the workers fight for their rights.[46] The framing is no longer the state moral responsibilities, but the enforcement of legal contracts or protection of labor rights. This is a back-and-forth process, which will eventually lead to equilibrium in the proper wage level.

The nonstate sector is a new entity born from market reforms. It has been facing growing pains. The government needs to learn to institute proper regulations. The investors have to learn to cope with the shrinking labor market and be prepared to face the increasing pressure from labor to raise their wages. The workers have been learning to organize their protests to maximize their gains. As Chan and Ngai argued, through these labor protests that transcend the hometown, ethnic and gender boundaries, we may witness the formation of a new working class.

Land-related disputes

With the official abolition of the agricultural tax in 2006 and the new government initiatives on building the new countryside (which means that the central government will offer appropriate funding to rural areas and the local governments need not invent schemes to collect fees from the farmers to fund their projects), protests against excessive taxation that were frequent in the past have completely disappeared. Yet the continued economic growth also brings another historical shift—the urbanization of a country that previously had 80 percent of the population in rural areas. The 2012 annual blue cover report by the Chinese Academy of Social Sciences revealed that the urban population had for the first time surpassed the rural population.[47] The reality beneath these figures is the expanding cities. Housing projects have been mushrooming in suburban areas, new industrial parks and shopping centers have been popping up, and golf courses have been emerging everywhere. All these projects need land. According to a report by the National People's Congress, China has lost 123 million *mu* of farmland between 1991 and 2011.[48]

Land ownership in China is a complicated system with some deliberate institutional ambiguity.[49] In principle, the state owns the urban land and the village collectives own the rural land, including the suburban land. Therefore, if the state wants to use the farmland owned by the village collectives, they have to negotiate a compensation package. In general, if the central state plans to construct national infrastructure projects, such as highways, high-speed railways and dams, there is not much room for bargaining by the rural collectives. However, there are also local projects sometimes directly involved and sometimes sponsored by the local government. It is the land use of these projects that oftentimes led to land disputes and, ultimately, mass protests.

88 *Subsistence expectation protests*

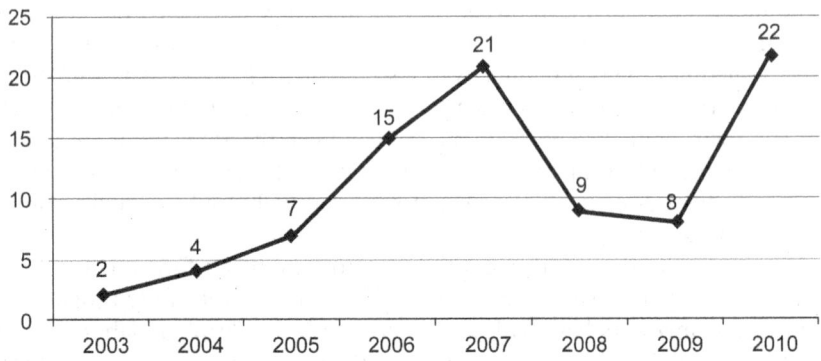

Figure 4.9 Large-scale land-related protests, 2003–10

From 2003 to 2010, we have recorded 88 protests over land-related disputes. By land-related disputes, we refer to the disputes over the compensation over land requisition and relocation, which often involves forced residence demolition. The major complaints are an unsatisfactory price tag and delayed payments. In this section, we will discuss a variety of protests over relocation compensation, disputed land prices and conflict between farmers and private companies. We also will take a look at the bloody conflict in Dongzhou village and a case where the farmers took the issue to court and won.

Relocation compensation

In the early stages of land requisition, the main cause of disputes was compensation for relocation. As relocation was mainly for national or provincial projects, farmers were relocated without much resistance but complained about the low compensation. For example, the construction of the Tankeng Power Station in Qingtian County (青田县), Zhejiang Province, involved 10 townships and 80 villages. All together the project had to relocate 50,000 people. From July to August 2003, there was a series of protests over the relocation with regard to unspecified compensation. In the end, the government issued new detailed compensation policies that responded to the interests of different groups of migrants, and the protests quieted down.[50]

A well-known case of land-related dispute occurred in Hanyuan County (汉源) of Sichuan Province. Hundreds of thousands of local villagers were forced to surrender their land and relocate to make way for the building of a hydroelectric plant. Many relocated farmers did not receive proper compensation and the newly allocated land was of lower quality. After futile petitions, a mass protest involving more than several tens of thousands of people eventually broke out in October 2004.

The angry peasants started to attack the electricity plant and government buildings. The crowd also detained the governor of Sichuan Province, who went to the scene in an attempt to reconcile the dispute, for more than 10 hours. The local government dispatched police to dispel the crowd. The peasants then faked a dead body (someone who had died in a car accident), claiming that he was killed by the police. The peasants carried the dead body to the government buildings and forced some government officials to kneel down to the dead body to show remorse.[51] The event startled the central government and an investigative group was dispatched. The investigative group announced that the electricity plant would be temporarily closed until the relocation disputes were settled.

Disputed land price

With the need for land skyrocketing, so did prices, with the value of land soaring quickly over a short period of time. Initially the farmers would agree to any decent price because it was much better than farming incomes. However, when the farmers later realized that their land was worth a ridiculously high price, they would recant their agreement. For example, the government of Yuling City (榆林市) in Shaanxi Province planned to build an industrial park in the suburb of Yulin. With land involved in the industrial park, Sanchawan village (三岔湾村) engaged in a serious land dispute with the local government. The deal was originally reached at about 500 RMB per *mu*. Yet after the government had built water and electricity supply to the land, its price soared to 500,000 RMB per *mu*. The villagers recanted. The government insisted on only giving minimum compensation (500 RMB per *mu*) for the land because it was barren and deserted. The farmers, on the other hand, demanded a much higher price for the land because it was now worth 1,000 times more. The confrontation lasted from March 2003 to October 2004—more than a year. During the confrontation period, the villagers blocked the construction of the industrial park. Angry farmers also destroyed some private property out of anger.[52]

There were many similar cases in which the villagers recanted their agreed selling price and demanded more. This is primarily because of an irregular land market. If well-connected speculators could make huge profits out of land transfers, why could villagers not void their previous agreement/contract and demand a larger share of the profits? No side (government, companies or villagers) had followed the market rules. In the end, such disputes were settled at a compromise price under the benevolent governance framework.

Conflict between farmers and companies

Sometimes the land disputes were between farmers and companies that purchased the use of the land. As local governments usually had close ties with these companies, they tended to turn a blind eye during the disputes and even acquiesced to violent solutions. For example, Shenyou village (绳油村) of Dingzhou County (定州县) is located close to a newly built electricity plant and 379 *mu* of land was designated to be the coal ash storage plot in 2003. Yet the villagers had not reached an agreement with the electricity plant on the price of the land, and kept interrupting the operation of the project. The villagers built 300 temporary sheds on the spot and determined to have a long-ter`m confrontation with the plant. In 2005, with the support of local government officials, the developer organized more than 300 thugs and attacked the villagers. Six villagers were killed. Then the villagers started to fight back, resulting in a great deal of violence.[53] The government arrested the core members of the group of attackers and decided to find another site for ash storage.[54]

The same thing occurred in Langfang in Hebei Province in October 2008. Villagers blocked the construction of a high-speed railway between Tianjin and Beijing in protest over compensation for the land taken. The compensation had been allocated to the local government, but the villagers insisted that they had not received the money. The construction company was frustrated by the blockage and hired organized criminals to attack the villagers, and finally got the construction moving.[55]

Disputes between farmers and companies are a gray area. Some companies are SOEs and some are private capital. They are not governmental, but they have close ties with the government. It is also in this gray area that a lot of corruption occurs.

The bloodiest conflict over land dispute

The bloodiest land protest during 2003–10 occurred in Dongzhou village (东周村), Shanwei County (汕尾县) of Guangdong Province. The electricity plant built in 2002 occupied a large land area in Dongzhou village. The villagers believed that they had not been properly compensated and protested. They built sheds outside the factory and attempted to stop the construction. The police arrested three villagers during the effort to demolish the sheds, which escalated the protest and the rank of protestors soared to several thousand. Armed police were dispatched. Tear gas was used to dispel the crowd and the riot became violent in December 2006. Villagers blew up the power station's equipment and threw fire bombs at the police. The police first opened fire into the air, but due to the chaos at the scene, nobody heard the shots and continued to attack the police. In order to defend themselves, armed police fired at the protestors, which resulted in several deaths and injuries.[56] This was the first time since 1989 that the government had opened fire during a citizen–government confrontation. Several major leaders of Shanwei City received disciplinary measures.[57] Since then, violent protests have recurred many times. The dispute has not been resolved so far.

Taking a dispute to court

Kaihua Township (开化镇), government of Wenshan County (文山县), Yunnan Province and a Xiazhai (下寨村) villagers' group signed two land requisition agreements in 2005 and 2006. According to the documents, the villagers' group agreed to let the government use two pieces of their land, all together 661.2 *mu*, and the government would pay a total amount of 37,027,704 RMB. The government moved on to build government buildings and housing projects. Yet the villagers later felt that the compensation was too low and refused to give up the land.

In October 2007, the local government dispatched 700 armed police to force the demolition of farmers' residences and confiscate 20 *mu* of farmland. Dissatisfied with the compensation, thousands of villagers tried to block the government's forceful demolition. Some 80 people were reportedly hurt, and some 20 were arrested. After the clash, the government issued several announcements demanding that the villagers hand over the requisitioned land.

The villagers' group then asked the Beijing Cailiang Law firm for legal assistance and launched a lawsuit against the government. The villagers argued that the initial agreements did not follow the procedure proscribed in "Land Management Law" and the "Implementation Procedures of Land Management Law," and therefore were invalid. With the legal assistance of the law firm, the villagers won the case. The High Court in Yunnan Province passed the verdict in November 2009, ruling that the government announcements were invalid and villagers' demands are partially legitimate.[58]

This is a case of a legal solution to the land dispute after violent confrontations. The crucial point for taking such an approach is that the villagers' dispute over the land price would need to have legal backing or there would need to be legal loopholes in documentation. The villagers in this case were fortunate to have the legal assistance of an experienced Beijing law firm.

Summary

The core of the land dispute has never been that the farmers want to hold onto their land. The central theme of the dispute is the perception of what is the fair price of the land. Sometimes the farmers did not get the full amount of money promised. Sometimes the farmers revoked the agreed price and wanted to raise the price. Most of the disputes are between companies (usually backed by the government) and farmers.

The land-related protests are inevitable friction in the process of urbanization. They are the pains of modernization. It is particularly the case in an irregular land market. Nobody (the government, companies or villagers) followed the market rules, and corruption is involved in many cases. As a result, corruption became the target or the justification for the peasants' protests for higher land prices.

Since the land is collectively owned, land-related protests are organized by the collectives (in most cases, villages), not by individual villagers. Bonded by kinship and driven by the expectation of higher returns, villagers are a cohesive unit and have a high fighting capability. However, because the farmers do not have many resources to voice their demands, they tend to adopt primitive and violent forms of protest, such as blocking construction or blowing up machines. A legal solution is one way of settling land-related disputes; however, because of the collective ownership of the land, farmers may not have a clear legal ground to their claims. Eventually the disputes have to be settled on moral grounds.

Other protests in the state sector

In addition to the labor protests in the SOEs, there are other protests in the category of the state sector. We made this distinction because the protest participants are different groups of people with different kinds of demands. Nonetheless, these protests also reflect the transitional pains and supplement the big picture of social protest in China. In this section, we will discuss veteran protests and teachers' protests.

Veteran protests

During 2003–10, there were eight large-scale protests by ex-servicemen, demanding material benefits. With the efforts to modernize the military forces, China has systematically reduced the size of costly ground units and increased the share of navy and air forces. The entire Chinese military has shrunk from 4 million in 1978 to 2.3 million in 2005.[59] The shift to high-tech equipment and emphasis on educational background inevitably discriminate against a large number of servicemen who had limited education. In the past, demobilized ex-servicemen were absorbed by local government agencies and state-owned enterprises through the planned system. Now all government recruitment is geared towards a better educational background. College education has become a necessary condition for any government job. Therefore, it was very difficult for the government to absorb the ex-servicemen who had middle-school education or lower. As the market reforms progressed further, efficiency-oriented enterprises were reluctant to take on unskilled ex-servicemen. This created a difficult situation for ex-servicemen and disgruntled veterans launched protests demanding better treatment. The following cases exemplify the social pains of this part of social transformation.

In 1982, after Shenzhen was designated a special economic zone, about 20,000 People's Liberation Army (PLA) construction corps members were dispatched to build the infrastructure for the new city. They were praised as the trailblazers of Shenzhen. After Shenzhen became a model of economic reform, these soldiers were demobilized and organized into several construction companies. With the rising demand for real estate, these companies have been making huge profits. However, SOE reforms transformed these companies into private ownership. As a result, thousands were laid off in the early 2000s. Many believed that they did not receive the full benefits that the central government prescribed for veterans. In November 2005, unable to reach an agreement on the lay-off subsidies, these veterans launched a protest and blocked the road. Eventually, the government issued compensation for the veterans.[60]

There was a series of veteran protests in 2007. In July, about 2,000 veterans gathered in front of the building of the People's Congress of Yantai City, Shangdong Province. The reason behind the protest was that the Yantai government had failed to implement the policies for demobilized military personnel. The protesters held out slogans like "it was glorious that we defended our country with blood, now it is sad that we have to demand justice and rights in tears" (想当年血溅疆场保国防吾辈光荣 而如今含泪维权讨公道国之悲哀), "we want policy, we want to eat, we want a way to live!" (要政策要吃饭要活路), and "harmonious society should resolve the veterans' problems" (和谐社会解决事业军转干部问题).

It was reported that since 2005, Yantai City has had several veteran protests, demanding solutions for employment, back wages, benefits, housing, subsidies and so on. The protesters argued that they protested for subsistence living. The local government did not follow the state policy on the veterans, which resulted in hard lives for the veterans. Angry about government attitudes, the veterans staged a large-scale protest. The veteran protesters were well organized and spirited.[61]

Most of the ex-servicemen were demobilized because of their low educational background and lack of skills. Therefore, they were not extremely welcome by local government or enterprises. In order to arrange the settlement, the Ministry of Railways held a comprehensive exam for 15,000 demobilized military personnel. After the exam, it admitted about 6,000 to its special railway schools for training. The Ministry promised that after two years of study, these ex-servicemen would receive a diploma and a job inside the national railway system.[62] Yet most of the railway schools did not provide a satisfactory education and living environment. There were complaints about the lousy conditions of dorms, meals and various fees. Then rumors circulated that they would not receive a decent job assignment unless they had connections or bribed the leaders.

In September 2007, about 2,000 veteran trainees in Baotou City, Neimenggu Province, waged a protest and confronted the police. A couple of days later, 1,000 veteran trainees in Qiqihar City, Heilongjiang Province, held another protest, smashing the classroom and dormitory buildings and burning vehicles. Some protests also erupted in Hubei and Shan'xi provinces, where these ex-servicemen held large-scale protests against the school authorities.[63]

The last veteran protest occurred on January 8, 2009. Over 1,000 ex-service officers gathered in front of the Shaanxi provincial government building, demanding a dialogue with the governor. These ex-officers joined the military in the 1950s and 1960s and transferred to enterprise later. However, once the enterprises ran into financial difficulties, they refused to take care of these ex-officers who were in their sixties. These ex-officers shouted slogans, sang military songs and attempted to get into the compound of the provincial government. The government officials had about three hours of negotiations with the protesters. In the end, the government promised to come up with a subsidy program to resolve the problem of ex-officers.

The disciplinary training in the military has obviously contributed to the effective mobilization of the protests. These protests were framed in moral subsistence terms with a strong sense of entitlement. The government awarded compensation to all six veteran protests, as veterans are a special social group and deservedly so.

Teachers' protest

We have recorded 21 large-scale teachers' protests in the period 2003–10. Here is an example. On March 26, 2009, more than 1,000 teachers from Henan rural school districts launched a petition in front of the Education Department of Henan Province. All the teachers were so-called "substitute teachers" (民办教师/代课教师). This type of teacher was hired because of teacher shortages in rural elementary and middle schools before the 1990s. Most of them have no teaching certificate but they devoted a major part of their lives to education in rural areas. However, with more and more normal school graduates on the job market, these substitute teachers were let go on the grounds that they did not have proper teaching qualifications. They did not receive much compensation and lost their pension and medical insurance. The Education Department of Henan Province declined their requests, which caused continuing petitions later.

This is an issue that is typically associated with socioeconomic transition. When there were teacher shortages in rural areas because of the educational lapses during the Cultural Revolution, many high-school or even middle-school graduates were recruited as "substitute teachers." Yet when normal colleges started to produce better-qualified teachers, the utility of the substitute teachers diminished. Many places simply decided to send them home. However, for those who had spent most of their lives in rural education, this policy was not fair treatment. Like most of the protests we have observed, this was a friction between the receding state moral obligation and the growing market rationality.

Conclusion

In this chapter we have discussed the large-scale labor protests in SOEs and nonstate sectors and the protests over land-related disputes, as well as some other types of protest in the state sector. As we have consistently pointed out, these protest incidents were the product of transitional pains—a transformation process from all-inclusive state responsibility to a mixture of state responsibility and market rationalism. As in any transition, this caused many structural displacements in which people lost their previous positions but either continued to hold onto the mentality of the past or complained about the unfairness of such changes, with the resulting tremendous social pains. This is most obvious in labor protests in the state sector. Labor protests in SOEs are the typical reaction to the structural changes caused by SOE reforms, at the core of which is privatization. As ownership was transferred to private hands, gone were all the state moral responsibilities. Workers who had developed a sense to belonging to an SOE were reluctant to give up their entitlement and continued to hold the state responsible for their subsistence living.

Land-related protests were the inevitable product of urbanization. The central issue in the disputes was the amount of compensation. In essence, it is about the right to land. In economic terms, ownership means that one has the right to sell or transfer the property at one's own decision. The vague collective ownership of land leads to many procedural loopholes. In some cases the compensation money was embezzled by grassroots cadres. In other cases the farmers retracted their previously agreed prices and demanded more. It is hard to pass judgment on who is at fault, as the land market has been very chaotic and involved too much corruption. The eventual solution to land-related protests was often a compromise settlement on moral grounds.

We have also discussed some of the less frequent protests—veterans' protests and teachers' protests. They are also spin-offs from the structural changes in the state sector. Demobilized ex-servicemen were formerly the beneficiaries of the planned economy, but were then thrown out into the cold to face market rationality, which is unfavorable to the less educated and less skilled. The fate of the substitute teachers, as we briefly discussed earlier, reflected the track of contemporary history of the Chinese educational system. These protests provided a fuller picture of social transformation that has touched various social groups and their lives.

Labor protest in the nonstate sector is a different story. It is the growing pains of a market-oriented economy. The diminishing labor supply has enhanced the bargaining power of the workers. New generations of workers volunteered to join the newly developed private sector on a contractual basis. They have fewer expectations of the government responsibility for their welfare and are taking matters into their own hands to fight for a better working environment and better pay. They engage in legal battles and use the Internet and cell phones as mobilizational tools. Nonetheless, if the owners fail to respond to their demands, they go to the government, as they continue to see the government as the ultimate caretaker.

When the protests involved the government, either directly or indirectly, moral claims seem to be a major framing strategy. There are two consistent themes in protests in the state sector. One is the right to subsistence living and the other is anticorruption. Protestors blamed their hardship partially on official corruption. However, the framing in protests in the nonstate sector is different, as there are no moral obligations for private or foreign companies. The claims are primarily based on contractual or legal terms.

Notes

1. Elizabeth Perry, "Chinese Conceptions of 'Rights': From Mencius to Mao-and Now," *Perspective on Politics* Vol. 6, No. 1 (2008): 45.
2. Ibid.
3. William Hurst, "Understanding Contentious Collective Action by Chinese Laid-off Workers," *Studies in Comparative International Development* Vol. 39, No. 2 (2004): 94–120.
4. Marc Blecher, "Hegemony and Workers' Politics in China," *China Quarterly* No. 170 (2002): 283–303.
5. Chen Feng, "Subsistence Crises, Managerial Corruption and Labor Protests in China," *China Journal* No. 44 (July 2000): 41–63; Lee Ching Kwan, *Against the Law: Labor Protests in China's Rustbelt and Sunbelt* (CA: University of California Press, 2007); Yongshun Cai, "The Resistance of Chinese Laid-off Workers in the Reform Period," *China Quarterly* No. 170 (June 2002): 327–44; and Hurst, "Understanding Contentious Collective Action by Chinese Laid-off Workers," ibid.
6. Hurst, "Understanding Contentious Collective Action by Chinese Laid-off Workers," ibid., 4.
7. "Buy-out" (买断) is a scheme in the SOEs reforms in China. In order to get reduce the excessive workforce, the enterprise would pay the workers a lump sum depending on the length of their employment with the enterprise. The employees then forfeited any future claims to income from the enterprise.
8. See, for example, Hurst, "Understanding Contentious Collective Action by Chinese Laid-off Workers," ibid., 20, figure 1.1, On-post employment in SOEs and urban collectives 1993–2004.
9. Mary Gallagher, *Contagious Capitalism: Globalization and the Politics of Labor in China* (Princeton University Press, 2005).
10. Haeyoun Won, "Withering Away of the Iron Rice Bowl? The Reemployment Project of Post-socialist China," *Studies in Comparative International Development* Vol. 39, No. 2 (2004): 71–93; and Marc Blecher, "Hegemony and Workers' Politics in China," ibid.
11. Mark W. Frazier, "China's Pension Reform and Its Discontents," *The China Journal* No. 51 (January 2004): 97–114.
12. William Hurst and Kevin O'Brien, "China's Contentious Pensioners," *China Quarterly* No. 170 (2002): 345–60.
13. www.chinese.rfi.fr/中国/20100606-湖北随州棉纺厂400工人堵路抗议.
14. www.china-labour.org.hk/chi/node/11560.
15. pioneer-worker.forums-free.com/topic-t349.html (accessed September 14, 2010).
16. www.caijing.com.cn/2009-07-27/110214831_2.html; news.bbc.co.uk/chinese/simp/hi/newsid_8160000/newsid_8169100/8169117.stm.
17. Personal interview.
18. All the cases were collected and confirmed by the authors' documentary study.
19. Hurst and O'Brien, "China's Contentious Pensioners," 349.
20. Ibid.
21. All the cases were collected and confirmed by the authors' documentary study.
22. www.gov.cn/ldhd/2010-12/22/content_1771062.htm.
23. Hurst, "Understanding Contentious Collective Action by Chinese Laid-off Workers," ibid., 99.
24. cn.reuters.com/article/chinaNews/idCNCNE85006W20120601.
25. Lee, *Against the Law*, ibid., 140.
26. Hurst and O'Brien, "China's Contentious Pensioners," ibid., 357.
27. www.nytimes.com/2010/02/27/business/global/27yuan.html.
28. Zai Liang, "Migration and Development in Rural China," *Modern China Studies* Vol. 17, No. 4 (2010): 48–74; and "Interprovincial Return Migration in Sichuan

Province in the 1990s: Individual and Contextual Determinants," manuscript, 2012.
29 Keith B. Richburg, "Labor Unrest in China Reflects Changing Demographics, More Awareness of Rights," *Washington Post*, June 7, 2010, A10.
30 www.clntranslations.org/article/65/short-term-work.
31 www.nytimes.com/2012/02/18/opinion/chinese-labor-cheap-no-more.html?_r=1.
32 Ching Kwan Lee has a detailed comparison of the labor protests in state sector and the private sector: Lee, *Against the Law*.
33 www.rfa.org/cantonese/news/china_labor_protection-20071023.html.
34 Chris King-Chi Chan and Pun Ngai, "The Making of a New Working Class? A Study of Collective Actions of Migrant Workers in South China," *China Quarterly* No. 198 (June 2009): 287–303.
35 Ibid.
36 Personal interview.
37 Anita Chan, "Labor Unrest and Role of Unions," *China Daily*, June 8, 2010, 9.
38 www.watchinese.com/article/2010/2248.
39 Chan and Ngai, "The Making of a New Working Class," ibid., 11.
40 Ibid.
41 Personal interview.
42 Yang Su and Xin He, "Street as Courtroom: State Accommodation of Labor Protest in South China," *Law and Society Review* Vol. 44, No. 1 (2010): 157–84.
43 Personal interview.
44 Our interviewees from Hainan government confirmed that they had several similar cases in which the government paid to cover the holes left by foreign investors.
45 www.maotianxia.com/ulwf804/1001-451651.aspx.
46 Lee, *Against the Law*, ibid., 22.
47 news.xinhuanet.com/2012-08/14/c_112722956.htm.
48 news.xinhuanet.com/politics/2011-02/24/c_121119918.htm.
49 Peter Ho, "Who Owns China's Land? Policies, Property Rights and Deliberate Institutional Ambiguity," *China Quarterly* (2001): 394–421.
50 www.sp.com.cn/zgsd/sdlt/200510/t20051024_19686.htm (accessed September 24, 2010).
51 Zhang Nandiyang, "Rumor and Mobilization in Chinese Contentious Politics," PhD dissertation, Chinese University of Hong Kong, 2009.
52 Authors' documentary study and interview.
53 news.sina.com.cn/c/2005-06-&13/02146151628;s.shtml.
54 news.sohu.com/20050720/n226385274.shtml.
55 Personal interview.
56 www.asianews.it/news-zh/%E8%AD%A6%E6%96%B9%E5%8C%85%E5%9B%B4%E5%B9%BF%E4%B8%9C%E7%9C%81%E4%B8%9C%E6%B4%B2%E6%9D%91%E6%8A%93%E6%8D%95%E5%8F%82%E5%8A%A0%E7%A4%BA%E5%A8%81%E6%8A%97%E8%AE%AE%E7%9A%84%E5%86%9C%E6%B0%91-4846.html.
57 Personal interview.
58 www.cai-liang.com/newsview.asp?ID=1310.
59 David Lampton, *Three Faces of Chinese Power: Might, Money, and Minds* (University of California Press, 2008), 39–43.
60 www.yzzk.com/cfm/Content_Archive.cfm?Channel=bn&Path=2198879092/47bn1a.cfm; and 何仲诗 [He Zhongshi], 互 網上的「深圳 荒牛」--以2005 11月初深圳退伍基建工程兵集會示威個案為，探討在網絡環境下研究社會事件的可能和局限 [Shenzhen Trail Blazers on the Internet: A Discussion of the Potential and Limits of Studying Social Incident on the Internet, the Case of Shenzhen Veteran Protest], www.youliguan.com/SZ%20Nov.pdf.
61 Personal interview with a police officer.
62 Railway schools are specialized technological schools equal to high school education.
63 Personal interview with a local reporter.

5 Benevolence violation protests

Disturbances and riots are an important part of social protest in China. Different countries have different definitions for such activities. For example, the British Riot Act of 1716 defined a riot as 12 or more people disturbing the public peace for a common purpose. In India, the law defines a riot as an "unlawful assembly" of five or more people using violence in pursuit of a common purpose. Most social scientists generally think of disturbances and riots as involving "an incident in which a crowd of fifty or more people damaged or seized property, assaulted someone or forced a victim to perform some action."[1] In this chapter we define large-scale disturbance as 500 or more people engaged in activities that disturbed the public order without a particular demand or direct interest. A riot is the more radical form of disturbance in which gathering crowds are committing acts of violence. Since violent acts are a matter of degree and there are no clear-cut boundaries between disturbance and riot, we will use disturbance and riot interchangeably in our general discussion throughout the book.

Disturbance is a form of social protest. Disturbing violence is the tactic of the protest. Because of the destructiveness of disturbances, Western scholars have long studied the phenomenon from the perspective of social psychology and treated it as a social illness. Some argue that the thinking logic and behavior of rational individuals, once they get together, would follow the crowd mentality and become irrational and uncivilized.[2] Others argue that the reason why people rebel is because of the "relative deprivation," a psychological gap between expectation and reality.[3] With the gradual institutionalization of the social movement in Western countries, the contentious protests were no longer studied as social malfunction, but as a rational political process. In contrast to the sociopsychological analysis, the political process model adopts a rational choice approach, focusing on the calculation of "interests" or "gains" and overlooking the emotional factors in a social movement. This has become the mainstream approach when studying contemporary social movement.

The political process model may be appropriate for the study of social movement in general, but not so much for disturbances. Participants in disturbances do not have any direct interest in the incident, some of them are simply influenced by the "square effect," and some have some sort of psychological identification with the victim of the minor incident that triggered the public rage. Contrary to the subsistence expectation protests in which protesters raised specific material demands, rioters often jumped in without any personal interest involved. To explain these emotional outbursts, we argue that the driving force behind rioters in contemporary China was the excitement over addressing perceived injustice and a fermented frustration over the perceived breach of benevolent governance. Most of the disturbances in China belong to the category of what we refer to as "benevolence violation protest."

From 2003 to 2010, there are 61 large-scale mass disturbances and riots, accounting for 11 percent of the total large-scale mass incidents. The occurrence of large-scale disturbances reached its peak in 2009 when all other major types of large-scale social protests declined. Compared to social protests triggered by specific economic grievances, the increase of social disturbances and riots that are not material interest oriented is startling. Alarmed by the serious threat mass disturbance poses to regime stability, the central government has strengthened the local government's responsibility system, which holds local officials accountable for such incidents. Consequently, the local governments had tried their utmost to prevent them from happening. The occurrence of riots declined in 2010.

These disturbances are often triggered by minor incidents, but rapidly become confrontational between citizens and the government. Tens of thousands of protesters, mostly mobilized by rumors, are just angry, discontent and take any opportunity to vent out their anger against the authorities. There is a strong "us" versus "them" sentiment in the crowd, which is one of the symptoms of profound social grievances. Just one minor spark could cause the cumulated anger to erupt. The increasing social disturbances may be a dangerous signal for the central government. First, this has reflected a

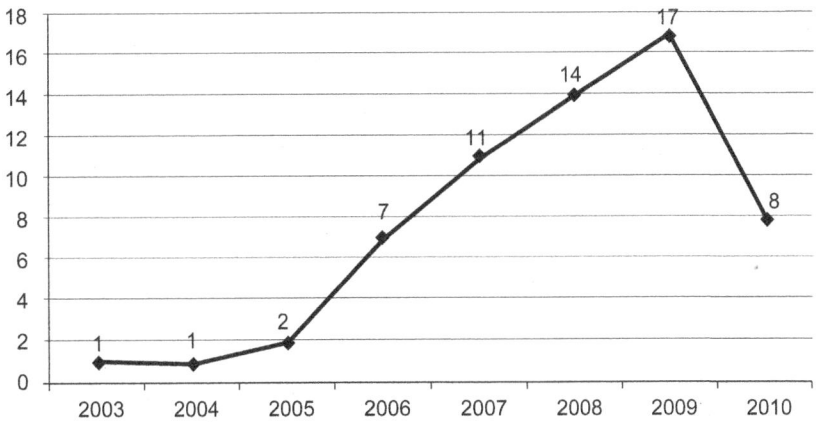

Figure 5.1 Frequency of large-scale disturbances by year
Source: Authors data

growing social frustration over the years of transformation. Second, noneconomic interest-driven social protests are not easy to appease. Disturbances are very destructive to property (public and personal) and social stability. Government officials who either caused or mishandled the disturbances are usually disciplined afterward.

Mounting social frustration

On the surface, large-scale disturbances are caused by minor incidents, such as an unnatural death, a confrontation between two strangers, or a car accident. However, the volunteer participants of the large-scale riot, who have no direct vested interest in the incident, are primarily driven by mounting social frustration.

"Pick up the rice bowl and eat meat, put down the chopsticks and curse the government" is a vivid description of a phenomenon that while people are enjoying a better standard of living they remain dissatisfied with the government.[4] These are precisely the people who would jump into a riot not to fight for their personal interests but to vent their frustration. A word of caution here: cursing the government does not equal the desire to overthrow the government. This dissatisfaction is less about the absence of any political freedom but more about the state of society in general.

Our explanation of this phenomenon is that while most people may have a much improved standard of living comparing with their past, they have other expectations not only in material terms but also in social terms. Most importantly their expectation of a benevolent government that could provide for a moral social order was wrecked during the reform era. As we have argued earlier, benevolent governance is an inseparable part of the foundation of Chinese regime legitimacy. People expect a benevolent government to provide for a more or less just social order and take care of its citizens, and its officials are moral role models—honest and uncorrupt. Reforms have created huge cracks in the image of a benevolent government.

We have pointed out that subsistence expectation protests are reflective of the disjuncture of the epochal economic transformations in China. So are disturbances and riots, which also exemplify the rugged process of the social transformation that was propelled by economic changes. Social disorientation, frustration and mobilization in a rapidly changing society inevitably create social raptures. Before the reforms in 1978, there were no rich or powerful classes in China. All the members of the society were more or less equal in their standard of living. There was a basic health care system in rural areas. In the urban cities, the work unit provided for social security and adopted the same standard salary system. Although the standard of living was very low, the state was able to maintain an egalitarian system and a clean image of the officials that continued the tradition of a benevolent government.

Since the implementation of the market-oriented economic reform in 1978, China's economy has developed at an astonishing pace. Its gross domestic product (GDP) surpassed Japan in 2010, ranking second in the world after the United States. However, while the standard of living is rising, the gaps between the rich and the poor and different regions have also increased dramatically. According to a *China Daily* report in 2010, China's Gini index has reached 0.47, surpassing the dangerous line of 0.4.[5]

During this transition process, the Chinese state has attempted to withdraw from many areas where they used to provide services, such as guaranteed housing, health care, public education and pension. As a result, people feel that they are no longer provided for and are left alone to brutal market forces. The basic collective system collapsed and a new security system has yet to be developed. In the cities, the work unit system is breaking up, many of those who were state employees suddenly lost any sense of security, exposed to the highly commercialized market environment. College graduates who used to be assigned jobs by the government, now might face unemployment upon graduation. Housing prices have skyrocketed to an unbearable level beyond the affordability of many middle-income families. The frustrations of having to struggle with market uncertainty on every front of life inevitably make people curse the government, despite the meat in the rice bowl. To make things worse, people can see that core government institutions have maintained their welfare with housing, health care and retirement for their own staff members. The new rich were able to deal with the market pressures with their wealth. These contrasts generate broad complaints in a society where the majority views egalitarianism as an ideal type of order.

China has attempted to establish rule of law in a society that was not used to the idea that law should be put above everything else.[6] There have been numerous conflicts in this regard. On the one hand, people attempt to evade rules that they determine to be unfair and thus need not be followed, such as setting up stalls without license or in places where it is prohibited. On the other hand, the government law enforcement that is trying to establish authority often behaves in a bullying manner and is perceived as related to some kind of corruption. The brutal law enforcement became a common complaint, especially when local governments started to employ "associate police" and "city management staff" who tended to be of lesser quality and lacked proper training.

At the same time, official corruption has become widespread. During Mao's era, taking a couple of kilograms of pork and a carton of cigarettes would be considered corruption. In 2010, it was revealed that the general manager of Sichuan Mobile alone had taken bribes of 2 billion RMB. In addition to pocketing huge amounts of money, news about officials seeking sex services and providing for illegitimate second wives was common. Corruption is the worst violation of a benevolent government. To be sure, many corrupt officials were punished by the law. However, the death sentence for corrupt officials is declining, while the corruption cases and amounts are ever increasing.

All together, the priority given to market efficiency, income discrepancy, state withdrawal from comprehensive public service, deviation from the sense of egalitarian tradition, and official corruption are considered violations of justice—a concept the Chinese people hold so dearly—and a violation of personal and public integrity of officials that is required by a benevolent governance. This has made the government and its officials appear to be losing their virtue, hence a betrayal of the expectation of benevolent governance. Chinese political tradition and Mao's legacies have fostered a popular belief that people have the right to constrain the state and its immoral officials by launching social protest. The compromising gesture by the government to some disturbances triggered by perceived injustice reinforces these cognitions.

As a general background, we explained the roots of social frustration in contemporary China. However, there are regional differences. Not all the social groups feel the same degree of frustration, nor do all locations have disturbances. For example, Solinger (2009) found that the poor in the cities, in fact, are more grateful to the government for low income subsidies. While her study was drawn from a limited sample, the conclusion may be valid in some other locations as well. A national survey also found that people become more tolerant of income inequality.[7] Our research found that the level of economic development and quality of local governance tends to account for the critical differences in whether or not riots erupt.

Political opportunity, mobilization and framing of riots

No regime endorses disturbances and riots and there is little political opportunity for such an act. Whenever there is a disturbance, police forces would be dispatched to control the violence and maintain order. Since the disturbances are usually triggered by a random incident and break out in an explosive manner, they do not need much political opportunity to explode. Nonetheless, despite little political opportunity, disturbances erupt. The Chinese traditional political culture has provided a larger political opportunity for disturbance, especially if the disturbance target is the misconduct of the government and perceived social injustice. Gamson and Meyer argued that some political opportunities are provided by the culture of mainstream values.[8] This type of cultural political opportunity is very stable. With the tradition of benevolent governance, "no country boasts a more enduring or more colorful history of rebellion and revolution than China."[9] Moreover, as disturbances are often framed in moral frustration over the breach of a benevolent government, the government tends to tolerate some of the less violent disturbances.

No organizations are needed for impulsive disturbances. Participants are strangers without shared material interest. Yet with some framing, they soon developed a common identity in the disturbance. The broad sense of "us versus them" would bring in more participants than any specific economic interest. Moreover, precisely because of the lack of organization, there is no control of the protest. Uncontrolled emotions breed radicalism. Minor incidents become an outlet to vent frustrations and soon escalate to large-scale smashing and burning. Participants become mobs.

The social and economic inequality brought on by the market mechanism and unprecedented official corruption translates into a perception that the moral obligation of the state for a just social order is absent. All social strata, while having different identities, share the same demand for a moral government, now become temporary allies. The weakening of state moral authority and official corruption has provided a common target for different social groups to come together. Crisis of government morality brings crisis of trust.

Without a shared material interest, the framing of the purpose of the disturbance most likely relies on the perceived moral injustice. Government corruption and official bias in favor of the rich or brutal law enforcement become the common frames that incite the crowd. Rumors also play an important role in exaggerating the perceived injustice.

Social riot in contemporary China[10]

Relative to other types of social protests, there are three general causes for large-scale mass riots. First, government staff, such as police or city management, using unnecessary violence to enforce regulations. Second are the abnormal deaths believed to be related to government agencies, officials and their relatives. The third cause is the conflict between the rich and the poor: most cases involved the accident in which a BMW automobile (a car brand that the Chinese new rich like to show off) hit pedestrians (often working-class poor people). We will discuss these types in this section.

Brutal enforcement of regulations

Zhengzhou incident

In Henan Province, on June 6, 2007, the city management of Zhengzhou City was cleaning up the illegal stalls on a major street and had a confrontation with a stall owner. Dongfeng road is located at the intersection of several universities in Zhengzhou. It was always crowded with stalls that did not have valid licenses. Some college students from humble family backgrounds liked to set up temporary stalls to sell petty crafts to subsidize their studies. When the city management was trying to clean up the illegal stalls, they had a dispute with a female student, which turned into physical pushing and shoving. The city management staff hit the student and broke her teeth. Other male students then called an ambulance and escalated the fight. One student used a brick to attack the city management staff, and soon attracted a huge crowd of onlookers.

The police arrived and put both the city management staff and the students involved into police cars. The crowd believed that the police should punish the city management staff on the spot, but seeing them being put into cars instead, when the weather was hot, the crowd shouted "don't let them sit in an air conditioned car, get them out!" The normal police procedure enraged the onlookers and turned the incident into a riot. Students overturned the vehicles of the city management. The police tried to separate the crowd from the police cars but failed. The police arrested the students who tried to overturn the police car, so the crowd surrounded the police car and chanted "release the students, release the students." In the end, the police released the students on-site under pressure. The gathering crowd stayed until midnight.

Anti-family planning incidents

There were two incidents protesting against the brutal measures to enforce the family planning policy by local governments of Bobai County and Rong County in Guangxi Province. China had adopted a one family-one child policy since 1979 in order to control the fast-growing population. Successful implementation of this policy has become one of the evaluation measures for local government performance. Bobai county government was under great pressure to control its population growth, as the county population had grown from 490,000 in 1949 to 1.6 million in 2002. The local governments used very harsh measures to enforce family planning, imposing a huge number of fines on violators. If the farmers were unable to pay the fines, the authorities would confiscate their property. On May 17, 2007, the township government officials had a conflict with them members of a household who failed to pay the fines, and got into a physical fight. The villagers went to the township government to protest. Farmers from other townships followed suit and a large-scale riot broke out.

In the following days, six other townships had mass sieges of local government buildings. There were about 3,000 participants at the peak. They started to destroy government buildings, gates, office equipment and official files. A few participants also burned government vehicles. The demonstration effect of the Bobai incident caused a chain reaction in its neighboring Rong County. Tens of thousands of farmers gathered and started to attack local governments and their buildings. In the end, the upper-level government had to send a work team of 2,000 officials to explain family planning policy and to calm down the popular rage against harsh implementation of the policy.

Family planning is not a popular policy. People were unhappy about the one-child policy, but accepted it as a legitimate state policy.[11] The brutal enforcement of the policy eventually enraged the peasants and they started to riot. These disturbances were slightly different from other cases. It targeted a particular policy enforcement and participants considered themselves victims.

Unnatural death perceived to have government connections

Guang'an incident

In Sichuan Province on November 7, 2006, a poisoned child was sent to a hospital in Guang'an and because the parents did not have enough money to pay the deposit, the hospital did not rescue the child in time to save his life. On November 9, the relatives of the dead child put up wreaths in front of the hospital to protest and demanded compensation. Because the hospital refused to pay the compensation demanded by the family, the confrontation escalated. Some citizens and nearby high school students went to the hospital to protest. The police dispatched forces to control the traffic, but more and more people flooded the hospital. Protesters tried to break through the police line, resulting in injuries on both sides. Then the rioters burned police cars. Some got into the hospital, smashed medical equipment and burned buildings. Others blocked the firefighting vehicles. The riot lasted until the early morning of November 10. It remained unclear whether the hospital was responsible for the death of the child. This incident was not necessarily related to government corruption, but to resentment over the marketization of hospitals, which resulted in the hospitals only caring about money and not much about poor patients.

Dazhu incident

In Sichuan Province in the early morning of December 30, 2006, the police station in Dazhu County received a report from a luxury hotel, saying that one of their female employees had died of unknown causes. On January 15, unhappy about the fruitless investigation, family and friends of the dead started to appeal to the public to put pressure on the government. Rumors online suggested that three high-ranking officials from the provincial government, who were good friends of the hotel owner, came to the hotel to drink. They forced the female employee to drink with them and then they raped her to death. The criminal acts were then allegedly covered up by the local government. Enraged by the rumors, crowds laid siege to the hotel and broke the windows, then set the hotel on fire. Tens of thousands of Dazhu citizens stood by and watched. The fire was finally put out by firefighters after two hours.

On January 22, the Mayer of Dazhu County promised to publicize the investigation result. According to the investigation, the waitress fainted in the hotel because of a combination of chronic pancreatitis and acute bleeding. Three male employees took her home and one stayed to care for her. The one who stayed then raped her. He then found that her face was pale and her lips had turned purple. The waitress was sent to the hospital and died there. The male employee was arrested for rape. As a piece of background information, this luxury hotel was owned by the director of the local police station. In a less developed county, that the director of a police station could own a luxury hotel worth 10 million RMB is outrageous, and this is why the local population was so disgusted by government and police corruption.

Weng'an incident

In Guizhou Province on June 22, 2008, a teenage girl, Li Shufen, drowned in a river while she was spending time with three other teenagers. The girl was from a poor peasant family and her parents refused to accept the police conclusion that their daughter committed suicide for no apparent reason. Several biopsies were performed by different agencies and the conclusion remained that the girl was drowned. Then a rumor started to circulate that she was raped. This soon turned into a riot with tens of thousands involved. The participants believed that the government was trying to cover up the rape case for the probable reason that some government officials were involved in the rape. The burning and looting lasted for about seven hours; the county government headquarters was destroyed and the police station was smashed up. About 150 people were injured during the incident. The incident caught the attention of General Secretary Hu Jintao, who issued several instructions for the resolution of the riot. Minister of Public Security Meng Jianzhu led the entire operation over the phone to quell the riot.

During the riot, various rumors rapidly circulated. One suggested that during the college entrance examination, a student sitting behind Li demanded help with the questions and Li refused, so that student asked Li out on June 21 and raped and killed her. Another rumor said that the deputy mayor's son and another teenager who also had a strong family background, raped and killed Li. The third rumor said that the victim's uncle went to the police station to report the case, but was badly beaten by the police, and then the police had the mafia beat her uncle to death.

The truth is that Li was a 16-year-old middle-school student. She did not take the college entrance examination. The teenagers she spent time with were her friends and none of their families had any official connections. Li's uncle was beaten by some unidentifiable people but he was sent to the hospital by the police and he was released by the hospital later.

This incident became a nationwide sensation thanks to the Internet. The development of the Internet has provided a strong platform for the dissemination of information. The Internet and cell phone messaging have become the channels for rumors. Only one hour after the incident broke out, photos and videos were circulated online. Rumors, therefore, snowballed to all corners of society.

Shishou incident

In Hubei Province on June 17, 2009, a man was found dead in front of the hotel where he had been working. The police determined that it was a case of suicide, but the relatives and the public were not convinced. There had been a similar case 10 years earlier in which a waitress was also found dead in front of the hotel. There was deep public suspicion about the background of the hotel. On June 18, the hotel issued a small amount of compensation and asked the family to accept the suicide conclusion. The hotel also announced that it would cremate the dead body. The victim's family refused this. The same day the police tried to send the body to the cremation site by force.

Sympathetic crowds blocked police efforts to remove the dead body, which led to a large-scale riot.

The government then dispatched a large number of police to the hotel, with armed police, antiriot and firefighting vehicles. Some protesting citizens were arrested. Contrary to government expectations, the protest was not quelled, but instead the enraged crowd escalated the riot. More and more people flooded into the street and confronted the police. Rumors about more bodies being found in the hotel were rife, fanning the imagination of the crowd. Rioters burned the hotel and police vehicles and injured some police officers. The incident lasted for more than 80 hours, with several tens of thousands of participants. This was the social disturbance with the most participants since 1989. In the end, because the scale of the riot was so large, both the central and provincial governments dispatched envoys to the scene, promised to investigate the incident and let the public know the truth. The crowd gradually dispersed.

Gancheng incident

In Hainan Province, this was a vicious riot caused by the improper handling of a dispute by the local police. On March 23, 2009, two middle-school students had a physical fight. One student was from Gancheng Village. The other was from Baoshang Village. The relatives of the student from Gancheng Village went to the township government demanding the punishment of the student from Baoshang. Failing to get what they were demanding, the angry villagers smashed the township government, burning the vehicles and buildings. Then the mob turned to the border patrol police station located just opposite the government building, throwing gas bombs at the buildings, police cars and some of the confiscated smuggled goods. After that, the mobs went to Baoshang village and smashed up a hotel in the village. The villagers from Baoshang then started to launch a counterattack. Several thousands of villagers had a large-scale fight, resulting in one death and six injuries.

The next day, Dongfang City dismissed the director of the local police station for mishandling the incident. However, the dismissal did not calm the situation. Gancheng villagers launched an attack on Baoshang village again. This time, a Gancheng villager was beaten seriously after being caught throwing a gas bomb. On the third day, Baoshang villagers intercepted a truck owned by a Gancheng villager and burned it. This triggered a second round of large-scale fights. Thousands of villagers threw bricks, rocks and gas bombs at each other. Routine life was disrupted; shops and schools were all closed. The fight was finally stopped by the riot police, who were then stationed in Gancheng Township for more than a month to ensure a peaceful resolution. This incident was not caused by unnatural death of any sort. It was triggered by a seemingly innocent fight among teenagers. Yet the mishandling of the incident led to the most vicious incident.

Perceived official bias in favor of the rich

Wanzhou incident

Wanzhou is a district in Chongqing City. On October 18, 2004, a porter accidentally bumped a woman, which led to a confrontation. The husband of the woman came over and assaulted the porter, claiming that he was a government official and he "could purchase your life with money." The quarrel attracted many onlookers. When a policeman arrived on the scene, the husband went over to shake hands him, indicating that he had wide connections. Even though the policeman did not know the husband, he did not refuse the handshake. Then the policeman heard both sides of the quarrel, putting all parties into a police car to take them to the police station for further investigation. The onlookers saw the husband shaking hands with the policeman and therefore believed that he had government connections. Then the rumor started to circulate that the police was going to let the husband off the hook and the beaten porter would not receive any justice. Convinced that the policeman was going to side with the husband, the crowd stopped the police vehicle for three and half hours before the policeman finally took the parties away.

Then the rumors about government officials beating poor people and being released spread quickly. At about 6 o'clock that evening, people started to gather in front of the government building, demanding that the official (attacker) be seriously punished. Some protesters had confrontations with the police and burned police cars, causing a serious traffic jam. The incident accelerated to a riot, which lasted until the morning. Several rioters got into the government building and started to loot property, such as computers. After police arrested the looters, the riot finally became quiet. Later it turned out that the attacker was not a government official but a private business owner, and he was charged accordingly.

Chizhou incident

In Anhui Province, this riot was caused by a car accident. On June 26, 2005, a Honda hit a pedestrian. Instead of making an apology, the driver got out of the car and attacked the pedestrian. Someone called the police, who came and took the driver to the police station. A large crowd gathered in front of the police station and waited for the conclusion. Then rumors flew. The Honda became a BMW (a symbol for the rich); the victim became a female high school student who died after being sent to the hospital; and the Honda driver supposedly claimed that "it only takes 300,000 bucks for a life." Because the driver was not locked up by the police when put into the police car, people believed that he was getting favorable treatment by the police. The incident escalated into a riot. Participants burned the car that caused the accident, then the police car, and smashed up the police station. The supermarket by the police station was looted. The supermarket looting was considered a serious criminal act so the police then stopped the riot in the name of protecting the property of the people.

Rui'an incident

In Zhejiang Province on August 18, 2006, a high school teacher, Dai Haijing, jumped from a building and died. The local police concluded that this was an ordinary suicide. However, her students and friends refused to accept the police conclusion. Dai's husband came from a billionaire family. Dai had broken marriage relations and she had recorded family violence in her diaries. The locals believed that Dai's husband's family had bribed the police and local media. An open letter written by the students of Dai's class started to circulate online: "Injustice Comparable to Dou'er, Snows in August—Will our teacher leave us in this manner?"[12] On August 19, thousands of students from the high school where Dai taught, gathered to mourn her death and paraded to cry injustice. Various rumors were circulating.

On September 7, two officials from the Bureau of Quality Control of Ruian City had a confrontation with peddlers when inspecting their scales. The incident, unrelated to Dai Haijing's death, ignited the fuse. Thousands of the protesters gathered in front of the local government building, protesting against brutal law enforcement and then demanding the thorough investigation of Dai's death. After futile dialogue with the government, mobs turned to the factory owned by Dai's husband's family, destroying the vehicles, machines and part of the factory buildings. The police arrested several protesters who were involved in smashing up property. The incident ended without any clear conclusion.

Causes of disturbance

How did minor incidents cause social disturbances of such magnitude? The riots we collected during 2003 to 2010 have revealed certain patterns and may be due to the confluence of several factors. We found that social tensions had been brewing for a long time in the locations where disturbances erupted. These social tensions were the product of low-level economic development and poor quality of local governance. Consequently, minor incidents would spark the fuse. Rumor played an important role in fanning and escalating the mass rage. We will elaborate on these factors in detail in the following sections.

Less developed local economy

The economy in the majority of the places where disturbances occurred was less developed. Table 5.1 illustrates the per capita GDP in all the counties, cities and districts where 61 disturbances erupted, in comparison with that of the provincial and national levels. GDP is not the only indicator, but is an

110 *Benevolence violation protests*

Table 5.1 Differences in GDP per capita

Location	Year	Per capita GDP	Provincial per capita GDP	National per capita GDP	Provincial	National
Hefei	2003	10,622	6,455	10,542	4,167	80
Yuxi	2003	13,860	5,841	10,542	8,019	3,318
Qujin	**2003**	**5,017**	**5,841**	**10,542**	**-824**	**-5,525**
Wanzhou	**2004**	**7,246**	**9,641**	**12,336**	**-2,395**	**-5,090**
Dongguan	2005	33,287	24,438	14,185	8,849	19,102
Chizhou	**2005**	**7,050**	**8,742**	**14,185**	**-1,692**	**-7,135**
Xiangyin	**2006**	**10,127**	**12,123**	**16,500**	**-1,996**	**-6,373**
Rui'an	**2006**	**24,380**	**30,991**	**16,500**	**-6,611**	**7,880**
Humen	2006	32,278	28,747	16,500	3,531	15,778
Lanzhou	2006	19,525	8,939	16,500	10,586	3,025
Bazhong	**2006**	**4,798**	**10,613**	**16,500**	**-5,815**	**-11,702**
Danzhou	**2006**	**7,454**	**12,499**	**16,500**	**-5,045**	**-9,046**
Guang'an	**2006**	**6,144**	**10,638**	**16,500**	**-4,494**	**-10,356**
Dazhu	**2007**	**9,154**	**12,997**	**20,169**	**-3,843**	**-11,015**
Guixi	2007	26,689	13,279	20,169	13,410	6,520
Bobai	2007	22,170	12,214	20,169	9,956	2,001
Rongxian	**2007**	**19,533**	**12,214**	**20,169**	**7,319**	**-636**
Chizhou	**2007**	**10,949**	**12,045**	**20,169**	**-1,096**	**-9,920**
Chongqing	2007	26,956	14,660	20,169	12,296	6,787
Yibin	**2007**	**10,505**	**12,997**	**20,169**	**-2,492**	**-9,664**
Huzhou	**2007**	**34,601**	**37,411**	**20,169**	**-2,810**	**14,432**
Zhengzhou	2007	37,679	24,671	20,169	13,008	17,510
Youyang	**2007**	**3,476**	**16,606**	**20,169**	**-13,130**	**-16,693**
Wusu	**2007**	**14,705**	**16,817**	**20,169**	**-2,112**	**-5,464**
Tianmen	**2008**	**11,561**	**19,837**	**23,708**	**-8,276**	**-12,147**
Wenchang	**2008**	**14,676**	**17,600**	**23,708**	**-2,924**	**-9,032**
Chengdu	2008	34,676	15,484	23,708	19,192	10,968
Yuhuan	2008	61,840	42,214	23,708	19,626	38,132
Taishan	**2008**	**18,557**	**37,195**	**23,708**	**-18,638**	**-5,151**
Yongshun	**2008**	**4,760**	**18,111**	**23,708**	**-13,351**	**-18,948**
Weng'an	**2008**	**6,000**	**9,904**	**23,708**	**-3,904**	**-17,708**
Fugu	2008	51,964	19,673	23,708	32,291	28,256
Huizhou	**2008**	**32,860**	**37,195**	**23,708**	**-4,335**	**9,152**
Menglian	**2008**	**6,154**	**12,530**	**23,708**	**-6,376**	**-17,554**
Binyang	**2008**	**8,023**	**14,578**	**23,708**	**-6,555**	**-15,685**
Wuxi	**2008**	**4,411**	**20,407**	**23,708**	**-15,996**	**-19,297**
Suqian	**2008**	**13,800**	**39,915**	**23,708**	**-26,115**	**-9,908**
Shenzhen	2008	89,800	37,195	23,708	52,605	66,092
Dejiang	**2009**	**6,149**	**11,062**	**25,608**	**-4,913**	**-19,459**
Guoluo	**2009**	**9,036**	**19,412**	**25,608**	**-10,376**	**-16,572**
Dongfang	**2009**	**15,625**	**19,150**	**25,608**	**-3,525**	**-9,983**
Pingxiang	**2009**	**23,287**	**15,921**	**25,608**	**7,366**	**-2,321**
Najing	2009	68,274	44,120	25,608	24,154	42,666
Huining	**2009**	**4,854**	**13,259**	**25,608**	**-8,405**	**-20,754**
Cangshan	**2009**	**15,780**	**35,794**	**25,608**	**-20,014**	**-9,828**
Lanzhou	2009	27,874	13,259	25,608	14,615	2,266
Shishou	**2009**	**10,591**	**22,659**	**25,608**	**-12,068**	**-15,017**
Yibin	**2009**	**13,475**	**17,289**	**25,608**	**-3,814**	**-12,133**

Table 5.1 (continued)

Location	Year	Per capita GDP	Provincial per capita GDP	National per capita GDP	Provincial	National
Nanchong	**2009**	**10,952**	**17,339**	**25,608**	**-6,387**	**-14,656**
Yuanling	**2009**	**11,973**	**20,387**	**25,608**	**-8,414**	**-13,635**
Lanzhou	2009	27,874	13,259	25,608	14,615	2,266
Kunming	2009	29,252	13,498	25,608	15,754	3,644
Ningbo	2009	73,811	43,575	25,608	30,236	48,203
Xi'an	2009	34,848	11,062	25,608	23,786	9,240
Datong	**2009**	**10,069**	**21,472**	**25,608**	**-11,403**	**-15,539**
Kunming	2010	32,991	19,038	29,992	13,953	2,999
Chenzhou	**2010**	**24,015**	**24,719**	**29,992**	**-704**	**-5,887**
Shenzhen	2010	94,296	44,736	29,992	49,560	64,304
Ma'ansha	2010	59,370	25,395	29,992	33,975	29,378
Zhengzhou	2010	46,840	28,716	29,992	18,124	16,848
Anshun	**2010**	**10,100**	**16,117**	**29,992**	**-6,017**	**-19,892**
Weiyuan	**2010**	**20,243**	**26,147**	**29,992**	**-5,904**	**-9,749**
Zhangjiagang	2010	12,828	61,022	29,992	-48,194	-17,164

Note: The per capita GDP (county, provincial and national) is the figure of the year when the protest occurred.
Source: (*China Statistical Yearbook*, various years)

important one of economic development. Some 37 out of 61 incidents (60 percent) erupted in less developed areas (highlighted in the table). Their per capita GDP was below both the provincial and national levels in the year the incidents occurred. There were also three cases that were below either provincial or national levels. We use the per capita figure because it best reflects the living standard of the locality and it is the situation about which people have the most acute feelings. A binomial test suggests that a disturbance is significantly more likely to occur in a county with its GDP below the provincial mean than in a county having a greater than the provincial mean GDP value ($p = 0.036$). In other words, disturbances are more likely to occur in relatively poor counties.

Why did mass riots usually occur in less developed places? First, the less developed economy means that the local government has fewer resources at hand to provide adequate social services, which are the minimum moral obligation of a benevolent government. Without resources, some of the important public services lapsed. For example, because Hainan's economic development was sluggish, it had insufficient funds to support local police. Therefore, in some of the remote areas, Hainan Province delegated the maintenance of local public security to the border patrol police, whose primary job was to prevent smuggling and illegal crossing of the border. The Gancheng police forces nominally belong to the border patrol police troops, which are under the direct charge of the Chinese Armed Police and have no connections with local governance. Even in this case, the police forces were understaffed. The ratio of police to population in Hainan Gancheng is 10,000:2, while China's average is 10,000:12 and the world average is 10,000:36. During the Gancheng incident, Gancheng Township had a 50,000 population and the police station only had 10 personnel.

The displacement of function (using border patrol troops for regular police tasks) has resulted in the negligence of normal government functions. Since the border patrol police station was located on the extreme periphery and was not subject to local government supervision, it did not care about the public security of the locals. According to the villagers, the police station would charge 1,000 yuan for each dispatch of forces. Even so, they did not solve any cases.[13] Local public order is very chaotic, and small gambling casinos were everywhere. Gambling disputes and robberies of casinos were common. Even the director of the police station had his own casino.

Second, official corruption tends to be more blatant in less developed areas and causes the most public resentment. A less developed economy means a low educational level for the region in general and, thus, a low level of official quality in local government in particular. Therefore, on top of inadequate public services, corruption, back door favoritism, mediocre skills in management and a lack of discipline become common practice in these local governments.

Third, public attention in less developed areas tends to be less diversified and more focused on government behaviors. In more developed areas, resources, information and opportunities are more pluralized, meaning that government positions are not the most desirable, so public sensitivity is not exclusively focused on the immoral behavior of government officials. In contrast, in less developed areas, job opportunities are limited, government positions are "iron rice bowls" for which the locals yearn. Government action thus becomes the focus of public attention. As a result, the public is more sensitive to official immorality, and is more likely to form a temporary alliance against such immorality. The Sichuan Dazhu incident, Hubei Shishou incident and Hainan Ganchen incident were all caused by government officials violating the rules and engaging in commercial activities. As they have controlled the major social resources and made huge profits in a meager economy, it would inevitably cause strong popular resentment. It is easier for social groups that have less diverse economic interests to develop temporary common identities and form a temporary interest community against corrupt officials when conditions allow.

Fourth, as economic development becomes the top priority for these less developed areas, the government-business relationship becomes colluded. Until 2008, the evaluation of local officials was directly related to their ability to attract investment and generate GDP growth. The relationship between government and business, therefore, became symbiotic. On the one hand, local government needed outside investment or local business to promote economic growth and generate tax revenues. On the other hand, the close relationship between government and business inevitably involved many secret deals, bribes and favoritism. These would convince the public that the government only cares about wooing the rich and neglects the poor people.

During the Chizhou incident, the reason why the locals could easily form a temporary alliance in the riot was because the driver was a businessman from outside. People believed that these outside businesspeople colluded with the corrupt government, took the money away from the locals and pushed up the housing price. They thought that the standard of living for local people had dropped as a result. Hence, after the outside businessman hit a pedestrian, many were convinced that the police would protect the attacker instead of the attacked.

Another example is that because of the discovery of mining resources in the Weng'an region, there were a lot of forced relocations and, consequently, a lot of disputes over the relocation. A large number of relocated migrants, forced out of their residences on unfavorable terms, had been grumbling and unsettled for a long time. Furthermore, the local mine owners had numerous conflicts with the locals, and the government always sided with the business interest, not the public interest, even to the extent of using the police force. This is why the people formed a temporary alliance against the government so quickly. As the new Party secretary of Weng'an County pointed out after the riot, on the surface, the death of the teenager was the cause of the incident. However, deep down, it was because of the violation of people's interests during the development of the mining resources and the settlement of the relocated residents. Behind the riots, we often discover political power-seeking rents, officials protecting officials and officials colluding with business, all of which were the most hated types of "loss of virtue" by the government.

As we discussed earlier, in less developed regions, government budgets could not support adequate police forces. This is one inducement for riot. The inadequacy of police forces led to expectations of government repression. A Haikou (capital of Hainan Province) police officer admitted that "Western Hainan has the lowest educational level. The villagers are quite barbarian. Don't mention the outsiders, even we have a strong sense of insecurity when going into these areas."[14] In contrast, the important economic or political center cities, especially the Centrally Administered Cities, because of their economic and political sensitivity, have abundant and very affective police forces. Protesters know what the bottom line is, so protests rarely escalate to riots.

Consequently we have found that with regard to the degree of destructiveness, riots that occurred in provincial capitals or big cities (Hefei, Lanzhou, Xi'an, Chengdu and Shenzhen) were limited to confrontations with the police and burning of police cars. At the county-level cities (Wanzhou, Shishou, Dazhu, Chizhou and so on), there were burnings of government buildings, smashing of equipment and looting of a supermarket. At the township level (Hainan Gancheng), we saw vicious fights and serious injuries. The lower the administrative level, the lower the economic development, the more destructive the riots.

A senior research fellow of the Ministry of Public Security pointed out that among all types of social protests, disturbances are the most destructive and exert the most pressure on social stability. Therefore, it is of utmost importance to prevent disturbances from erupting in Beijing and its neighboring areas. As a result, Beijing has the biggest police force and the most advanced police equipment, and hence, the highest administrative efficacy.[15] In contrast, the governments in remote areas usually do not have effective control over society owing to lack of resources. Low levels of economic development severely constrain the budget of the local government and tend to lead to low administrative efficacy.

Some of the disturbances occurred in developed areas. Yet, they were not necessarily local residents who participated. For example, the disturbance in Humen of Guangdong Province was caused by the conflict between city management and the rickshawers who came from Hubei Province. Most rickshawers in Humen were from Hubei. Therefore, when the conflict occurred, all the Hubei rickshawers and other outsiders participated in the riot. No Humen local residents participated in the riot.[16]

Poor quality of local governance

The root cause of the social tension and riots in contemporary China is the poor quality of local governance. The central government's emphasis on GDP growth has forced the local government officials to concentrate on economic development and, as a result, overlook the social management and the rights of ordinary citizens. Local governments lost the desire and ability to manage and coordinate pluralizing social interests. Consequently, they developed a tendency to rely on coercive power to deal with social discontent.

The most blatant feature of coercive management is the excessive use of the police. Using the police is the common method to maintain social order in many societies, but there is a lack of respect and obedience to police in the tradition of benevolence. Excessive use of police power ran contrary to the benevolent tradition of Chinese society. For example, in the Shishou incident, the early dispatch of police was unable to maintain public order, but became the symbol of tyrannical rule and escalated the conflict. The Party secretary of Weng'an County, Shi Zongyuan, pointed out that the Weng'an government had a tendency to use the police whenever there was a problem, which intensified police-civilian relations, added to which, corruption within the police force was the cause of the riot.[17]

Another feature of coercive management is the brutality of city management staff when enforcing city regulations. Lacking a rule of law tradition, the regulation enforcement of city management, a basic function of city management, has become the symbol of a government without virtue. In some incidents, it was the disputes that originated from city management that led to a temporary alliance of a diverse group of people and, eventually, riot. Several large-scale disturbances were triggered by conflicts between staff members of the city management agency (*chengguan*, 城管) and illegal vendors on the street. The cleaning up of the illegal street peddlers was prescribed by official regulations and legitimate, but the public sympathy was with the illegal vendors, as the *chengguan* staff is perceived as bullying and rude.

The third feature of coercive management is excessive fining. In less developed areas, local officials' efforts to stimulate economic development far exceeded government responsibility for social management and service. Fining became one of the important sources of government revenue. Local governments used fining to replace actual management. In some places fining became the only management. This often became the trigger of riots, if fining became a widespread method and produced a critical mass of victims. For example, the riots caused by family planning measures in Guangxi were triggered by coercive fining, including demolition of houses, confiscation of property and forced abortion.

In addition to coercive management, the local government also lacks crisis management skills. In public administration theories, crisis management is divided into three stages: prevention, management and responsibility. Contemporary crisis management is complementary to the traditional Chinese idea of benevolent governance. Yet the local government in less developed areas lacked crisis management experience and the skills to communicate with the media.

In the first stage of crisis prevention, local governments were insensitive to social grievances. Some of the crises were caused by extreme incidents, such as the unnatural death of the victim. Preservation of life is the bottom line of a benevolent government, yet the local government in less developed areas often overlooked this bottom line. When the unnatural death of a waitress caused a social uproar in Dazhu County, the Party secretary of the county remained puzzled: "isn't it just the death of a person, how come it caused such a fuss?"[18] He was dismissed later, partially because of his insensitivity to human life.

Lacking the experience of crisis prevention, in almost all the riots the local government missed the best opportunity to calm down the crisis. For example, when the public were upset at the death of a waitress in Dazhu County, the government agencies were busy engaging in official government elections and neglected the investigation of the death incident. In the eyes of the population, if a government does not care about life, it is typically a loss of virtue.

During the second stage of crisis management, local governments were rigid at best. According to benevolent tradition, the highest official in the local government is the parent official. In general people have less faith in the court system, but believe in upright and clean officials. However, during these crises, local government did not follow the moral principles of benevolent governance. The highest official in local government was often absent from the scene, either because he thought it was not important or lacked the courage to face the angry crowd. As a result, he became a moronic official in the eyes of the public and further enraged the riots. The use of the police force reinforced such images and escalated the conflicts. In contrast, all the eventual conclusions of such riots were accompanied by the public appearance of the highest official of the local government and him making relevant promises.

Moreover, local government officials lacked communication skills. The government was awfully ineffective in communicating with the masses in times of crisis. For example, during the Shishou incident, amid a plethora of rumors the government statements about the incident were few and vague. This does not help the authorities to subdue the angry population. Many local governments lacked the skills to deal with the news media. They refused to give interviews, restricted the reporters' access to the scene and cut off Internet connections. All of which reinforced the impression that the government was covering up something. Even if there were halfhearted press conferences to declare the government position, the long-lived habit of rigid propaganda style also greatly reduced the efficacy of a public relations effort by the government. The dogmatic phrase of "a small portion of ill-intentioned people agitated the masses who do not know the true facts" had fostered an adverse public psychology that questioned everything the government stated.

Responsibility system is a tradition of benevolent governance. "If an official does not take care of the people, he should better go home to sell sweet potatoes." This phrase has circulated for thousands of years in China. It is true that some officials were dismissed after the riots. However, the dismissed officials were often reinstated elsewhere later, making the government lose credit. The public finds it difficult to trust the government.

Local governments and police forces were generally perceived as either corrupt or incompetent, or both. The fact that the police were often dispatched in favor of the capitalists who have a close relationship with the government whenever there was a dispute between peasants and the companies reinforced the public perception. It is very obvious that in many riots, when the police took the disputing parties away for investigation, the crowd would immediately assume that the police were siding with the guilty party. There was a profound distrust of the government.

As a counterexample of the poor quality of the governance, the governments in the important economic and political center cities, especially the Centrally Administered Cities are more capable of dealing with the protests. For example, during the fire incident of November 2010 in Shanghai, the government showed great flexibility. At the fire scene, citizens were making speeches accusing the government of ignorance and immorality, and demanding democracy. The police showed tolerance. The top government officials appeared on the scene to mourn the dead of the fire incident and because the Shanghai government was able to take the moral high ground, the public accepted the benevolent government behavior. Thus, the Shanghai government successfully turned a potential social protest into a government-authorized mourning activity. This ability to assuage public anger by occupying a moral position is something that local governments seriously lack.

After the Chizhou incident, the Chizhou government official remained baffled that the riot occurred. "Police treated it as a normal social dispute. Only two security guards hit people, and you can only detain these two guards. Who would know this turned into such a large-scale riot?"[19]

A factor that is closely related to both the low levels of economic development and poor quality of governance is the distance from central cities. In his book, *Disorder under Heaven: Collective Violence in the Ming Dynasty*, James Tong argues that the remote regions, "being less penetrable by imperial control, would have the higher level of collective violence." He finds that "the further away the county is from Beijing (the capital city of the Ming Dynasty), the more rebellious they were."[20] Distance is a rough measure. It does not take into consideration the difficulty of transportation nor the size of the province. For example, 80 kilometers from Haikou City would put a city into mountainous areas, while 80 kilometers from downtown Beijing is barely outside of the sixth beltway. Given the tremendous work needed in measuring distance and administrative efficacy in contemporary terms, this hypothesis has to be tested later.

Rumor as mobilization and strategic framing

The typical feature of riots is the lack of effective leaders and organizations, which are critical for social movements. Precisely because of the lack of leadership and an organizational network, protests easily become uncontrollable and even deliberately commit crimes. That is why we call such actions riots. In order to get hundreds, thousands, or even tens of thousands of people to the street, there has to be a mechanism to compensate for the lack of leaders and organization. In all these riots, we found that rumor played a much larger role in fulfilling the lack of other mechanisms. This is not to say that rumors did not play a role in other protests, but it played a much more significant role in instigating, mobilizing and enraging riots.

Some scholars argue that rumor is a compensation mechanism in an opaque situation where there is insufficient information. Others believe that rumor is a weapon for the powerless, since it does not require many resources to spread. There is no argument that no riot ever occurs without rumors to incite, accompany and intensify the violence.[21] With the introduction of cell phones and text messages (SMS), rumors travel fast, and help to create a temporary identity for the participants.

In other forms of social protest, effective leaders would employ rumors as instruments to frame and mobilize the movement. Yet at the same time, they would also curtail the most outrageous rumors so the protest remains under control. In a riot, outrageous rumors run wild but are easy to refute, hence deflating the emotionally charged rioting activities.

Rumor performed two major functions in riots. First, it created a position of "us" versus "them." They are the "evil," powerful, corrupt officials and inhumane rich people. We are the powerless, humiliated and oppressed. This kind of frame would naturally induce people to side with or join the powerless. People were eager to accept the rumor and pass it onto others because they know that there are plenty of corrupt officials and arrogant rich people, and these stories might be true.

The second function is to frame the incident in terms of moral injustice. Rumor is a fabrication of a fact, but framing is to promote and enlarge the fabrication. Moral injustice is more likely to incite emotional anger than other wrongdoing. Emotionally charged actions tend to be violent. Let's look at some of the rumors created during these riots. For example, in the Zhengzhou incident, city management staff were rumored to be drunk, and broke the front teeth of the poor female student; in the Weng'an incident, the victim was rumored to be raped to death by the deputy mayor and the son of the public security bureau chief, and her lower body was a bloody mess; in the Dazhu incident, the high-ranking provincial officials were said to have used drugs and raped the waitress, and her body had dark bruises and her private parts were messy; and in the Chizhou incident, the rumor goes that the new rich drove a Mercedes Benz and hit the victim, whose bones were exposed. All these rumors framed a morally decadent "them" and served to mobilize a large number of sympathizers to riot.

The broad categorization of us versus them and moral injustice tend to attract broad participation in the protests, larger than some of the material-based protests. The long-fermented social frustration then found an outlet for venting. Sometimes, "counter"-rumor may divide the temporary alliance on the street and help to pacify a protest. On April 29, 2010, in Jiangsu Taixing, a man ran into a kindergarten and stabbed several dozen little children. Taixing citizens held a protest the same night, demanding that the government seriously punish the murderer. Their slogans were "Killing corrupt officials is heroic, Killing innocent kids is cowardly!" While the government may have no connection to the murderer, the angry crowd believed that the government was responsible and thus the immoral "them." The news media also joined the framing process against the immoral government as a part of "us." However, the framing process could serve as a double-edged sword: it can accelerate the formation of identity, and also divide the temporary protest alliance. When the Internet started to circulate another rumor that this kindergarten was a government institution and all the children were offspring of corrupt officials, suddenly public opinion turned around and bulletin boards were full of "great!" comments. The obscure boundary of "them" and "us" deflated the protest, and some of the protesters left.

Conclusion

Ever since China established Confucianism as the official doctrine, the mandate of heaven has become the basis of regime legitimacy. The stability of the regime depends, to a large extent, on the moral function of the state and the moral quality of its officials. Frustration over the loss of virtue by the officials and the state would accumulate and wait for an outlet to explode. Even though China was the first country to establish a professional civil service system, it never resolved the issue of effective supervision.

The consequence of the loss of virtue by the government and its officials is the formation of a temporary alliance of all social strata, using riots to express disgust for the official corruption and sometimes malign governance. In contemporary China, socioeconomic transformation has produced broad displacement and increasing social frustration. Disturbances are not about poverty, but about relative deprivation in terms of both wealth and justice.

As we have discussed earlier, there are three general triggers of large-scale disturbances. The first is that government exercises its authority in a malign manner. This is a direct violation of benevolent governance. The second is the unnatural death of individuals, which are suspected to be related to corrupt government officials. The third is the dispute between the rich and the poor and the suspicion that corrupt officials are under the influence of the rich. Altogether, it is always about violation of benevolence and about corrupt officials. This is the reason why we labeled disturbances the benevolence violation protest.

Riots are more likely to break out in less developed areas. This is because the less developed areas lack resources to provide satisfactory public services and government corruption is more blatant. The quality of the governance in less developed areas tends to be low as well. The government officials lack crisis management skills and tend to rely more on coercive power to deal with social discontent, which is more often than not counterproductive.

Rumor is a part of any social protest, but it is an essential part of a riot. In the absence of organizations or organizers, rumor mobilizes the masses by framing injustice and providing temporary riot identities. As the masses have long been frustrated by official corruption, they are gullible and tend to believe everything in circulation except the official versions.

Looking at the geographic location of disturbances (Table 3.5), one may notice that disturbances are more frequent in some regions than others. For example, Sichuan and Chongqing together have 12, about one-fifth of the total. It is the place historically at the peripheries of central China. It is also the place where there were large-scale mass fights during the Cultural Revolution. Without much empirical evidence, we may speculate that a tradition of rebellion or feisty folk customs has played a role in such disturbances. This speculation definitely needs to be substantiated by further empirical research.

Notes

1 Steven I. Wilkinson, "Riots," *Annual Review of Political Science* No. 12 (2009): 330.
2 Gustave Le Bon, *The Crowd: Study of the Popular Mind* (New York: Dover Publications, Inc., 2002), chapter 1.
3 Ted Gurr, *Why Men Rebel* (Paradigm Publishers, 2011).

4 Being able to eat meat is considered a symbol of a comfortable life in Chinese tradition. The original Chinese did not specify the target of the cursing, but everyone understands it is the government.
5 "Country's Wealth Divide Past Warning Level," *China Daily*, May 2, 2010.
6 e.g. Stanley Lubman, *Bird in a Cage: Legal Reform in China after Mao* (Palo Alto: Stanford University Press, 2002); and Randall Peerenboom, *China's Long March Toward Rule of Law* (Cambridge University Press, 2002).
7 Martin Whyte, *Myth of the Social Volcano: Perceptions of Inequality and Distributive Injustice in Contemporary China* (Palo Alto: Stanford University Press, 2009).
8 William Gamson and David Meyer, "Framing Political Opportunity," in Doug McAdam *et al.* (eds) *Comparative Perspectives on Social Movements* (Cambridge University Press, 1996), 283–84.
9 Elizabeth Perry, *Challenging The Mandate of Heaven—Social Protest and State Power in China* (New York: M.E. Sharpe, 2002), ix.
10 All the cases are collected by the authors' field work and documentary studies.
11 Yanqi Tong, "Dispute Resolution Strategies in a Hybrid System," *The China Review* Vol. 9, No. 1 (Spring 2009): 17–44.
12 Dou'er is a legendary figure in a classical drama opera. She was wrongfully accused and executed. To validate her innocence, snow fell in the hot June summer.
13 lw.xinhuanet.com/htm/content_4520.htm.
14 Personal interview.
15 Personal interview.
16 Personal Interview.
17 news.xinhuanet.com/legal/2008-07/05/content_8493365_1.htm.
18 Author's interview with an onsite CCTV reporter.
19 "安徽池州打砸抢烧'6·26'群体性事件调查" [Investigation of Anhui Chizhou 6.26 Mass Incident], 《南方都市报》, 2005年7月1日 [*Southern Metro News*], July 1, 2005.
20 James Tong, *Disorder Under Heaven, Collective Violence in the Ming Dynasty* (Palo Alto: Stanford University Press, 1991), 129–30.
21 Gordon W. Allport and Leo Joseph Postman, *The Psychology of Rumor* (New York: H. Holt & Co.), 193.

6 Protests over developmental syndromes and identity

We have put all the cases that do not fall into the four major categories into the "other" category. The main consideration is that they do not occur as frequently. However, even these infrequent eruptions reflect the pulse of China's bumpy transformation. When we say bumpy, it does not mean "troubled" or "problematic," which implies failure. Instead, it implies rough, but forward movement. In this chapter, we will discuss two categories of these other large-scale social protests. One is what we termed developmental syndromes, which include environmental protests and protests over illegal fundraising. The other is protests over various identities, such as national, ethnic, local and lineage.

Developmental syndromes

China has experienced rapid economic development. There have been problems associated with this phenomenal development. One is environmental pollution. Increased use of energy and insufficient facilities and technologies to treat industrial and life waste cause serious air and water pollution and other environmental problems. Large-scale protests against pollution have become more common. Another problem was born out of the lack of market regulation—illegal fundraising. In an immature financial market, companies would invent various schemes to grab money out of the pockets of those who want to strike it rich. The bankruptcy of such schemes would lead angry victims to the street.

Environmental protests

High economic growth in China brought with it the degradation of the environment. The resulting environmental degradation increases the public environmental grievances. Yanqi Tong has clarified two types of the environmental movement. One is pollution-driven grassroots protest, and the other is world view-oriented environmental nongovernmental organizations (NGOs).[1] The pollution-driven grassroots protests tend to be large-scale, since the victims are many and the threat is immediate to human health. The world view-oriented environmental NGOs are more sustainable but only involve a small minority of activists. Since pollution threatens the subsistence of the people and the state is officially committed to green policies, there is enough political opportunity for antipollution protests. Here we mainly discuss the grassroots large-scale environmental protests. During the period of 2003–10, we recorded 20 large-scale environmental protests. The years of 2008 and 2009 had five of those each, and all are primarily pollution driven.

Subsistence antipollution protest

The Changsha Xianghe Chemical Plant was a private enterprise introduced by the Gaotou Township government (in Hubei Province) in 2003. In 2004, the plant purchased a production line to produce indium—a kind of soft metal that is crucial in the electronics industry. Ever since that, according to nearby villagers, trees around the plant started to die. Villagers started to feel fatigue, dizziness, and joint and chest pains. Some villagers and children went to the provincial hospital and found that their bodies had excessive cadmium. Then there were two cases of sudden death (one 44 years old and the other 61 years old) in the summer of 2009, both bodies found to have four times the normal level of cadmium.

For months, villagers had reported the pollution problems, but the government only issued pamphlets to explain what cadmium poison was, hoping to dissuade people's fear. On July 30, 2009, thousands of villagers took the street to express their concerns about the pollution. This time the government responded promptly. On August 1, the head of the chemical plant was detained on criminal charges. The bureau chief and vice-chief of environmental protection were suspended pending further investigation. The government then purchased and destroyed crops and other products within 1,200 meters of the plant. Farmers also received a temporary government stipend for 37 days.[2]

The other case occurred in Jiangsu Province. On October 21, 2009, 10,000 residents of Pingwang Township of Wujiang City took to the street protesting against the operation of a waste-burning power plant. The trial operation on October 19 had produced an unbearable smell over the entire township. Residents were afraid that the waste-burning facilities might cause serious damage to their health. This waste-burning power plant is located in a densely populated area. The closest residential complex is only 50 meters away. Within 1,000 meters, there are kindergarten, elementary and middle schools.

It was rumored that the former Party secretary received a bribe from the power plant and signed off on the project. The official version was that the plant had passed the state inspection and was constructed according to state standards. Nobody believed it. The demonstrators questioned: "if it is not harmful, why didn't you build it next to your office building?" They also complained that there were no public hearings about the project and people had little input into the decision. On October 22, the government announced that the project would be temporarily suspended.[3]

These two cases are very telling of the current situation of China's social and economic transformation. In the first case, the local government was only interested in economic growth and did not take people's complaints seriously. Once the people took to the street and pollution was determined to be seriously harmful, the government did react swiftly. In the second case, Wujiang is located in the most developed region of China. The idea of a waste-burning power plant is an environmental protection effort to deal with the increasing waste produced by industry and modern lifestyles. However, there lacked a thorough evaluation of the proper distance between waste-burning facilities and human residence. Most importantly, the public is demanding a more open policy process and more public participation in the matters important to their livelihood.

Protests from the middle class

Most of the mass incidents were launched by disadvantaged social groups, such as laid-off workers and peasants. They were fighting for their right to subsistence. Yet there were a couple of large-scale mass incidents that were mainly participated in by the new middle class in the cities. Two were related to environmental protection (an anti-maglev protest in Shanghai and anti-PX plant protests in Xiamen) and the other was the anti-dog killing gathering in Beijing.

The protest in Xiamen was against the building of a para-xylene chemical plant near Xiamen city. A chemistry professor at Xiamen University warned that the chemical might cause cancer among nearby residents. On June 11, 2007, citizens of Xiamen launched a "walking" protest against the project, eventually forcing the government to relocate the project.[4] There were complicated interests behind the protest. For example, the land developer was afraid that the pollution threat might scare away potential house buyers. However, the ordinary citizens who participated in the protest were genuinely concerned about their living environment.

In 2007, the Shanghai government planned to build a magnetic transit railway to Hangzhou. It was met with opposition from those who resided along the proposed transit lines. They worried that the radiation effect from the magnet would be harmful to their health. They refused to accept the conclusion in the proposal that the magnetic transit posed no harm to nearby residents. In order to minimize the political sensitivity of the protest, citizens of Shanghai created a form of "collective strolling" to oppose the project.

On January 12, 2008, more than 1,000 Shanghai citizens took a stroll on the People's Square in front of the Shanghai government, protesting against the potential harms that could be brought by the project of a magnetic railway. Some strollers held out slogans like "magnets harm health," and shouted "we oppose the magnetic railway!" The police questioned several dozen slogan holders, but released them immediately. Then the police closed the square. The protesters did not confront the police and turned to the Nanjing

Road shopping areas. Shanghai police avoided having direct confrontation with the protesters and followed the crowd at a distance. Since it was raining and the temperature was low, the peaceful protesters dispersed.[5] Shanghai government did not take a stand on whether or not it would continue the project, but publicized the email address of the evaluation office of the project and asked citizens to participate in the consultation. The project is still pending.

The anti-dog killing protest in Beijing was a different case and hardly qualifies as environmental protest. We discuss it here because animal protection is a part of broader environmental concerns. In October 2006, Beijing government issued a policy that each household could only have one dog and prohibited any large and aggressive dogs. The government also required families to register their dogs and confiscated dogs that had not received immunization shots. On November 11, 2006, thousands of dog owners gathered in front of the Beijing Zoo to protest against this policy. This was the first time that Beijing citizens protested against a single government policy. Protesters held out slogans such as "against killing," "against height limit" and "civilize policy enforcement, raising dogs is innocent." Police forces continued to advise the protestors to end the event, but did not run into confrontation. The police took away a dozen protesters, but released them after inquiries. After three hours, the police agreed to inform the government about the protesters' demands. The protest ended.[6] Beijing government did not explicitly remove this policy, but quietly adjusted its implementation. All the television programs that advocated such a policy were withdrawn from airing. As the protesters chose to stage the protest in front of the zoo, it did not symbolize any political implication. The purpose of the protest was clear and the protesters came from the middle class. The process was peaceful. The government did not trace the organizers and did not arrest any participants.

It is true that the participants of these protests had their interests at stake. Yet these protests also reflected certain postmodern values of citizens. Environmental awareness usually emerges when a society has reached a high stage of economic development.[7] The new middle class are the beneficiaries of the economic boom in China. Therefore, their concerns are primarily about quality of life. Unlike the protests against pollution that directly threatened the survival of the affected population, the protests in Shanghai and Xiamen were against a potential future threat, reflecting the education and knowledge levels of the urban middle class. These types of protests are rare, but have demonstrated different features to mass incidents in China. All three mass incidents were peaceful in style. Thousands of people were mainly mobilized by cell phone or Internet messages.

Illegal fundraising

There were seven such cases during this period. The two typical cases are the Shengyang "Yilishen" incident in 2007 and the Hunan Jishou incident in 2008. Both were caused by illegal fundraising.

Yilishen incident

Yilishen Group was a company that sold health products made from ants. It adopted a production model of "contracted production." Households that paid a minimum of 10,000 RMB deposit could raise ants at home. In 14 months, the company would buy back the ants and return the households their investment plus a profit of 3,250 RMB. The return rate was 32.5 percent. The consistent high return rate for several years had encouraged more investors. Retired workers sold their houses to invest in this company. The Yilishen products were among the bestsellers on the market and even got into the United States.

In 2005, the US Federal Drug Administration (FDA) issued a warning that the Yilishen health products contain an element that is the main component of Viagra. Taking too much of this element would cause serious heart problems. The FDA, therefore, banned the Yilishen products on the American market. After they were banned in the United States, Chinese consumers started questioning Yilishen products as well. As a result, Yilishen products started to lose their market in China.

On October 11, 2007, investors found that their expected profit return did not appear in their bank account as promised. Rumors started to circulate that Yilishen Group was in financial problems. On November 20, 2007, tens of thousands of ant-raising households laid siege to the Yilishen building in Shengyang. Some households also believed that the government was responsible because it issued the license to Yilishen. The police took away the protesters in trucks. A dozen protesters who attempted to get into the government building, were detained and later released. On November 29, Yilishen Group officially filed for bankruptcy. The bankruptcy affected 30,000 ant-raising households and their 20 billion RMB investment. Police immediately arrested the chairman of the board of trustees of the company and other managers and prosecuted them on the charge of financial swindling. The property of the company was frozen and sold at a discount to pay back the investors. The incident was gradually pacified over a year.[8]

Jishou incident

In 2004, a couple of developers in Jishou City of Hunan Province started fundraising with interest returns several times higher than the banks. Most families in Jishou invested, lured by the high returns. Jishou City government also encouraged citizens to invest out of concern for improving the governing record on economic development. In 2008, the fund totaled 16.8 billion RMB. However, since Jishou is an underdeveloped area, it could not digest this amount of investment. The development projects were unable to profit and the financial chain broke. All the housing projects, on which the government pinned its hopes, went into bankruptcy and collapsed. On September 4, 2008, tens of thousands of protesters laid siege to the government building in

Xiangxi Autonomous Prefecture in Hunan. Protesters also crowded the Jishou railway station and blocked the traffic.

Under the direct intervention of the provincial government, some 90 involved developers and government officials were arrested. This lessened the anger and concern of the protesters. The government then worked hard to clean up the debt and minimize the damage to the ordinary investors. After 15 months of work, most of the investors got their money back.[9] The 90 arrested suspects were put on trial. No protesters were punished.

These two cases of illegal fundraising have reflected the chaotic situation of a financial market (or the lack of) in China. First, there are bold speculators who would take advantage of an imperfect market to strike gold. Second, there are gullible people who dream of making quick and easy money. Together with the lack of regulation in the financial market, there were many financial swindling cases in China. These two cases developed into large-scale mass protests because of the huge number of victims.

Protests over identities

We have put some cases into the "other" category because they are hard to classify. However, after going through the cases in this category, we find some cases share an interesting theme: protest over the expression of self-identity. Stuart Hall pointed out that identity is something that people hold onto in an uncertain world. In a changing world, people need something that is not changing—a true self.[10] This self-identity has multiple layers, ranging from national identity to ethnic identity to local identity to lineage identity. The characteristics of these protests are: 1 their targets were not the Chinese government; 2 the major demands were the expression of self-identities; and 3 they usually were accompanied by violence to different degrees. These protests include anti-Japanese protests (three), ethnic conflicts (eight), disputes over local dialects (two), and clan feud (one).

Anti-Japanese protests

Historically China had been the strongest country in East Asia. In modern times, China was surpassed by Japan and fell behind. Ever since the Sino–Japanese War in 1894 until the end of World War II, Japanese invasion and massacre had been a nightmare for the Chinese. The two countries normalized their relationship in the 1970s. The frictions in the relationship continued, such as official visits to the Yasukuni Shrine, the revision of textbooks that removed passages on the aggression, insincere apologies for the war crimes, and the dispute over Diaoyu Island.

The relationship between the countries has remained quiet for most of the time since World War II. Only at certain particular moments, such as the official visit to the Yasukuni Shrine by Japanese prime ministers, does the hatred for Japan flare up in China. There were anti-Japanese protests every year in the 1990s, and such protests reached their peak in 2003, 2005 and 2010.

Northwest University student anti-Japanese protest

In 2003, when Koizumi became the new prime minister of Japan, he adopted a hawkish China policy, and insisted on visiting the Yasukuni Shrine. In August 2003, it was discovered that the chemical weapons abandoned by the Japanese in Northeast China had leaked and led to many local residents having serious illnesses. Then in September 2003, a Japanese firm sponsored a collective vacation in the Zhuhai special economic zone and its employees had a party with prostitutes. All these events, reported by the media, started to build up public rage against Japan.

On October 29, 2003, Northwest University in Xi'an was holding a foreign language festival, and Japanese students at the university participated in the performance. Three Japanese students led by their Japanese teachers performed a program with sexual elements. Three male students were naked, put paper cups on their private parts, and threw out paper pieces from their bras.[11] The performance was interrupted and cancelled following objections from the audience. Then rumors went around that the Japanese students also had "this is Chinese" written on their bodies.

The next morning, a large crowd of students surrounded the foreign students' compound on campus and demanded apologies from the Japanese students. The president of the university promised that he would expel the three Japanese students and the Japanese teacher. However, the angry students continued to demand an open apology. They threw the staff members who were trying calm the protest into water ponds and tried to enter the residential building. Some students were detained by the police.

Since there are many colleges and universities in Xi'an, the news about the Northwestern University protests circulated quickly. Students from other campuses started to gather and support students at Northwestern University. In the evening, students took to the street and handed out pamphlets. Students gathered in front of the government building of Shaanxi province, and delivered their letters to the government, demanding an apology from the Japanese students. At the same time, students from all over the universities entered the campus of Northwestern University, asking for the release of the detained students. After their demands were declined, students rushed into the foreign student residential building and dragged the Japanese students out. The riot police finally got the event under control.

On October 31, all the campuses in Xi'an closed their gates and students were asked to stay in. However, thousands of students got out and destroyed a restaurant that served Japanese cuisine. Armed police were at the scene. Finally the chief of the Provincial Education Bureau showed up and promised to deal with the Japanese students. Students then went back to campus.[12]

Multicity anti-Japanese protests in 2005

In 2005, Japan started to apply to become a permanent member of the United Nations (UN) Security Council. At the same time, the Japanese Ministry of Education was reportedly approving a revised history textbook that covered up the Japanese invasion of China. In March 2005, citizens in Chongqing, Guangzhou, Shenzhen, Zhengzhou, Shenyang, Chengdu and Harbin initiated a signature campaign to oppose Japan's bid to the UN Security Council.

On April 9, 2005, students from Peking University and Qinghua University gathered in front of the Hailong electronic market building, holding a signature campaign to boycott Japanese products. As more and more students assembled, some students suggested that they should go to the Japanese Embassy. The demonstration snowballed along the way. Some demonstrators vandalized shops that were selling Japanese products and threw stones at the Beijing offices of Nippon Air and Mitsubishi Bank. Beijing government dispatched a large number of armed police around the Japanese Embassy. Some protesters were able to break through the line and threw bricks at the embassy building, burned Japanese flags and a portrait of Koizumi, and overturned Japanese-made cars. As the Japanese embassy building was a new building, there was nobody inside. The protesters then turned to the old Japanese embassy, which all the Japanese staff had already vacated. The protests ended late at night.[13]

On April 10, tens of thousands of Guangzhou citizens went to the Japanese Consulate to protest against the revision of textbooks. Armed police separated the protesters from the consulate. Angry protesters turned to the main streets in Guangzhou, and destroyed the bulletin boards that advertised Japanese electronic products.[14]

On April 16, college students in Shanghai assembled on the Bund and People's Square to hold a demonstration. The crowd then moved to the Japanese Consulate. Demonstrators demanded that Japan face its war history and stop revising textbooks. Students held out slogans such as "oppose Japan's bid for UN Security Council," "defend Diaoyu Island," and "down with the Japanese." As the demonstration was not approved by the authorities, the Shanghai government took a hard-line position against protesters. Universities banned their students from leaving the campus and declared that students who ignored the ban would be expelled. The government also arrested those who vandalized Japanese businesses and planned to sue the demonstration organizers.[15]

On April 17, citizens from Shenzhen had an anti-Japanese protest. They threw eggs at all Japanese-made cars. The demonstration lasted until late at night.[16] Other cities, such as Tianjin, Nanjing, Wuhan, as well as Hong Kong, also had different scales of anti-Japanese demonstrations.[17] The government tried very hard to emphasize the importance of stability, and all the universities had programs to convince students to stay on campus. The waves of anti-Japanese protest gradually died down. Although the demonstrations broke out in multiple cities, we counted them as one incident.

Anti-Japanese protest over the Diaoyu incident in 2010

On September 7, 2010, there was a collision between a Chinese fishing trailer and a Japanese naval ship near Diaoyu Island. Japan then detained the Chinese captain and all the fishermen.[18] On September 8, the activists of the Defending Diaoyu Movement initiated demonstrations in front of the Japanese Embassy against the actions by the Japanese government. Demonstrators claimed that the detention of the Chinese captain was not an insult, but an act of invasion. They demanded that the Japanese government apologize, release the detainees and make compensation. Shanghai, Shenyang, Tianjin, Chongqing, Shenzhen, Xi'an, Changsha and Wuhan all erupted in anti-Japanese demonstrations. Some of the demonstrators vandalized businesses that sell Japanese products or cars.[19]

On September 18, the date that Japan invaded Northeast China 79 years before, another anti-Japanese demonstration erupted in Beijing. The authorities approved the demonstration application, but forced the demonstrators to go to the embassy in small groups and in different time slots. Therefore, the demonstration was orderly and peaceful.[20]

Since the Japanese government took a hard position on Diaoyu Island, the right wingers threw smoke bombs at the Chinese Consulate in Nagasaki, and anti-Japanese demonstrations flared up again in many Chinese cities in October. On October 16, university students in Xi'an held anti-Japanese demonstrations. Several thousands of university students marched to the center of the city, shouting "boycott Japanese goods," "return our Diaoyu Island," and "down with Japanese devils!" They also sang "March of the Volunteers" and other anti-Japanese songs. The demonstration clogged the traffic in the city center, and some Japanese-made cars were smashed. After hours of talks with the students, the government eventually convinced the demonstrators to return to campus late in the afternoon. All universities in Xi'an issued an order requiring students to remain on campus for two weeks. The protests died down.[21]

Major features of anti-Japanese protests

The anti-Japanese protests in China have several features. First, relations between the two countries are very fragile and easily tipped over by sensitive events. Even the result of a soccer game could trigger waves of anti-Japanese demonstration. The second feature is the endurance of hostility on the Chinese side. This is a typical victim mentality with a humiliated arrogance. Since the Japanese unapologetic official attitudes toward its war crimes and the actual occupation of Diaoyu Island, which are the issues that cannot be resolved in a short time, anti-Japanese protest may erupt at any time. Third, the protests are likely to spread nationwide. Almost all the big cities have had anti-Japanese protests, the protests even extending to Chinese communities in the United States and Taiwan. Fourth, university students are the main participants of these demonstrations. The size of the demonstration is comparable to the size of the university student population in the given city. The student anti-Japanese demonstration in Beijing was the largest protest since the 1989 Tiananmen student movement. Shanghai, a city that was regarded as an apolitical city, had a large anti-Japanese protest in 2005 and broke the stereotype of Shanghai. Lastly, the Chinese government tended to adopt a "use" and "restrict" approach to the anti-Japanese protests. On the one hand, the government used the protests to put pressure on Japan. On the other hand, the government also prevented the demonstrations from turning into other protests that target the government.

Ethnic conflict

Ethnic conflict in China includes both the conflict between Han and other ethnic groups, and the conflict among different minority ethnic groups. After 1949, ethnic conflict among minority groups rarely exceeded 500 participants. Therefore, this book will focus on the ethnic conflict between Han and other ethnic groups. From 2003 to 2010, there were eight large-scale ethnic conflicts between Han and Hui, Tibetan and Uyghur groups. In the following section, we will discuss three major incidents.

2004 Henan Zhongmu County Han–Hui ethnic conflict

Zhongmu County is located in the middle of Henan Province, about 50 kilometers away from the provincial capital Zhengzhou. It was a less developed area with a per capita income of 2,000 RMB. On October 29, 2004, a Hui taxi driver hit and killed a girl who was from a Han family. The victim's family went to the taxi driver's family and asked for compensation, which resulted in dispute. Villagers from the taxi driver's family stood up and tried to protect the taxi driver and beat the member of the victim's family. All the nearby Han and Hui crowds gathered around and broke into large-scale fights. Both sides had some thousands of participants, fighting with farming tools. Since the Hui group had more participants and was more physical, they beat the Han crowd badly and robbed the Han families and their shops. Even the police who were attempting to maintain order were beaten badly.

When the news about the ethnic conflict spread, thousands of Hui people from neighboring counties came over in truck loads to support their ethnic members in Zhongmu. Henan Province government immediately imposed martial law and dispatched armed police to Zhongmu. The police blocked all the roads to Zhongmu and forced Hui volunteers to return to where they were from. Those Hui volunteers then used bricks and stones to attack the armed police, which resulted in police casualties. The situation was brought under control when more armed police were dispatched. According to the report by *The New York Times*, this conflict led to 148 deaths, including 18 police officers.[22] The local government denied these reports and only acknowledged some 20 deaths.

The police arrested around 20 Han villagers who were involved in the killing, but did not arrest any Hui. This caused strong resentment from the Han population. Governor of Henan Province Li Chengyu was a Hui, and Han people believed that he was protecting his own ethnic group. The angry Han population staged a confrontation with the police who were enforcing the martial law. The majority of the voices on the Internet demanded the dismissal of Li and denounced the perceived unjust treatment of the Han group in the incident.

The Hui ethnic group are the descendents of the ancient Arabs, Persians and Mongols. They believe in Islam. Contemporary Hui speak Chinese, but Arabian and Persian are also used in many areas where the majority population is Hui. Traditionally the Hui prohibited marriage with outsiders.[23] According to the census of 2000, there are 9.8 million Hui in China, comprising the third largest minority group in the country. It is also the minority group that spread all over China. There are Hui temples and communities in every provincial capital city in China. There are no physical differences between Hui and Han, and there are no disputes over national identity. At most times, "the Huis have coexisted with the Han for the past 1,300 years, but they are far from being invisible on China's radar screen of ethnic conflict."[24] Two scholars vividly described them as 'familiar strangers.'[25]

The rapid economic development in China has led to the enlarged gap among different regions. Even in the poorer regions, Han tend to live better than the Hui, and the wealth gap between Han and Hui was one of the major causes for ethnic conflict. During this conflict there was no separatist demand or international support for the Hui. However, the sense of ethnic identity is very strong inside the Hui group. In order to avoid the impression that the Han government is mistreating the Hui, local government tended to be more accommodating to the Hui than to the Han. While avoiding the radicalization of Hui, the government took the brunt of the Han rage over government ethnic policies.

Lhasa 3.14 incident and the protest against Carrefour in 2008

In March 2008, there were several violent conflicts triggered by the Tibetan demonstration in Tibet, Sichuan and Gansu. The conflict in Lhasa of Tibet Autonomous Region on March 14 was the most serious. There were several casualties and many shops were destroyed. Following the Lhasa incident, Aba Tibetan Autonomous Prefect in Sichuan Province and Gannan Tibetan Autonomous Prefect in Gansu Province also saw the demonstrations and violent conflicts.

China was about to host the 29th Olympic Games in 2008 and was under the scrutiny of the world media. Tibetan exile groups organized various activities in order to attract international attention to the Tibetan issue. On March 10, the Tibetan exiles in India called for the "Going Home on Foot" campaign, attempting to walk to Tibet from India and Nepal and express the desire to return home. This activity was blocked by the Indian and Nepali police forces. At the same time, some lamas in Tibet had started demonstrating. Some even held out the flag of the snow lion, which is the symbol of Tibetan independence. They chanted "free Tibet" and "Tibet independence." Some were arrested by the police.

On March 14, the protest in Lhasa escalated. Some lamas and Tibetans started to attack and burn the shops owned by Han and Hui.[26] Others poured boiling water onto the police who were trying to maintain order. Many shops were looted. Still others got into the Muslim mosque in the chaotic crowd, and burned the Koran. On March 15 and 16, Tibetans and clergy in Aba Tibetan Autonomous Prefect and Gannan Tibetan Autonomous Prefect also launched violent protests. Tibetan students in Beijing Central Nationality University organized protest activities on campus asking for a free Tibet.

According to the official government report, the protests led to 18 deaths and 382 injuries. Several hundred shops were burned down and looted. Armed police and local security also suffered 242 injuries and deaths.[27] The Chinese government then dispatched a large amount of armed police and military forces to Lhasa and controlled the major pathways in Tibet. At the same time, the police started to round up those who participated in the violence. The firefighting forces moved into all Tibetan temples in the name of preventing fire incidents. This 3.14 incident had led to protests from Tibetans all over the world. Chinese embassies in many countries were attacked and protests were staged.

The Tibet 3.14 incident was the first incident after the June 4 incident that created tremendous international pressure on the Chinese government. At the same time, nationalist sentiment inside China and among Chinese students abroad was at an all-time high. Nationalist posts and messages flooded the Internet forums. Overseas Chinese students organized activities to defend the passing of the Olympic torch. One of the nationalist outbreaks was the protest against Carrefour.

In April 2008, when the Olympic torches for the Beijing Games were delivered to Paris, Tibetan protesters tried to grab the torches. When the news was reported in China, many students were furious. Then there was a rumor online saying that the biggest shareholder of Carrefour, Louis Vuitton Group, had donated a large amount of funding to the Dalai Lama and other Tibetan independence groups. The French Carrefour is the largest foreign retail company in China. Slogans like "boycotting French goods, starting with Carrefour" appeared on the Internet. On April 16, the French ambassador to China commented that "boycott will not produce anything, ... it is against common sense."[28] His words provoked more rage from Chinese "netizens" (Internet citizens). On April 17, a photo of a Chinese national flag at half mast in front of a Carrefour store in Wuhan appeared online. Netizens believed that Carrefour did it intentionally to humiliate China. On April 18, several thousand college students went to a Carrefour store in Hefei to protest and forced the closure of the store. Louis Vuitton Group immediately issued a statement, claiming that it "has never supported any organizations and activities that are against the interests of Chinese government and people."[29] Carrefour also took some measures to restore its image, such as hanging the Olympic and Chinese national flags outside their stores. However, the protest activities continued all over China. In Beijing, Tianjin, Wuhan, Qingdao and Xi'an, young students protested in front of Carrefour stores. They threw water bottles at those who went there to shop, calling them collaborators, and forced some stores to close.[30]

The French government sent several envoys to Beijing to restore bilateral relations. The Internet had calls to hold a national boycott of Carrefour on May Day. Under government pressure, all the colleges cancelled the May Day long holiday if there were Carrefour stores in their cities. College authorities also worked hard to prevent students from going to Carrefour to protest. The Carrefour store in Zhongguancun Beijing is located right in the universities in Beijing. It became the most protected place during May Day. Police blocked and detained some protesters. The protest movement gradually died down.

Xinjiang 7.5 incident

A vicious mass killing incident occurred on July 5, 2009, in Ulumuqi, the capital city of the Xinjiang Uyghur Autonomous Region. There were 197 deaths and more than 1,600 injuries. This is the most deadly ethnic conflict in Xinjiang since 1949. The origin of this incident was the June 26 Shaoguan incident in Guangdong. In order to improve the living standard and job opportunities for the Uyghur, the Xinjiang government had organized labor exported to Guangdong. The Shaoguan City of Guangdong had accepted a large amount of Uyghur workers to work in their local factories. In May of 2009, Keshi City of Xinjiang sent 800 young Uyghur workers to Shaoguan. All of them started working at the Xuri toy factory. Since that time, there were increased cases of theft in the factory, and several female Han workers were reportedly being harassed.

On June 16, 2009, an Internet post "Xuri is true garbage" reported that two Han female workers were raped by six Uygur workers. On June 25, when a female worker was screaming for help when harassed by Uyghur workers, Han workers gathered and beat the Uyghur workers. One of the Uyghur workers ran back to the dorms for help. Then a large crowd of Uyghur workers assaulted the quarter where Han workers reside. Both sides used bricks and iron bars to fight until dawn. Armed police finally brought the situation under control. There were 120 injuries, of whom 81 were Uyghur workers. Two Uyghur workers died in the incident.[31]

Criminal cases involving ethnic conflict have always been very thorny for local government. Police immediately arrested the person who issued the false message that Han female workers were raped by Uyghur workers, and arrested those who participated in the incident, most of whom were Han workers. The Xinjiang government also tried to calm down the relatives of the Uyghur victims to prevent further escalation of the conflict.

On July 5, 2009, several hundred Uyghur gathered on a square in Urumqi and held a protest about the Shaoguan incident. Some protesters held out slogans for an "East Turkestan." When the police tried to disperse the crowd on the square, another thousand Uyghur started to slaughter Han and Hui residents in a highly populated downtown area, using military knifes, bricks and bayonets. They also burned buses and some public facilities.[32]

When the authorities realized that the protest on the square was only a lure to the police attention while the real purpose was to slaughter innocent citizens, they redirected police forces to round up murderers. However, by then, more than 100 innocent citizens were slaughtered, and 1,000 injured. Later, the chief of the Provincial Public Security Bureau and the mayor of Urumqi were dismissed because of the misinformation and the mistakes made in dispatching police forces late.[33] Urumqi declared martial law and cut off cell phone and Internet connections.

On July 7, having realized that the 7.5 incident was an intentionally plotted and organized ambush against the Han, Han people decided to retaliate. Crowds of people started to attack the Uyghur area with shovels and sticks. They were stopped by the police. After the Party general secretary of Xinjiang Autonomous Region promised onsite that the government would guarantee the safety of the life and property of ordinary citizens and punish murderers, the crowd then dispersed.[34] On July 8, Hu Jintao, who was attending the G8 summit in Italy, returned home early and more police forces were dispatched to Urumqi. The situation quietened down, but the tension continued.

Ethnicity issues

China is a multi-ethnicity country. Before 1949, the definition of ethnicity was very vague. In the 1950s, the Chinese government confirmed that China has 56 ethnic groups, with Han being the majority. Therefore, all the non-Han groups are called minority groups. According to the 2010 census, the Han population accounts for 91.5 percent of the population, and minority groups take the other 8.5 percent. Within the minority groups, Zhuang is the biggest group. Hui, Uyghur and Tibetan ranked fourth, sixth and tenth, respectively.[35]

For most of history, Han were the major power holders in the government structures. Han lived in the developed regions of China, and minority groups lived in relatively underdeveloped Northwest and Southwest regions. Even though minority groups were smaller in proportion of the population, they tend to live together in their regions and spread all over the Han regions. Therefore, there is a demographic structure of "concentrated in small areas, mixed in large areas." Within the places where minority groups concentrated, their numbers are much larger than the Han. Within the Han areas, minority groups tended to live together and formed a tight community.

Ethnic issues are important because they are relevant to national security, territorial integrity and social stability. The specific characteristics of an ethnic group make the ethnic issues tough to handle. Ethnic groups have their own cultural traditions and strong sense of identity among their members. They are bonded together, not by economic interests, but by their cultural and religious identities.[36]

The ethnic groups that often collided with Han usually have their own languages and religions, inhabit relatively independent regions, have a history outside of the central control, and have some international connections. However, because of the common languages and religious beliefs, these minority groups have distinctive identities from those of Han. The international connections refer to the ability to generate international pressure, or connections with fundamentalist movements, such as "East Turkestan Islamic Movement." These groups have strong separatist tendencies.

The rapid economic growth led to the widening gap among different regions. Regions of minority groups tend to lag far behind. This has created a strong sense of relative deprivation for the minorities. We have previously argued that economic inequality is not necessarily a direct cause for social protest or instability. However, if economic inequality coincides with ethnic groupings, it becomes a much deeper grievance and generates stronger frustrations. This is why Uyghur and Tibetans, those groups that have their own language, coherent ethnic identity, strong religious beliefs and international connections, clashed with the Han population in vicious violent conflicts.

In the history of the People's Republic of China (PRC), there are two stages with regard to ethnic relations. Mao's period was the most peaceful period. Ethnic issues were defined as class issues. Each ethnic group was divided into different classes. The poor comprised the majority of each ethnic group. They were "liberated" and enjoyed a better social status. The government also had preferential policies for the ethnic poor. Ethnic relations during Mao's period, therefore, were the most harmonious. For example, the land reform and religious reform freed slaves from the slave owners and religious leaders. The concept of class struggle divided the wholeness of the Tibetan group. The lower class of the Tibetan population became the allies of the Communist Party and basis of social support. The Communist Party recruited many young Tibetan serfs to the Party and government. The same policy was also practiced in Xinjiang and Ninxia. During this period, minority groups had the strongest identity with the nation, even surpassing their own ethnic group and tradition. For example, Hui in Ninxia were willing to raise pigs to support the government policy.[37] This would be beyond imagination in China today.

Since the reform of the 1980s, Mao's ethnic polices were revised. His populism was replaced by "elitism." Many Han cadres in Tibet withdrew inland. Religious authorities were restored. Lamas became the full-time clergy and received government stipends. Ordinary Tibetans also revived the tradition of making donations to temples. With the restoration of ethnic elites in Tibet and Xinjiang, ethnic issues started to emerge. The ethnic elite, with the control of important positions in society, manipulated the ethnic identity issue. Starting in 1986, there were scattered protests in Tibet. In 1987, the largest protest since 1957 erupted. In 1989, there was the Lhasa riot. These protests and disturbances promoted the development of the "Free Tibet" movement.

Ethnic issues bring violent conflict. The central government issued a document in 1984, stipulating that the authorities should arrest fewer and execute fewer and give lenient treatment in general to criminals of ethnic minorities. This is the so-called "two fewers and one leniency (两少一宽)."[38] This is a policy guide for ethnic criminal issues. It has played a positive role in maintaining public security order in ethnic regions. It is a typical policy of benevolence. Yet, it also violated the principle of rule of law. In any criminal cases, regardless of who is guilty, minority members would always receive more lenient treatment. Many believed this policy had indulged criminals with a minority background and furthered the violence against the Han population, such as the 7.5 incident. This policy also alienated the Han people, who started to believe that the government was on the side of the ethnic minorities and lost confidence in the government's impartial position. This is why on July 7, three days after the 7.5 killing, the Han crowd decided to take matters into their own hands, and tried to retaliate.

Defending local languages

"Defending local languages" is another type of social protest in China today. In 2010, there are two such occurrences with more than 1,000 participants. The first one was the "defending Cantonese" demonstration in Guangzhou in July 2010. The other was "defending the Tibetan language" in the Tibetan areas of Qinghai and Gansu provinces in October 2010.

"Defending Cantonese"

Guangzhou was the host city of the 2010 Asian Games. In order to serve the guests from all over the continent, the City Political Advisory Committee of Guangzhou had set up 17 subcommittees to study the soft environment of Guangzhou. One of the subcommittees submitted a proposal on July 5, suggesting that the city radio comprehensive channel increase program broadcasts in standard Mandarin. The main suggestion was that the ratio of Cantonese programming was too high and outsiders did not understand. This was not good for news media communications. Increasing Mandarin programs would help outsiders better understand the new development of Guangzhou.

A native Guangdongnese Han Zhipeng, who was a member of the Political Consultative Committee, posted a microblog claiming that "our mother language is in danger! Our local culture is in danger!" His microblog was widely circulated among Guangzhou citizens. Then the Cantonese broadcasters of Guangzhou City Radio also called for "defending Cantonese" in their microblogs. After being re-posted millions of times, the message became that Guangzhou City Radio was going to cancel all Cantonese broadcasts and adopt Mandarin instead. Moreover, "all the kindergartens and elementary schools will prohibit Cantonese on campus and violators would be fined."

Debates over "the superiority of Cantonese or Mandarin" and "should we preserve Cantonese" were all over the paper media in Guangzhou. The mainstream views were to defend Cantonese. Major news media in Guangzhou used phrases such as "the death of Cantonese" and "Guangzhouers are facing collective amnesia" to incite the public. On July 9, a newspaper in Guangzhou published a report saying that grandparents were unable to communicate with their grandchildren, and the younger generation wanted to learn Cantonese but had no language environment. Then there was a collective panic that Cantonese would soon become extinct.[39]

The debate also extended to the news media in Hong Kong and Macao. Cantonese communities in the United States, Europe and Australia expressed their concerns. An official of Guangzhou government commented that "this is the first time in history that a proposal from the Political Consultative Committee has triggered such large-scale public participation."[40]

On July 11, several hundred youth held a "flash mob" on the people's square of Guangzhou City. They sang Cantonese songs in an attempt to raise the attention of Guangzhou citizens on the campaign of defending Cantonese. On July 25, several thousand Guangzhou citizens gathered on the Beijing Road of Guangzhou City, and held another demonstration to defend Cantonese, in an attempt to express a sense of crisis about the survival of the language. The demonstration was peaceful and ended when police expelled the crowd.[41]

"Defending the Tibetan language"

This refers to a series of protests against the "official neglect of education in Tibetan riot of 2008, local governments in Tibetan areas redesigned their educational policy. In September 2010, Qinghai province passed the "Guidelines of Educational Reform and Development in Mid- and Long-Term Perspectives (2010–20)."[42] The guidelines cancelled the bilingual education with Tibetan as the main language and changed it to bilingual education with Mandarin as the main the Tibetan language" in Qinghai, Gansu and Beijing in October 2010. After the language, and required that the transition be completed in 2015. The province started to hold Mandarin training sessions for Tibetan teachers. The policy change was interpreted as a restriction on the use of Tibetan language on campus.

After the Defending Cantonese campaign in July 2010 the Tibetan activist Tsering Woeser commented that if Guangzhouers could take to the streets to defend Cantonese, what about Tibetans? As a member of a minority, they saw slogans like "I am a Chinese kid, I like to speak Mandarin," and "Mandarin is our campus language" and dared not speak up. She encouraged Tibetans to use the same methods to defend their own language.[43]

Tibetan teachers were worried that once this policy was implemented, Han teachers would replace them in schools. Driven by a sense of crisis, Tibetan teachers and students from the Huangnan Tibetan Autonomous Prefecture took to the street on October 19, 2010, protesting against using Mandarin as the teaching language. Then Tibetan students from Hainan Prefecture, Guoluo Prefecture and Gannan Prefecture of Gansu Province and lamas took the street. On October 23, hundreds of Tibetan students from Central Nationality University also launched a campus protest. All these protests were peaceful and ended peacefully.

Interpreting the conflict over language

Defending Cantonese is not an isolated case. We could observe the same crisis about the identification of local culture in Shanghai. On February 4, 2009, *Xinmin Evening News*, the largest newspaper that reports local social news, published an article entitled "New Heroes in Shanghai, all are Elites without Household Registration."[44] It argued that "speaking Shanghai dialect has no cultural taste." It triggered an uproar among Shanghai locals, especially the youth. Many protesting voices were posted on the Internet and street protests were planned in front of the *Xinmin Evening News*. In order to pacify the angry youth, the executive editor responsible for the article was removed by the newspaper.[45]

The conflict over Cantonese is a microcosm of the outside culture pounding the local culture in a transitional society. Beijing, Shanghai and Guangzhou are the most developed cities in China with the most resources and job opportunities. Therefore, they became the most popular destinations for all the bright, young talent. With time passing, young people from outside became the main group in the local society. They have higher education levels, work harder and occupy important positions in all walks of life. The most successful would purchase better housing, cars and provide their children with the best possible education.

In contrast, the local youth, having grown up in an environment with easier access to education and employment, were not as competitive. Facing the fact that outside people have become more successful, they started to become resentful. The ability to speak a local language becomes the last advantage the local youth enjoy. Language is the ultimate link of cultural and psychological identification. Behind the conflict over local language is the fear of losing local identity.

The protests for the Tibetan language in Qinghai and Gansu are not for Tibetan independence, but originated from the sense of subsistence crisis by the Tibetan teachers. It is fundamentally different from the Lhasa riot in

2008. It is similar to the debate over Cantonese, which originated from the fear that they would fall from the economic development track. Occupational pressure from outsiders and job competition between Mandarin and Cantonese broadcasters led to the campaign to defend local languages. Of course, because of the complication of the Tibetan issue, political sensitivity and international attention are very different between the Tibetan and Cantonese protests.

China has had thousands of years of history. However, some local identity is always stronger than the national identity, especially in the Guangdong and Shanghai areas.[46] As the most developed cities, the locals on the one hand are very proud of being the Guangzhouers and Shanghainese, but on the other hand they have to face increasing competition from outside populations. The Tibetan language is related to ethnic conflict. In both language debates, the teachers and news media have dominated the voice of public opinion and played a central role.

Lineage conflict

From 2003 to 2010, we have only recorded one large-scale lineage conflict. We decided to discuss it here because lineage is an important issue in state-society relations. In Chinese history, the power of the central government never effectively reached below the county level until 1949. Rural areas had always been outside the centralized power structure, and primarily relied on the gentry and lineages to play the linkages with the dynastic administration. The gentry were the educated local elite, usually the head of lineages, which commanded well-connected networks. The lineage is a cultural symbol, as well as a social power institution.[47] Prasenjit Duara argues that "lineage" is a corporate group demonstrating descent from a common ancestor, usually through some corporate property and ceremonial ties, and often residing together.[48]

Before 1949, even though lineage organizations existed in most rural areas, the power relationship between lineage and central government varied in different locations. Generally speaking, lineage organizations were not well developed in the north. As the capitals of dynasties were most often located in the north, the central government had been able to penetrate into rural areas, resulting in weak lineage institutions. When natural disasters hit, the central government was able to deliver relief service and coordinate various interests effectively. Therefore, the northern lineage organizations tended to remain a cultural concept based on blood-related kinships.

In contrast, rural areas in the south were far away from the central government. Central power was unable to reach villages. It had to rely on the lineage organizations to maintain social order. Once natural disasters occurred, the central government had to rely on the well-connected lineage organizations to provide disaster relief. As a result, lineage networks developed into social power organizations in some places, such as Hunan, Guangdong, Jiangxi, Anhui and Fujian. They had their own punitive laws that superseded the national legal codes. Individuals had to attach to lineage networks to survive the harsh agricultural life. The power balance between the southern lineages and central government primarily depended on the strength of the central power. When the state was weak, local lineages controlled their own affairs and eroded the national authorities.[49] When the state was strong, the two sides reached a balance and the lineages were sanctioned by the central government.[50] In addition, the lineages would exercise self-restraint and help to maintain local order.[51]

The Communist revolution significantly weakened the power of the lineages.[52] Since 1949, the Communist regime has been the first in Chinese history that has successfully penetrated into rural areas. With the entrance of the state power, lineages declined. Two campaigns played important roles in dismantling the foundation of the lineages. One was land reform, which cut off the linkages of the landowning class to the land and its involvement in lineage activities. The other was the Cultural Revolution, which destroyed lineage documents, genealogies, lineage temples, lineage cemeteries and many cultural symbols of lineages. All lineage activities were banned.[53] However, even during the peak of these political campaigns, the regime only promoted the transfer of power from social lineages to the state, but did not wipe out the lineage tradition entirely.[54]

The Household Responsibility System introduced in rural China in the 1980s brought the collective system to ruins. The weakening of the central power in the rural areas resulted in the rise of the lineage authorities. At the same time, farmers lost their sense of security in the competitive market environments. The resurrection of the lineage networks in southern China reflected the restoration of lineage rituals and massive donations to restore lineage chronologies and lineage temples. A dual power structure emerged in the rural south. On the one hand, there are village committee and township governments. On the other hand, there are the lineage networks with the most senior male exercising actual control. Grassroots Party officials also possess dual identities of being on the government payroll and members of the local lineages.

Under this dual structure, the local lineages would support village elections, conscription, family planning and state grain procurement. The state power would retreat from routine social life in the localities, delegating interest coordination, management of property disputes and traditional festivities to lineage organizations. During our fieldwork in the Boyanghu area of Jiangxi Province, we found that lineages coexisted with the state power peacefully and never challenged the government. They even voluntarily cooperated with the government in some public infrastructure projects. For example, the construction of the Beijing–Kowloon railway needed to relocate 2,277 graves in this area in 1993. With the coordination of local lineage networks, there was not a single "nail household."[55]

Submission to state authority does not mean compromise among lineages. There are organized competition and confrontation among lineages. As the power of lineages derives from the symbols of the bloodlines of lineages, the legitimacy of the lineage authority is based on the control of the ancestral hall, ancestral cemetery, genealogies and various ceremonies, such as wedding, funeral, baby shower and lineage rituals, such as ancestral cemetery worship. Ancestral cemeteries are especially important for the solidarity and identity of lineages. Lineage members self-consciously identify themselves as part of a group distinctive from outsiders.[56]

The confrontation between lineages tends to take the form of organized violence. These confrontations are generally triggered by three causes. First, the scramble for symbols of lineage power is the scramble for control of the lineage. The restoration of lineages depends on the reconstruction of the ancestral hall, genealogies and ancestral cemetery. Because of the loss of documents in past political campaigns, the work has to be done through the vague memories of the elderly. More often than not, the conflicting memories led to violent confrontations among lineages. The second cause was the competition in festival ceremonies, such as the dragon dance, to show the power and influence of the lineages. For example, in the rural areas of Lianyuan City of Hunan Province, there were 30 to 40 lineage feuds caused by the dragon dance annually from 1978 to 1987 (the period in which lineages were resurrected).[57]

The third and most important cause were the disputes over land and property. Southern China is situated in a network of rivers, lakes and streams. Frequent floods tend to cause changes of landmarks and lead to disputes. Lineages usually use violent means to solve these disputes. After 1978, with the decollectivization of farming, such disputes accelerated, increasingly with some deaths. There were four such cases in Taihe County of Jiangxi Province in 1992.[58] Our fieldwork in Jiangxi found that the local security offices usually arrested the major participants of the fights, but never investigated the chief of the lineage. If both sides suffered deaths, the court would not hand out the death penalty.[59] In this way, the state power attempted to limit the vicious conflict within the boundaries of the lineages, and avoid the lineages aligning themselves and challenging the state.

In April 2005, a lineage-related feud over an ancestral cemetery broke out and was finally contained by the Wangzai County government, Jiangxi Province. There are two major lineages in Chixi village—the Long family and Ding family. Both families believed that a nearby hill was the ancestral cemetery of their lineages. The Long family claimed that before 1949, they would visit the ancestral cemetery every year during memorial day. After 1949, with the decline of the lineage, the cemetery was deserted. Now they had found their ancestral cemetery on the hill. The Ding family countered that this hill was located within the Ding lineage property boundaries. A 94-year-old member of the Ding family argued that he did not recall the Long family ever visiting this place before 1949. Ding lineage asserted that this place was their "dragon pulse," a crucial geographical line that determines the fortune of the lineage. According to tradition, there should not be any activity to remove dirt or ignite fireworks on the dragon pulse, which would ruin feng shui.

Around Tomb Sweeping Day, the Long lineage planned to hold a worship ritual on the disputed hill. The ritual would involve firecrackers and the Ding lineage believed it would disrupt the dragon pulse. Both lineages organized more than 1,000 members with knives and sticks in preparation for the fight. The Ding lineage submitted a report to the government in the name of the village committee, claiming that the Long lineage had raised more than 1 million yuan and purchased 2 tons of gunpowder to prepare for the violent dispute. Wangzai County dispatched around 800 police officers and officials to disperse the conflict. The police officers were able to separate the lineages at the beginning. However, later on about 600 Long lineage members crossed the line and started to attack the police. The police then arrested several villagers and lineage leaders. Then the Ding family and Long family started violent fighting among themselves. The conflict was finally brought under control. Jiangxi Provincial government then declared that all the lineage organizations were illegal and all the ancestral memorial temples should be closed down in the area.

On April 27, the heads of the Long and Ding lineages turned themselves in. The Public Security Bureau arrested some 20 villagers and issued orders for those who had fled. The police confiscated about 900 iron sticks, steel tubes, knives, bamboo spears and 30-odd lineage banners. Wanzai County government also dispatched work teams of 1,000 officials to every family of the two lineages, requiring them to sign a promise that they would not participate in future lineage feuds.[60]

This incident is interesting in the way it related to grassroots governance in China. Lineage networks have traditionally supplemented the grassroots government in many areas, such as taking care of the elderly and supporting young students to get to college. Will the resurrected lineage networks resume their traditional functions? To what extent will the lineage networks cooperate with the government? These are the questions that remain to be answered.

Conclusion

In this chapter we have discussed some of the other large-scale social protests. While they are less frequent than the major types of protests, they are nonetheless equally reflective of the transitional pains of China. Pollution and illegal fundraising are the typical symptoms of development, which are the product of the lack of regulation on environmental protection and of the financial market. To a certain extent, these protests belong to the subsistence expectation protests, as pollution and illegal fundraising affect subsistence living. The government is held responsible for the pollution produced by enterprises. Even though individuals are responsible for losing money to illegal fundraising schemes, the victims hold the government responsible for getting their money back. Their expectations were partially met.

Protests over identities include anti-Japanese nationalist protests, ethnic conflicts, defending local languages and lineage conflicts. On the surface, these are discrete incidents. However, these seemingly disconnected protests reflect the search for, and hold onto, some identities (national, ethnic, local and lineage) during the confusing time of transformation. Recurring anti-Japanese nationalist protests are the effort to reassert a Chinese identity when many are disappointed with government corruption and incompetence. Local and lineage identities provide some comfort and support for struggling individuals in a confusing market environment. Ethnic identities have much deeper cultural and religious roots. Economic development has no doubt strengthened some ethnic cleavages, as minority groups were left out of the economic boom.

Notes

1 Yanqi Tong, "Environmental Movements in Transitional Societies: A Comparative Study of Taiwan and China," *Comparative Politics* Vol. 37, No. 2 (January 2005): 175.
2 news.sohu.com/20090804/n265704190.shtml; and news.sina.com.cn/c/2009-08-01/014016047310s.shtml.
3 www.canyu.org/n10227c6.aspx.
4 news.bbc.co.uk/chinese/simp/hi/newsid_6710000/newsid_6714400/6714425.stm.
5 Personal interview with a Shanghai police officer.
6 Personal interview of an onsite CCTV reporter.
7 Ronald Inglehart, *Cultural Shift in Advanced Industrial Society* (Princeton University Press, 1990).
8 王奉友挪用侵占养殖户保证金实录 [Records of Wang Fengyou Embezzling Deposit Money] (沈阳电视台新闻调查节目 [Shenyang TV Investigation Program]).
9 "湘西非法集资案详情" [Details of Illegal Fundraising in Xiangxi], 《瞭望东方周刊》2010年02月02日 [*Liaowang Oriental Weekly*, February 2, 2010], finance.ifeng.com/news/20100202/1788658.shtml.
10 Stuart Hall, "Ethnicity: Identity and Difference," in Geoff Eley and Ronald G. Suny (eds) *Becoming National: A Reader* (Oxford University Press, 1996), 339–49.
11 The performance may well be part of Japanese culture, as the Japanese students claimed, but the performers seemed to be insensitive to other cultures.
12 news.xinhuanet.com/newscenter/2003-10/31/content_1154032.htm.
13 Personal interview of a participant from Peking University.
14 CCTV reporter onsite video records.
15 news.enorth.com.cn/system/2005/04/26/001012398.shtml; and news.enorth.com.cn/system/2005/04/26/001012828.shtml.
16 www.bbc.co.uk/zhongwen/simp/chinese_news/2012/09/120915_china_japan_violent demo.shtml.
17 www.nytimes.com/2005/04/17/international/asia/17cnd-hong.html.
18 www.ft.com/intl/cms/s/0/a09e651a-bb04-11df-9e1d-00144feab49a.html#axzz27c9A ffSl.
19 Ibid.
20 Personal interview with a Beijing police officer.
21 Personal interview with a reporter from *Huashang Newspaper* (a local newspaper of Xi'an).
22 "Martial Law Declared as Nearly 150 Die in Clashes in Central China," *The New York Times*, November 1, 2004.
23 Gladney Dru, *Muslim Chinese, Ethnic Nationalism in the People's Republic* (Harvard University Press, 1991).
24 Wenfang Tang and Gaochao He, "Separate but Loyal: Ethnicity and Nationalism in China," *Policy Studies* No. 56 (2010): 15.

25 Ibid.
26 James Miles and Michael Sheridan, "Fears of Another Tiananmen as Tibet Explodes in Hatred," *Sunday Times*, March 16, 2008.
27 新华社拉萨3月28日电, China News Agency, March 28, 2008.
28 news.sina.com.cn/c/2008-12-08/092116804318.shtml.
29 news.sina.com.cn/c/2008-04-17/160113753055s.shtml.
30 finance.sina.com.cn/focus/webjlf/.
31 Personal interviews with the media reporters covering the incident.
32 Ibid.
33 Ibid.
34 Personal interview with a CCTV onsite reporter.
35 中国国家统计局 [State Statistical Bureau], 人口统计年鉴 2010 [*Population Yearbook, 2010*].
36 Colin MacKerras has a very good account of ethnic issues in China. See his: "Tibetans, Uyghurs, and Multinational 'China': Han-minority Relations and State Legitimation," in Peter Hays and Stanley Rosen (eds) *Chinese Politics: State, Society and the Market* (Routledge, 2009), 222–42.
37 Personal interview with Ningxia local residents.
38 张济民, 张竹萍 [Zhang Jimin and Zhang Zhuping], "对少数民族中的犯罪分子必须实行'两少一宽'" [We Must Adopt 'Two Fewers and One Leniency' to Minority Criminals], 《青海民族学院学报（社会科学版）》1991年第1期 [*Journal of Qinghai Ethnic College* No. 1 (1991)].
39 gd.news.sina.com.cn/news/2010/07/09/942799.html.
40 Personal interview, September 2011.
41 paper.wenweipo.com/2010/07/26/CH1007260009.htm.
42 news.xinhuanet.com/edu/2010-09/23/c_12598473.htm.
43 woeser.middle-way.net/2010/08/blog-post_05.html (Woeser's official homepage).
44 "新英雄闯荡上海滩, 不限户籍个个精英" [New Heros in Shanghai, All are Elites without Household Registration], 《新民晚报》2009年2月4日B6版 [*Xinmin Evening News*, February 4, 2009, B6].
45 news.sina.com.hk/cgi-bin/nw/show.cgi/9/1/1/1027191/1.html.
46 Personal interview with the lieutenant governor of Guangdong Province.
47 Maurice Freedom, *Linage Organization in Southeastern China* (Athlone Press, 1965).
48 Prasenjit Duara, *Culture, Power, and the State, Rural North China, 1900–1942* (CA: Stanford University Press, 1988).
49 陈支平 [Chen Zhiping], 《清末民间抗粮与乡族势力》[Resistance to State Grain Procurement and Rural Lineage in the End of Qing Dynasty], 《厦门大学学报》2006年第1期。[*Journal of Xiamen University* No. 1 (2006)].
50 常建华 [Chang Jianhua], "近代闽台族正制考述" [Investigation of Mintai Lineage System in Modern Times], 《中国社会经济史研究》, 2006年01期 [*Studies of Chinese Social Economic History* No. 1 (2006)].
51 陈支平, 《清末民间抗粮与乡族势力》, ibid.
52 谢庐明、曾小锋 [Xie Luming and Zeng Xiaofeng], 《20世纪二三十年代赣南乡村宗族与苏维埃革命 – 兼论中国共产党对宗族的认识和政策》[Rural Lineages and the Soviet Revolution in the 1920s and 1930s—The Perceptions and Policies of the Chinese Communist Party on Lineages], 《江西行政学院学报》2006年第1期, [*Jiangxi Administration College Journal*, 2006]; and 傅建成 [Fu Jiancheng], 《新民主主义革命时期中共宗族政策、行为分析》[Analysis of the Policies and Behaviors of the Chinese Communist Party During the New Democratic Revolution], 《安徽史学》(合肥)2009年期第3期, [*Anhui Historiography* No. 3 (2006)].
53 钱杭 谢维扬 [Qiang Hang and Xie Weiyang], *传统与转型：江西泰和农村宗族形态* [Tradition and Transition: Rural Lineages in Jiangxi Taihe] (上海社会科学院出版社, 1995年 [Shanghai Social Science Academy Press, 1995]), 24.

54 Ibid., 25.
55 Ibid., 45.
56 Lily Tsai, *Accountability without Democracy* (New York: Cambridge University Press, 2008), 150.
57 钱杭 谢维扬 [Qian Hang and Xie Weiyang], ibid., 268.
58 Ibid., 31.
59 Personal fieldwork notes.
60 "江西万载县发生大规模宗族械斗" [Large-scale Clan Feud Fight in Jiangxi Wanzai County], 《南方都市报》, 2006年5月18日, [*Southern Metropolitan News*, May 18, 2006].

7 Creating public opinion pressure
Large-scale Internet protests

Internet mass incidents (网络群体性事件) are a different species of social protest. Our data set of 548 large-scale mass incidents does not include any Internet protests. However, as Internet protests have become a popular form of protest in China, it is impossible to depict a full picture of social protest without giving an account of Internet protest in China. We have generated a different list of large-scale Internet protests. In accordance with our other data set, we limit the Internet protests to the same time frame: 2003 to 2010. By large-scale Internet mass incidents, we refer to the Internet discussion critical of government (including government officials) behavior with more than a 1 million click rate. For large-scale microblog-based mass incidents, our criteria are that they must involve at least three opinion leaders, each with at least 100,000 followers, and each with issues of at least 10 microblogs daily during the incident.

This chapter will first give a background brief of the Internet population in China. Then we will investigate the Internet mass incidents, their development and consequences. We would like to position our analysis in the framework of moral politics. Unlike the real world social protests, where the majority of them are over economic subsistence issues, the Internet mass protests focus on issues of injustice. In order to generate public opinion pressure, moral appeal is the most effective means of mobilizing support.

Netizens in China

According to the China Internet Information Center (CNNIC), by the end of 2010, the number of Chinese Internet users had reached 457 million (Figure 7.1). This is a net increase of 73 million compared with the end of 2009. The Internet penetration rate is 34.3 percent, which means that more than one-third of the Chinese population has access to the Internet. (The world average is 25.6 percent.)

In the meantime, mobile Internet users more than doubled from 117 million in 2008 to 303 million in 2010. The combination of wired Internet with wireless cell phones has qualitatively changed the scope of Internet coverage. People can now communicate with the Internet while on the go. First-hand

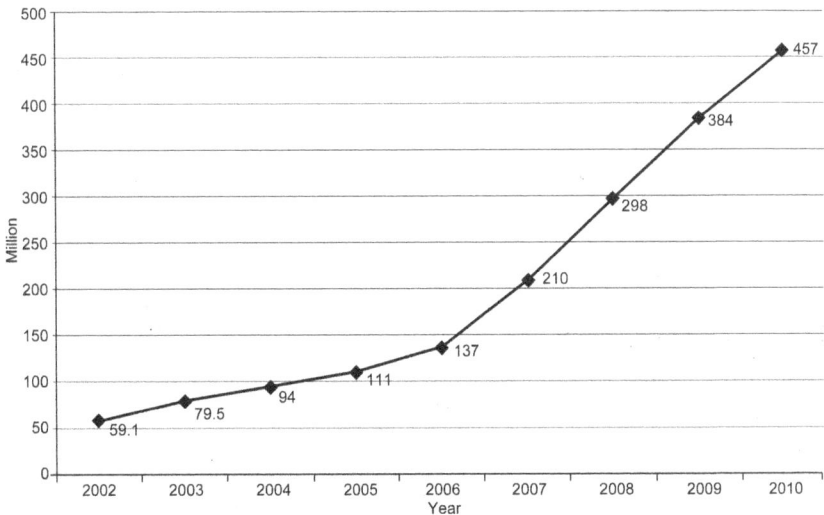

Figure 7.1 Number of Internet users by year (million)
Source: All data on the Internet users in China come from the China Internet Information Center, The 27th Survey Report on the Internet Development in China, www.cnnic.cn/research/bgxz/tjbg/201101/P020110221534255749405.pdf

information delivery (both in text and in video) is much faster and more efficient with mobile phones as the terminal.

A brief break down of the Internet population would inform us about the potential participants of Internet protests or the actual users of "liberation technology."[1] The age of Internet users spreads from 10 years old (or under) to 80 years old. However, the bulk of users are 10 to 30 years old (Table 7.1).

Corresponding to the age groups, the education levels of Internet users concentrate on middle school and high school levels (Table 7.2). It is interesting to note that the percentage of netizens with middle school and high school education (68.5 percent) goes way beyond that of the comparable age

Table 7.1 The age composition of Internet users (%)

Age group	%
Under 10	1.1
10–19	27.3
20–29	29.3
30–39	23.4
40–49	12.6
50–59	3.9
60 and over	1.9

Source: (All data on the Internet users in China come from the China Internet Information Center, "The 27th Survey Report on the Internet Development in China," www.cnnic.cn/research/bgxz/tjbg/201101/P020110221534255749405.pdf)

Table 7.2 Education levels of Internet users (%)

Education	%
Primary school	8.4
Middle school	32.8
High school	35.7
Technical college	11.8
College and above	11.4

Source: (All data on the Internet users in China come from the China Internet Information Center, "The 27th Survey Report on the Internet Development in China," www.cnnic.cn/research/bgxz/tjbg/201101/P020110221534255749405.pdf)

group (10–19 years old, 27.3 percent). This indicates that more than 40 percent of the adult netizens with middle school and high school education are not currently students.

If we divide up Internet users by profession, the two largest groups of Internet users are students and professional white-collar workers, each taking a 30 percent or so share (Table 7.3). Self-employed and unemployed groups are a distant third and fourth in ranking, respectively. It is worth noting that in 2010, farmers took up about the same share of the Internet population as government employees, and more of a share than workers in the manufacturing sector.

If we divide the netizens by income level (see Table 7.4), the majority are at the lower-middle level. This is understandable since 30 percent of them are students who tend to have no or very low income. The other striking phenomenon is that the percentage of high-income Internet population is low. If according to the State Statistical Bureau's definition of a 5,000 RMB monthly income as middle class, only 6.6 percent of the netizens belong to the middle class. We could also move down a bracket to include those who have 3,000 RMB or more monthly income as middle class, as the State Statistical

Table 7.3 Internet users by profession (%)

Profession	%
Student	30.6
Professional/white collar	29.2
Self-employed	14.9
Unemployed	4.9
Government staff	5.8
Migrant worker	3.5
Worker (manufacturing)	2.9
Farmer	6.0
Other	2.2

Source: (All data on the Internet users in China come from the China Internet Information Center, "The 27th Survey Report on the Internet Development in China," www.cnnic.cn/research/bgxz/tjbg/201101/P020110221534255749405.pdf)

Table 7.4 Income structure of Internet users (%)

Income	%
above 8,000	2.9
5,001–8,000	3.7
3,001–5,000	10.5
2,001–3,000	16.2
1,501–2,000	14.5
1,001–1,500	13.2
501–1,000	15.1
below 500	19.4
no income	4.6

Source: (All data on the Internet users in China come from the China Internet Information Center, "The 27th Survey Report on the Internet Development in China," www.cnnic.cn/research/bgxz/tjbg/201101/P020110221534255749405.pdf)

Bureau's standard refers to family income rather than individual income, though realistically one can barely survive on a 3,000 RMB monthly income in the big cities. In this case, 17 percent are middle class.

These distributions by age, education, profession and income of the Internet population indicate the composition of the participants of Internet discussions. Internet public opinion is primarily representative of young students (the majority of them may be in high school) and professional white-collar workers. The portion of self-employed/freelancers is also significant. The overwhelming majority of Internet discussion participants also belong to the low-income population. While it could be argued that Internet users are not representative of Chinese society as a whole, the fact is that political changes are always initiated and promoted by the most vocal and active minority.

Large-scale internet protests

Increasing Internet access has provided millions of people with a broad public space in which to voice their opinions and instantly communicate with other Internet users. It empowers ordinary people to participate in discussions of public concern. Since Internet protests operate in a virtual space, people can participate from anywhere and at any time. You don't have to take leave from school or the office as you would to protest on the street; you can protest from home at night when you are alone. This greatly reduces the cost of participation. In addition, the anonymous nature of Internet participation reduces the political risks associated with street protests. The Internet makes it much easier to formulate a consensus, ferment emotions and provoke action in a short time period. As a result, we have observed a strong surge of Internet opinion groups in recent years. This new public opinion source has become increasingly effective at exerting its influence over public affairs and public policy making.

Table 7.5 The number of large-scale Internet protests by year, 2003–10

	2003	2004	2005	2006	2007	2008	2009	2010
Internet mass incident	2	1	1	0	3	5	12	24

Table 7.5 shows the number of the large-scale Internet mass incidents from 2003 to 2010. We can see an upward trend of the occurrence of these incidents. The strong showing of 2009 and 2010 probably indicates the deepening social frustration over rampant government corruption and misbehavior on the one hand, and the growing effectiveness of the new social media (especially the development of microblogging).

The development of Internet protest

The development of Internet protest has gone through several stages. The first stage began with what we call *reactive* protests. Usually a protest starts with the exposure of certain incidents by the traditional news media. Then the Internet provides cyberspace for public discussion. Typical cases are the Sun Zhigang incident and the BMW accident in 2003. In both cases, the traditional media first exposed the incidents, and then the discussion forums on the Internet reacted and exploded into heated public opinion pressure. In the end, the overwhelming public opinion pressure forced the central government to take action.[2]

The second stage is *initiative* protest. Since the traditional news media has limitations on its news coverage, the publicly accessible Internet, thus, becomes an independent source of revelation. The representative example is the relocation incident in the Nanjing downtown district in 2005. It was first reported online by a graduate student from Peking University that the local government was destroying historical sites, which eventually led to an Internet protest campaign.[3] In the past, people had to seek media exposure to generate public opinion pressure or get the attention of central government. Now, more and more people publicize government corruption cases or individual suffering on the Internet, which is much more accessible than the traditional media, in order to generate public opinion pressure or sympathy.

The third stage is characterized by *interactive* protests. The Internet and the traditional news media feed off each other and shape public opinion about particular incidents. Either one could start to report an incident, and then the other joins in and escalates public opinion to new heights. This has become the major pattern of Internet involvement in public affairs. Journalists and TV hosts often go to the Internet looking for newsworthy clues. Internet opinion leaders are also eager to write columns for newspapers or appear on TV programs.

One example is the so-called "fishing law enforcement" (钓鱼执法) incident in Shanghai in October 2009. In an effort to wipe out unlicensed taxis, plain-clothes police officers pretended to be customers and tricked private car drivers into taking passengers. Those who were caught would be fined heavily. One victim who fell into this trap put up a protest post on the Internet. Then the traditional media got involved and dug out more such cases. The interactive process immediately created a public opinion storm and forced the government authorities to make a public apology.[4]

The fourth and current stage coincides with the development of microblogging in China. Twitter was developed in 2006 and became very successful in the American and European markets. Fearing its political implications, the Chinese government blocked Twitter in China. As a replacement, Sina—the largest Chinese Internet portal—opened its microblog (Weibo) service in August 2009. Weibo combined the functions of both Facebook and Twitter. The main impact of Weibo is that while anonymous Internet discussion remains overwhelming, we have real name opinion leaders with millions of followers. With fast dissemination, Weibo now can broadcast events live. By the end of 2010, Sina's microblog had 60 million users, and issued an average of 25 million messages daily. Many Internet protests in 2010 originated on Weibo. In addition, because of the emergence of the opinion leaders, there are heated debates over issues of public concern. Many Internet mass incidents were initiated by these opinion leaders. We will have a detailed discussion of this new social media later in this chapter.

Types of Internet supervision of government behavior

The main function of Internet protest is to wage moral campaigns against government misbehavior. Specifically, these campaigns can be grouped into several types: exposing corruption cases, supervising officials' behavior, generating public opinion pressure on the judicial process, and pressing for policy adjustment.

Exposing corruption cases

Corruption is secretive. Yet, the Internet enables more watchful eyes on government officials and provides channels to bring corruption cases out into the daylight. For example, in December 2008, netizens spotted that Zhou Jiugeng, the bureau chief of housing management of Jiangning District of Nanjing City, was wearing a US$14,500 Vacheron Constantin watch and smoking extremely expensive cigarettes when he appeared on a TV program. This kind of lifestyle is well beyond his means. The videos and photos were circulated online and generated huge public opinion pressure on the Nanjing City government. The City Disciplinary Committee had to launch an investigation and found that Zhou indeed had taken a huge amount of bribes. Zhou was later arrested.[5]

In 2010, a series of incidents were exposed that showed that the processes of recruiting local government staff members involved corruption. The main feature of the corruption was that the second generation of the officials received special treatment and the entire process was unfair. For example, a unit under the Bureau of Human Resources and Social Security of Sanya City, Hainan Province, had a job opening in May. One applicant received 99 points (the maximum being 100) in the exam and got the job. None of the rest of the applicants received more than 79 points. This "outstanding" student turned out to be the daughter of the Bureau Chief of Social Insurance of Sanya City. Many believed that she either got special treatment in grading or she had seen the questions beforehand. After preliminary investigation, her qualification was void and her father was suspended.[6]

Another public opinion explosion was caused by a recruitment advertisement for a staff member at the county office of fee management, which is part of the Bureau of Finance of Pingnan County, Ningde City, Fujian Province. The requirements for eligible applicants are described thus: "College graduate from domestic college, bachelor degree from a foreign country, specialize in international accounting, English proficiency college grade four, household registration in Pingnan County, female, under 25 years old." There was only one applicant who met these requirements and she was the daughter of the deputy mayor of Ningde City. After the exposure of this case, the chief of the Bureau of Finance had to resign.[7]

Obviously, these randomly exposed corruption cases are only a small tip of the iceberg. Official corruption runs much wider and deeper then the few cases being revealed. The ultimate solution to China's rampant corruption depends primarily on the central government's willingness to enforce strict measures and establish institutional arrangements against corruption. However, the sporadic Internet exposure has served as a deterrent to such behavior.

Supervising government behavior

In a similar fashion, government officials' behavior and words are closely scrutinized. Misbehavior or "slips of the tongue" would be quickly disseminated online. In November 2008, several documents surfaced on the Internet showing that local government officials from Jiangxi, Zhejiang and Jiangsu were using public money to fund their "foreign country exploration tours [出国考察]." The pressure of Internet opinion propelled official investigations and the officials in question were disciplined. The central government also issued new regulations that took back the approval power of local governments' "foreign country exploration tours."[8]

In June 2009, Lu Jun, the chief of the planning bureau of Zhengzhou City, participated in a TV program. When answering a question about why land that was originally appropriated for affordable housing was being used for building expensive villas, he retorted, "are you speaking for the Party, or are you speaking for the masses?" His comment caused a mighty uproar on the Internet. The government of Zhengzhou City was forced to suspend Lu.[9]

In 2010, there was a series of incidents involving government procurement. For example, the Bureau of Finance in Fushun City Liaoning Province purchased iPod Touches to be used as flash disks. The Public Security Bureau in Suzhou purchased iPhone 4s for work-related communication tools. In addition, the Public Security Department in Heilongjiang Province was exposed as having purchased notebook computers priced at 41,000 RMB (more than $6,000) each. Netizens questioned the necessity of government agencies having to purchase all these luxury items in order to function. Many commented that this was taxpayers' money and the government should not go on a shopping spree.[10] All these government procurements were suspended under public opinion pressure. Since all these cases occurred in December, it seems likely that these government agencies were finding ways to spend money that they otherwise would have had to return. This is common in many bureaucratic settings, but the watchful eyes of netizens exposed the improper behavior.

Generating public opinion pressure on judicial process

The rule of law is central to modern society, democratic or harmonious. The Chinese government has also declared its desire to pursue the rule of law in their political system. There are many obstacles on China's long march to the rule of law, one of which lies in the Chinese tradition of emphasizing moral justice rather than procedural justice. Such conflict is typically reflected in Internet protests.

In February 2009, the police in Danfeng County, Shaanxi Province, arrested a high school student for the death of his girlfriend. The suspect died during the interrogation. Internet opinion pressure forced the arrest of the police officers involved and all received one- to two-year sentences after a speedy trial.[11]

In May 2009, Deng Yujiao, a karaoke parlor waitress, fatally stabbed one of the three local government officials who were forcefully demanding her sexual service. She was arrested for involuntary manslaughter. As the news broke out online, a cascade of posts overwhelmingly supported Deng as if she were a national hero. The Internet frenzy drove a quick ruling and Deng was released without charge. Many believe that without the landslide Internet support, Deng might have languished in prison for life.[12]

In 2008, Xu Ting, a migrant worker in Guangzhou, found that an ATM machine accidentally recorded his withdrawal of 1,000 yuan as 1 yuan. He therefore withdrew 171,000 yuan from his account, which contained only 171 yuan. After being on the run for about one year, Xu was apprehended by the police in 2009. In court, the only law applicable to his case was theft from a state financial institution, for which the punishment is severe: life in prison or the death sentence if the amount is more than 100,000 yuan. Xu received life imprisonment. This sounded extremely unfair and triggered public uproar. Those who had embezzled millions only received limited prison terms, and Xu received life for 171,000 yuan! The law was obviously outdated, as while

100,000 yuan was a huge amount of money at the time the law was drafted, this was no longer the case. The intermediate court in Guangzhou in the second trial decided to reduce the sentence to five years.[13] Moral justice finally won over procedural justice.

Pressing for institutional adjustment

Individual cases may result in the fall of certain officials. More lasting impact, however, would come from institutional change. Some large-scale Internet mass incidents have achieved such a goal. A typical case is the Sun Zhigang incident. In 2003, a college graduate from Hubei, who was seeking job opportunities in Guangzhou, was sent to the detention center because he did not have a temporary residence permit. He was beaten to death by other inmates there. An Internet uproar ignited a debate on the plight of migrants unable to obtain proper urban registration and the inequity of the long-standing Custody and Repatriation system. The system was subsequently abolished.

Two prison incidents occurred in February 2009. In one case, a prisoner was killed by fellow inmates and the other case was the aforementioned death of a suspect during police interrogation. Both triggered heated Internet reaction, especially the former, wherein the prison authority first claimed that the person died while playing peek-a-boo with other inmates. "Playing peek-a-boo" thus became a popular online phrase denoting sarcasm. Under the pressure of public opinion, the police involved received prison terms. More importantly, the government has also started to overhaul the prison system and investigate systematic abusive police practices.

In an effort to tighten Internet control, the Ministry of Industry and Information Technology announced that all personal computers sold in China are required to install the filtering software "Green Dam-Youth Escort [绿坝.花季护航]" from July 1, 2009. Internet users rallied against this move and finally forced the indefinite suspension of the initiative.

We should not exaggerate the impact of Internet protests on institutional and policy adjustment. So far, these adjustments are rare and ad hoc at best. However, these Internet protests have exposed the loopholes in and deficiencies of the current system, cumulatively, and they may push for further institutional and policy adjustment.

Microblogging and contentious politics

Microblogging and Internet protests in China

In recent years, microblogging has developed rapidly as an information exchange platform for Internet users following the creation of blogs. In 2006, Twitter came into being as the first microblog platform. With messages being limited to 140 characters, Twitter has become the most popular form of microblogging and the second largest information and social network after Facebook. By allowing anonymity and reposting, Twitter provides a platform that is much more open than Facebook, which is a more or less closed circle of friends and acquaintances. The traditional blogosphere requires writing skills and a reasonable amount of logic for the expression of opinions and ideas. Producing a blog consumes a lot of energy. Microblogging is different. With only 140 characters, you can simply make a statement without evidence or reasoning, not to mention polishing of style. It is fast food communication.

Twitter has achieved great success in the European and American markets, but is unable to enter the Chinese market. The Chinese government strictly forbids any comments that openly support overseas dissidents or Falun Gong, or call for the overthrow of the communist regime. As it could not force Twitter—a US company—to delete such comments, the Chinese government blocked access to it in China soon after Twitter came into existence. A large group of faithful Chinese Twitter users, using sophisticated techniques to break through the government blockade, is able to access and use Twitter. However, there are a couple of problems with Chinese Twitter. First, like any platform, Twitter has designed mechanisms to filter out undesirable language once a message is "reported" by readers. This only applies to English content, however. Twitter has no mechanism to filter obscene Chinese language. As a result, the Chinese messages on Twitter can be quite filthy. The "dirty" language environment has deterred many potential Chinese users. Second, if not many Chinese are able or can be bothered to access Twitter due to technical difficulties, Twitter becomes a less desirable place for increasing popularity or getting information.

Seeing the great potential of the microblog market, Chinese Internet companies have emulated Twitter and introduced a group of microblog platforms, such as Fanfou (饭否), Jiwai (叽歪), Digu (嘀咕), and Tengxun (腾讯). Alarmed by the mobilizing effects of microblogging during the general elections in Iran, the Chinese government closed these platforms in July 2009. At around the same time, Sina opened its own microblog service in August 2009. Sina is one of the biggest commercial Internet corporations in China, with close relations to the government. It conveniently has a dual identity. For the government, it is an "insider" and therefore is easy to control. For users, however, it is a commercial institution and has market credentials. This dual identity enabled the Sina microblog service to monopolize the microblog market. The government subsequently has allowed other companies to provide microblog services, but Sina has already taken the largest share of the market, and netizens are already used to the Sina service and its network. The number of microblog users with other companies is far behind that of Sina.

According to the "White Paper on Year One of China's Microblog Market," a report by Sina, 60.9 percent of all microblog users in China is using Sina's service. From March 2010 to June 2010, the number of monthly microblog users increased from 54.5 million to 103 million. During the same period, Sina's microblog monthly visits increased from 71.6 million to

211.9 million. By the end of 2010, Sina's microblog had 60 million users and posted an average of 25 million messages daily.[14]

On account of the nature of microblogging—fewer words and more information—it can be used on computers as well as on mobile communication devices, such as cell phones. This "quotation" type of information dissemination is much speedier and fits into the rhythm of modern life, which makes people impatient at lengthy commentary. As the design of Twitter allows the summary of the number of followers, it enables ordinary people to enjoy the "star" effect and realize the dream of being in the social spotlight. Social celebrities soon realize this effect and open their own microblogs. Twitter quickly became a popular public communication platform.

If the content of information is no longer the point of attraction due to word limit, then the "name" becomes the substitute. Microblogging changed the anonymous method of posting in Internet discussion forums. On the one hand, those who set up their microblog accounts might use their real name in order to achieve the celebrity effect and gain followers,[15] on the other hand, the host companies want to have "real people" to attract users to register with their microblog services. This has had a great impact on the nature of Internet discussion. If the blogger is a real person, his or her followers will be more faithful, following everything and every piece of information from and about the blogger. The followers, therefore, become a group with cohesion and solidarity. They would fight to protect the one they are following.

One of the advantages of microblogging is its re-posting function. If you like a post, you can click the re-post button and send it to all of your microblog followers. The former president of Microsoft China and Google China, Lee Kai-fu, once described this speedy re-posting function as "virus contagion." The information could be disseminated in a very short time period to the largest possible population. For example, suppose one blogger has 100 followers. If one's message is reposted by 10 of his/her followers who also have 100 followers each, then there will be 1,000 readers. If 10 percent of these 1,000 re-posts the message again, after several clicks the number of readers of the message may reach hundreds of thousands or even millions.[16]

According to Lee Kai-Fu, Chinese microblogging is functionally more informative. A limit of 140 characters in English allows only one or two sentences, while 140 Chinese characters can deliver more information.[17] As a result, Twitter users only use the microblog as a tool for personal or social communication, while the Sina microblog has provided a new media platform that is more informative and effective.

The microblog service in China has mixed the best features of both Twitter and Facebook. It can post pictures, videos and web links, like Facebook, and also is open and fast like Twitter. Once the host company has verified the identity of the blogger, it will attach a "V" after the blogger's name (meaning verified). Once the users see a celebrity's name with a "V," they know that this is the real celebrity, not someone taking the name. By the same token, media outlets with a "V" also affirm their authenticity and increase their credibility.

The ability to accelerate information dissemination is reflected in the design of the microblog account. In the past, one had to visit each individual blog or forum to see what people were saying. Now, the first page of one's microblog account will display the latest posts of all the microbloggers one is following. In this manner, one will not miss any important messages.

With the ability to upload pictures and video clips, the microblog's real time live broadcasting function has surpassed TV media. For example, after the mudslide in Gansu Zhouqu in August 2010, all the news media used pictures taken by a netizen at the scene. Even if you are creating false information, you need to make it appear logically convincing. In another example, within an hour of the fire on Jiaozhou Road in Shanghai, there were several hundred photos of the fire in the microblogosphere, far exceeding the speed of traditional media. The ability to broadcast live has broken through official censorship and has demonstrated the potential of microblogging in Internet protests. As a result, there has emerged a scene where all netizens are journalists, commentators and detectives.

The nature of microblogging has not only made it a platform for individuals and organizations to spread information, but also given it great potential to mobilize social movements. In the past, organizers used loud speakers to lead protesters. If there is broad participation, the scene will be very chaotic and noisy. The government could easily identify the organizers and suppress the protest. Mobile phone messages could serve as a communication instrument among potential participants, but it is a limited and closed network. During the process of the protest, it is difficult for organizers to use short cell phone message to lead the movement. Microblogs changed this. Organizers are able to give orders in a prompt fashion on the microblog, and participants can see these messages immediately. The organizer can become a "shadow" leader, even giving orders from thousands of miles away. Unable to identify the leaders onsite, the government is less likely to suppress the protest.

Despite sophisticated technical control and blatant Internet censorship, the Chinese Internet remains surprisingly open. On account of this openness, the Internet has become a public sphere in which various criticisms against the government are voiced and public opinion pressure is generated. In order to understand the landscape of Internet discourse in China, we need to be aware that this is not a straight state versus society dichotomy. As Joseph Fewsmith has shown, Chinese intellectual elites are divided by very different ideological orientations.[18] These divisions have been further consolidated by the development of the Internet. Several major forums dominate public Internet discussion in China. The major liberal Internet forums are Tianya (天涯), and Kaidi (凯迪). The famous Maoist forum is Wu You Zhi Xiang (乌有之乡). The radical New Left goes to Siyue Qingnian (四月青年&mdash] the English web name is Anti-CNN). The Moderate New Left uses Zhonghuawang Luntan (中华网论坛). Before 2010, Internet protest could be labeled "positional warfare." That is, netizens would visit the forums in line with their opinions. When consensus over a particular incident occurs, such as happened in the Sun Zhigang incident, all the forums join forces and criticize the government. These are the cases from which most scholars are drawing conclusions about the functions of the Internet in China. However, when a particular incident is controversial, netizens fight with each other in their forums and are somewhat overlooked. Because of the anonymity of the posters, there are no leaders and organizers; all the Internet protesters are protesting on their own.

The development of microblogging has changed this ecosystem. Now Internet protests could be called "bayonet warfare." As the Sina microblog service has the majority of microblog users, different factions and groups now come together on one battlefield from various forums. Again, if consensus is achieved regarding a particular incident, netizens protest together. More often than not, we have observed controversy between different camps over particular cases. The real name verification system by the microblog service has enhanced the role of the opinion leaders who are crucial in microblog-based Internet protests. Netizens use the re-post function of the microblog, promptly spreading the comments of the opinion leaders, and thus push public opinion on certain incidents to the peak. The positions of the opinion leaders usually influence the opinions of their followers and determine the direction of certain events. Therefore, by 2010, the format of Internet protest had changed greatly. Different factions now have their own temporary opinion leaders. Followers form their opinions by following their opinion leaders' positions rather than forming their own thoughts or finding their own facts.

In an oversimplified fashion, there are two major camps in the microblogosphere with regard to debate over public affairs. One camp is composed of liberal intellectuals who advocate Western-style democracy and freedom. This is the camp that has the largest following. For example, Li Chengpeng, who was a sports commentator, has a follower base of 5.8 million.[19] The famous writer Zheng Yuanjie has about 3.4 million followers.[20] The other camp, which is less influential, is the so-called New Left. The leading New Left spokesperson Ran Xiang, who has a sharp tongue, has 589,000 followers.[21] Another leading spokesperson, Sima Nan, has about 510,000 followers.[22] (All the numbers of followers are as of August 2012.) The bloggers from this camp are more sympathetic toward, but do not necessarily support, the government. Yet they consistently attack the pro-West tendency of the liberal camp. The liberals accuse the New Left camp of being a "50-cent" party: rumor has it that they receive 50 cents for each post supporting the government.[23] As a countermeasure, the New Left accuses the liberal camp of being a "direction-guiding" party (带路党), a label derived from the collaborators during the Anti-Japanese War who helped the foreign invaders by giving them directions for attacking the locals.

Microblogging is a "quotation" type of writing. It does not require serious reasoning and analysis, and one can finish a message within 10 seconds. As there is no effective way to prevent dissemination of false information, the cost of doing so is very low. Sina's microblog has become a field in which netizens attack each other and sources of rumor mongering. To a certain extent, the messages resemble the "big character posters" during the Cultural Revolution, only they appear in electronic form with a much faster speed of dissemination. For example, on January 28, 2011, a famous TV series playwright, Chen Wanning, issued a microblog complaining that his friend had been strangled at Cairo airport, but that Chinese embassy personnel there did not take care of Chinese citizens, but "just run for their own lives." Within 30 minutes, the message had been re-posted 26,000 times, with 5,000 comments, all criticizing the uselessness of the Chinese Embassy in Egypt. Chen Wanning issued another message 40 minutes later, explaining that he did not know what was going on, and he was only making a casual complaint out of concern for the safety of his friend. However, the false information had already spread out like a virus, and public opinion continued to attack the Chinese government regardless of Chen's clarification.

In microblog-based Internet protests, public intellectuals play decisive roles by acting as societal opinion leaders. They are university professors, journalists, lawyers, writers and artists. Their opinions affect netizens and have public appeal. The government in general takes a conciliatory approach toward microbloggers who disseminate false information. Any punitive measures against these social celebrities would trigger a new round of criticism toward the government. The microblog protests led by these opinion leaders, therefore, generate greater public opinion pressure on the government, and this is called "micro revolution [微革命]."[24]

The features of microblogs have convinced social opinion leaders that "microblogging changes China."[25] They claim that to "surround and watch is power." These two statements, thus, become the core principles of the "micro revolution." The ability of "real time live broadcasting" and generating "public attention" has changed the process of Internet mass incidents. Opinion leaders have become the leaders of Internet protest participation. Internet protests have moved from individual to organized collective action. The microblog's real time live function has surpassed the TV media, as shown by the earlier examples of the mudslide in Gansu Zhouqu and the fire on Jiaozhou Road in Shanghai. The ability to broadcast live has broken through official censorship, and demonstrated the potential of microblogging in Internet protests. In many instances, the government was forced to change its policies under the pressure of Internet public opinion. This in turn reinforces the belief that "microblogging changes China."

Case analysis of microblog Internet mass incidents

In this section, we will trace the major microblog protests that occurred in the Sina microblogosphere in 2009 and 2010. In this short time, there have been many heated public "surround and watch" incidents. Some of them are not directly related to government behavior, such as the fake educational credentials of a CEO from a private company. As mentioned earlier, the criteria we used to select the cases are: 1 they must be related to government behavior; 2 at least three opinion leaders must be involved; 3 the opinion leader must have at least 100,000 followers; and 4 during the events, opinion leaders must have issued at least 10 microblogs a day. In this way, we ensure that the incidents are large enough to warrant analysis. All the information is derived from various microblogs on the Sina microblog service and individual interviews with media reporters involved with particular incidents. For each incident, we will provide the microblog addresses of the major opinion leaders. One word of caution here: Sina registration is required to access these microblogs, and some of the earlier comments may no longer exist.[26]

The first case of the micro revolution

The Feng Zhenghu returning home incident does not fit strictly within our criteria. This incident occurred on Twitter and did not have a large following inside China. It is regarded as the first case of China's "micro revolution," however, as the Twitter report of the ongoing event forced the eventual resolution of the incident.

Feng is a dissident based in Shanghai. On June 7, 2009, Feng returned to Shanghai Pudong airport from a visit to Japan. He was denied entry on the grounds that his documentation was incomplete, and he was deported back to Japan. Over six months, Feng tried to return seven times, but all of his attempts failed. In November 2009, after failing to board the plane in Narita airport, he refused to leave and lived in the airport. For more than 80 days Feng used Twitter to publicize all his activities in the airport.[27] He also gave out his bank account number, asking for donations from sympathizers. Some of his supporters re-posted his messages to domestic forums. This incident attracted international media attention. On November 18, 2009, United Nations (UN) refugee officials visited Feng in Narita airport. They were willing to help Feng stay in Japan legally. Feng declined their offer. He issued several messages daily with photos. Under international public opinion pressure, officials from the Chinese Embassy in Tokyo paid a visit to Feng on January 25, 2010. Eventually, Feng ended his protest in the airport and returned to Shanghai on February 12, 2010.

Interestingly, Feng Zhenghu did not know anything about Twitter before this incident. Therefore, in the first 10 days of the protest, he did not attract much public attention. His friend helped him get a Twitter ID and advised him to use it. Within a month, Feng's Twitter ID acquired 7,000 followers, and that number increased daily. In addition to getting attention from the UN, the international media, and nongovernmental organizations (NGOs), his sympathizers in China also re-posted his microblog on Chinese Internet forums. Since the Chinese government blocked access to Twitter, the Chinese netizens' reaction was limited. Twitter did play an important role in the final resolution of the incident, however. Some opinion leaders labeled the Feng

Zhenghu returning home incident the first case of micro revolution in the first year of microblogging in China.

Generating public opinion pressure

The Li Mengmeng college entrance exam incident is a more authentic demonstration of the powerful effect of microblog-based mass protest. It is a case where Internet public opinion pressure forced the local government to reverse an administrative decision. Li Mengmeng was a high school graduate from Kaifeng City in Henan Province. In 2010, she achieved a passing score on the college entrance exam, but she did not receive an admission notice from any college. After tracking down her record, it was found that the county college admission office had mistakenly not submitted her application documents to the provincial office. The provincial office insisted that, as a matter of principle, they would not accept the late submission. Li issued an appeal in her microblog.[28] The message was re-posted 20,000 times within a day and generated 4,000 comments. One netizen even wrote a "micro letter" to the Party secretary of Henan Province, asking him to intervene.[29] He also asked all the netizens to re-post his micro letter: "just a click away, we may help someone to realize her dream." His letter was re-posted 100,000 times within three days, generating 20,000 comments. Comments were re-posted at the speed of 10,000 per hour. The traditional media also followed the story as it developed and reported the incident on their platforms.

Facing tremendous public opinion pressure, the provincial college admission office convened a meeting and admitted Li Mengmeng to Henan Finance and Law College. Within a week, several hundreds of thousands of netizens had participated in the Li Mengmeng incident, to overthrow the decision by the provincial college admission office, and changed Li Mengmeng's life. This is called a victory of microblogging and a victory of netizens. "Surround and watch is power, microblogging changes China," thus, has become a popular quote on Internet forums.

Live broadcasting

The Yihuang incident is a case that exemplifies the "live broadcast" function of the microblog. On September 10, 2010, the Zhong family in Fenggang village, Yihuang County of Jiangxi Province, set themselves on fire to protest the forced demolition of their house. One person died and two were injured. On September 16, 2010, two sisters from the family, by invitation of the Phoenix TV station, planned to take a plane to Beijing for a media interview.[30] At the airport, they encountered county officials who tried to prevent them from leaving. The sisters called Liu Chang, a journalist from *New Century Weekly* who had been covering this incident, for help. Liu Chang issued a microblog for public help "crying with blood [泣血求助]."[31]

At first, the message did not attract much attention. Then, an Internet opinion leader, Murong Xuecun, re-posted it.[32] The message spread immediately. At the airport, the Zhong sisters hid in the ladies' room and locked the door, using their cell phones to contact Liu Chang. Liu then contacted another reporter, Deng Fei, from the *Phoenix Weekly*. Deng Fei then broadcast the situation live from Nanchang airport and called for other media to get involved.[33] Some of the Zhong sisters' audio clips in the ladies room were broadcast online. Various media reporters flooded Nanchang airport, all writing their own microblogs and comments. Public opinion leaders and some university professors, scholars and celebrities also became involved and made comments. Several hundreds of thousands of netizens gathered on the Sina microblog to "surround and watch" the developments.

In the end, the Zhong sisters negotiated with the county officials and returned home. The same evening, Chengdu TV station and Phoenix TV station aired a program about the Yihuang incident. The following day, the Guangdong newspaper media issued a long report on the incident. The Party secretary and mayor of Yihuang County and the deputy mayor, who was in charge of relocation, lost their jobs a month later.[34]

Another microblog live broadcast event was the aforementioned Shanghai fire incident. On November 15, 2010, a residential building in the Jing'an District of Shanghai caught fire while undergoing renovation. Workers accidentally triggered the fire while operating electrical welding equipment. The fire resulted in 58 deaths and 56 disappearances. Within the first hour of the fire, several hundred original microblogs appeared with many photos of the fire scene. When the traditional media reporters arrived, they also used their institutional microblogs to report the disaster. Eight workers were detained for the accident. Netizens argued, however, that the migrant workers were scapegoats, and demanded that the city government investigate the officials who were in charge of the project, as well as the contractors. In early December, the city government officially arrested the director of the construction committee of Jing'an District and the relevant suspects.

On November 21, 2010, the seventh day after the fire, 100,000 people went to the scene to mourn the dead in accordance with Chinese tradition. Media reporters were there as well. The ability to broadcast live by microblogging was once again being demonstrated. Reporters from Southern Media kept issuing microblogs about seeing police onsite, warning that there was a possibility that the police would clash with the crowd: "There may be conflict between the police and people," "the situation may go out of control," and so on. Then, surprising the media that anticipated confrontation, the Party secretary and mayor of Shanghai appeared and joined the mourning crowd. The official Shanghai Orchestra also came and performed mourning music onsite. Everything proceeded in an orderly manner and the mourning activities ended peacefully. Those reporters who were guessing that a police–civilian conflict would take place quietly deleted their microblogs. Many opinion leaders characterized this microblog live broadcast as "microblog witnessing the growth of citizen power."[35]

Framing injustice

In order to mobilize Internet public opinion, the initiator has to frame an unjust event in a short message. The most convenient way is to fan public anger against the immoral behavior of government officials. The "my father is Li Gang" incident is a typical case.

On October 16, 2010, a black Passat hit two female students on the campus of Hebei University. One died and the other was seriously injured. Traffic accidents are common and this one was just one of the millions that happen every year, but what made this incident famous is the way the media framed it. According to *China Management Time* reporter Wang Keqin's microblog, the driver was under the influence of alcohol and did not stop after the accident. When he was stopped by the security guards, he was indifferent and arrogant, claiming "my father is Li Gang, take me to court if you dare."[36] The driver was Li Qiming, a student at Hebei University. His father Li Gang is the deputy chief of the Public Security Bureau of a local district.

Immediately, "my father is Li Gang" became a popular Internet phrase. The Sina microblog exploded with millions of comments. It became the code word for the "second generation of officials [官二代]." Many netizens started to form sarcastic sentences using the phrase. Some artists made sculptures to express the meaning of "my father is Li Gang." The infamous phrase immediately became a form of expressing criticism of the government. Then all kinds of false information started to circulate online, claiming that Li Gang was the vice-governor of Hebei, had five villas, and that his son would only get three months of prison time.

Another reporter who was on the scene together with Wang Keqin had a different account of the incident. According to her microblog, Li Qiming was drunk and hit two students. Yet after the accident, Li was very scared and nervous. He begged the security guards, "I just hit people, please don't let my father know, his name is Li Gang."[37] Later in the court trial, the security guard testified that Li Qiming looked scared, and the phrase "my father is Li Gang" was uttered in the context of asking him not to contact his father. Li did not show any kind of arrogance as described by Wang Keqin's microblog. Yet nobody was interested in this alternative account of the accident. On January 30, 2011, contrary to all the speculation that Li would escape punishment, Li Qiming was sentenced to six years in prison. Now, most netizens have accepted that the original report by Wang Keqin was not accurate, but "my father is Li Gang" continues to be a code word for the second generation of officials.

The Fudan Huanshan 18 donkeys incident is a case of erroneous framing that eroded public trust in the media in China.[38] In December 2010, 18 students from Fudan University ventured into an undeveloped area in Huanshan, a famous mountain resort in China. They got lost and used their cell phones to call for help. Police searched and found them, but when escorting the students back, one police officer fell off a cliff and died. After getting back to the campus, none of the students wanted to take moral responsibility for the accident, and they started to blame each other. Netizens were enraged by the unappreciative students and accused them of being "cold blooded" and labeled them the "Fudan 18 donkeys."[39]

On December 21, 2010, the Sichuan *Chengdu Commercial Daily* published a report titled "The Truth behind the Fudan 18 Donkeys Stranded in Huanshan." The reporter claimed that the students called the police three times, but failed to get any response. Then, one of the students sent a short message to his uncle in Shanghai. His uncle then contacted the Shanghai government, which in turn contacted the police station in Huanshan. Only then were the police dispatched. The reporter also implied that this "uncle" was a high-ranking official with extensive connections.[40] Internet criticism then turned from the students to the Shanghai government, the mysterious "uncle" and the Huanshan police. Netizens condemned the Huanshan police for being interested only in serving the government and for ignoring ordinary citizens.

After some "human flesh search,"[41] netizens found that one of the students did send a message to his uncle in Shanghai for help. His uncle, however, is a laid-off worker; the *Chengdu Commercial Daily*'s report proved to be false. This incident set off a crisis of trust in the media. The newspaper found that the report was only based on rumors, which the reporter never verified. The reporter was dismissed. The significance of the Fudan 18 donkey incident is that traditional media started to reevaluate the effect of false information on the public, and the microblog users became more mature in their own judgment when facing the information explosion.

Internet controversy

Most Internet incidents that are studied by scholars are primarily framed as state versus society. As we mentioned earlier, these were the cases where there was a consensus among netizens that the government/officials were wrong. As more and more cases vie for public attention, however, it is more difficult to reach a consensus in the microblogosphere. Opinion leaders argue with each other. Followers fight with each other. The Qian Yunhui incident is the best example of such Internet controversy.

This was the last major microblog-based Internet incident in 2010. There was broad involvement of social celebrities and the incident expanded from virtual space to the real world. Qian was the leader of Zhaiqiao Village, Leqing City of Zhejiang Province. He had led villagers in repeated petition visits over the requisition of the village land and, as a result, had served prison terms three times. On December 25, 2010, Qian was hit by a construction truck outside of the village and died. His death was immediately alleged to be murder by the government. Some villagers claimed that Qian was beaten by five special police officers who then held him down and let the construction truck run him over. Villagers clashed with the traffic police who were onsite to handle the accident. After throwing bricks at the police and injuring some, several villagers were detained. The Sina microblog immediately published the pictures and video clips of villagers being taken away. The same evening, 300,000 netizens watched the development of the incident. Internet opinion leaders, well-known scholars, media reporters, lawyers, artists and social activists all appeared on their microblogs, leading their followers and shaping public opinion on this incident.

There was heated debate online. The core of the debate was whether this was an ordinary traffic accident or a cold-blooded murder. Yu Jianrong from the Rural Development Institute of the Chinese Academy of Social Sciences (CASS) supported the "murder conspiracy" thesis,[42] and opinion leader Ran Xiang and reporters from the Xinhua News Agency insisted that it was merely a traffic accident. Their respective followers began fighting intensively. The majority of netizens was inclined to believe that this was a murder case.

The Qian Yunhui incident attracted nationwide media attention. Reporters from various media flooded into Zhaiqiao Village. Qian's wife complained: "Qian had been sending various complaint documents and letters everyday when he was alive, and you guys never paid any attention. Now he is dead, and you all showed up?" On December 27, 2010, Leqing police held a press conference and declared that the Qian incident was an ordinary traffic incident, presenting photos and experts' evaluations. This did not change the opinion of those who advocated the murder conspiracy theory. Internet opinion leader Zhang Ming, a professor at Renmin University, questioned on his microblog, "I don't understand, Leqing officials thought that they were releasing their statement to a bunch of dummies? They cannot even make a convincing story."

Several voluntary investigation groups were formed. The NGO Citizen Alliance also got involved in the incident. Lawyers Xu Zhiyong and Wu Danhong organized a Citizen Alliance investigation group and went to Leqing as an independent third party.[43] Their report, published online, concluded that there was no evidence of murder. In the meantime, another media investigation group, led by Chen Min from the Southern Media Group, gave a vague account that the incident might not be murder.[44] Since Xu Zhiyong and his Citizen Alliance are symbols of the rights defender in China, their report undermined the murder conspiracy camp. These s, once the leaders of the liberal camp in China, were now accused of being bought off by the government.

As a side story of this incident, on January 5, 2011, a microblog claimed that Beijing lawyer Zhu Xianli had received 400,000 yuan from Qian Yunhui in a lawsuit over the land dispute. It claimed that, since Qian had lost the case, Zhu must be a con artist. On January 7, *New Beijing News* published an interview with Wu Xin (one of the microblog opinion leaders), with the headline "Beijing Lawyer Exposed to Cheat Qian Yunhui out of 400,000 yuan."[45] Other media followed, all accusing Zhu of cheating when referring to his legal fees. Internet accusations flooded in. Under pressure, Zhu returned 200,000 yuan. Ran Xiang, the opinion leader of the other camp (traffic accident), commented that those who attacked Zhu had no sense of the legality of a contract. The result would be that no lawyers in the future would be willing to take the case for farmers.

On January 27, 2011, CCTV aired an investigative program on Qian Yunhui's case, showing evidence that all the rumors about murder were fabricated. Then the reporter Wang Xiaoqin, who produced the program, became the target of criticism.[46] Reporters from *Southern Weekend* and *Southern Weekly* led the charge. Their criticism was focused mainly on Wang Xiaoqin's moral standards as a person, not evidence that would prove his conclusion was wrong.

On February 1, 2011, the court in Leqing City held the trial on the accident. The prosecutor demonstrated Qian Yunhui's watch video (Qian had a watch with a video camera function. The watch was first taken away by a villager and then confiscated by the police), which recorded the process of the accident. There was clearly no beating or holding the victim under the wheels by special police. The opinion leader of the "murder" camp, Li Chengpeng, continued to question the authenticity of the video and insisted that it was a case of covering up murder. The same day, a netizen reposted Li's pieces in a Falun Gong newspaper, *Epoch Times*; some of Li's supporters started to accuse Li of being a helping hand for the Falun Gong. In fact, Li did not submit his articles to *Epoch Times*; the editor of *Epoch Times* just included Li's blogs in the newspaper without his knowledge. This somewhat distorted information discredited Li and harmed his reputation. Most netizens have now accepted that Qian Yunhui's case was a traffic accident, and public attention regarding the case has died down.

Features of Internet protests

What have we learned from the discussion of the major Internet protests from 2003 to 2010? These cases demonstrate that the Internet has become an important platform to generate public opinion pressure on the government. Some protests have resulted in the government's reversal of its erroneous decisions and have held officials accountable. This aspect of Internet protest has been studied quite extensively and we will not dwell on it. In this section, we are going to elaborate on some of the unique features of the Internet mass incidents.

The emergence of opinion leaders

The most salient feature of microblogging is the emergence of opinion leaders, which has altered the ecosystem of Internet discourse. On the one hand, the opinion leaders are able to frame the protests more eloquently and theatrically. Their followers, while a loose collection, have some common bonds. Internet protests, therefore, have become more coherent and sustainable. On the other hand, different thought camps have become more personalized and fragmented.

Fragmentation is a serious threat to a healthy civil society and democracy. Cass Sunstein believes that blogs and forums do not promote social solidarity, but instead "create a high degree of social fragmentation." He argues that "people are likely to move toward a more extreme point in the direction to which the group's members were originally inclined" with blogs and forums, a phenomenon he calls "Group Polarization." Since netizens would only visit the blogs and forums that express the same opinions as they do, their minds would become more closed, and in order to distinguish the opinion differences from other groups, netizens would become more and more radical.[47]

The emergence of opinion leaders has furthered the phenomenon of group polarization. For example, during the Qian Yunhui incident, opinion leaders started to attack each other, and their followers would follow their leaders and attack each other. A surround and watch originally targeted at the government evolved into fights among different camps, with the worst possible insulting language. In place of a civil society, we saw a mass society. Charismatic opinion leaders would instigate mass "riots" online and the threat of revenge. The more personalized the Internet division became, the more abusive comments would be to attack each other. The language violence has seriously damaged the image of a virtual civil society, and furthered Internet group polarization. More advocation of hatred instead of solidarity will not create a healthy civil society but tear society apart.

One positive aspect of the emergence of competing opinion leaders is the direct rebuttals among rival groups. While you can only convince the convinced, the coexistence of the opposing opinions could have some influence on those who are undecided. For the convinced, this is a radicalization process. For the undecided, they are at least presented with alternative perspectives. Moreover, once false information is disseminated online, there would be some effort by the opposing camp to clarify, which at least casts doubt on the credibility of such information.

Media involvement

The other important feature of Internet mass incidents is the intense, even inseparable, involvement of the traditional media in cyberspace. All of the news media have their institutional microblogs, and all the reporters have their own personal microblogs. Some of them have even become opinion leaders. Readers follow news media microblogs closely, and the news media follow the public microblogs even more closely for sources of news. Once the microblogosphere reveals something newsworthy, the traditional media follow up and give extensive coverage. In some cases, it is the media microblogs that initiate the Internet protests. In principle, the government controls the media. There are official directives issued regularly on what events and phrases cannot appear in the media. However, in reality there is a gray area in which the media has flexibility. As we indicated earlier, the Chinese media and its reporters have different ideological orientations. The more liberal-leaning ones may choose to report specific incidents involving specific local government agencies within the general propaganda directives. The extensive involvement of traditional media in Internet protests will amplify public opinion pressure and accelerate the resolution of a given incident.

Another aspect of this media involvement is the commercial factor. The ongoing market reforms have forced all news media to operate on a profit-driven basis.[48] Reception rates (sales, audience share and clicks) have become the priority of editorial consideration. Many young reporters are surviving on a thin line between maximizing sales and not crossing the official limit, as they are paid by piece work.[49] Focusing on incidents of injustice inflicted by local government misbehavior is a safer bet, as they attract public interest and do not directly challenge the central government. As the central government would like to have a watchful eye on local officials, such reports are tolerated.

Sometimes over-zealous reporters exaggerate or alter the facts to fan public opinion. Taking the Yihuang incident, for example, the reporter from Phoenix TV acted as a general manager, directing the activities of the Zhong sisters, which helped to intensify the conflict rather than reduce the tension, therefore getting more netizens to surround and watch. The reporter became a household name in the microblogosphere overnight. During the "my father is Li Gang" incident and the Fudan 18 donkeys incident, reporters took words out of context or even made up news, emphasizing the connections between the people involved in the accident and the government background in order to achieve name recognition and newspaper sales.

Moral framing

What mobilizes people to join an Internet protest? Particular economic grievances that led to mass incidents on the street do not have much appeal to a broad Internet population. Such a population is too diverse to share any common economic interests. In order to mobilize a diverse group of netizens, the most effective approach is to frame the grievances in moral appeals—antigovernment corruption or a cry of injustice. With the minimal cost, more people would be willing to participate in Internet mass protests.

All the cases we have discussed in this chapter were framed with moral appeals. The case of Sun Zhigang, in which a college graduate was mistreated and beaten to death, was an example of extreme injustice. There was also a series of corruption exposures (an expensive watch, backdoor recruitment, extravagant budget spending and so forth). The most resented cases were the perceived abuses of government privilege, of which "my father is Li Gang" was the most notorious.

Moral framing can also be found in the calling for nonviolent gatherings by the so-called "jasmine organization" in early 2011. The organizers did not encourage the crowd to carry banners or shout slogans. Nonetheless, they provided a list of slogans. On top of the list were: We want food! We want jobs! We want justice! All these suggested slogans were clearly framed in subsistence moral terms. The main theme of other slogans was antigovernment corruption.[50]

Not only do the targeting of government corruption and cry of injustice have moral appeal, but using moral sensation is also an effective way of getting public attention. Here is an example. Peng Baoquan, a rights activist, was locked up for six days in a psychiatric hospital for taking photos of local protests in Shiyan County, Hubei Province, in April 2009. Peng ran into Guo Yanrong, who had been in the same psychiatric hospital for 14 years. In the early 1990s, Guo reported that his bureau director had taken bribes. The official investigation did not find enough evidence and dismissed the case. Guo persisted in his accusation and was put into a psychiatric hospital for "obsessive schizophrenia of a hereditary nature." Peng decided to help Guo after he was released from the hospital. Peng posted Guo's case on the Internet, but the response was disappointing.

Then Peng took a different approach. Peng wrote in the name of Guo's daughter, claiming to be a 24-year-old teacher, and that she would be willing to give up her virginity to whoever could save her father. A daughter selling herself on behalf of her father has been a persistent theme of the filial piety teachings in traditional China. People rarely practice it today, but they have a soft heart for it. This post set off an outpouring of sympathy from thousands of Internet users. Guo was released three days later. In reality, Guo does not have a daughter, but a son. This is a case of moral sensationalization by fabrication. Netizens debated over whether this fabrication itself was moral or not. Some strongly believed that at least it achieved its goal: getting Guo released.[51]

The limits of Internet protest

The essence of Internet mass incidents is the power of "surround and watch," which generates tremendous public opinion pressure on the government. To evaluate the impact of "surround and watch" on further political changes, we need to understand who is watching and what they are watching.

Pippa Norris raised the concept of the "digital divide" between rich and poor countries.[52] The same would apply within a single country. In China, it is not necessarily a divide between the rich and poor population, since Internet access is inexpensive. It is more a divide between better- or less well-educated, younger or older generations, and those with or without much leisure time. The ever-changing Internet technology is a hassle for less-educated and middle-aged users. Lack of time is a critical Internet access barrier to middle-aged and middle-class persons who have to shoulder social and familial responsibilities.

According to a Data Center of China Internet (DCCI) report on the Internet microblog and community, the majority of microblog users are students (32.5 percent high school students, 23.6 percent college students, and 21.1 percent graduate students), who are using microblogs to kill time. If we divide them by age, we can see that 45.7 percent were born in the 1990s and 40.8 percent in the 1980s.[53] This means that the majority of those who "surround and watch" in the microblogosphere are high school and college students. It is certain that the middle class in China is not the backbone of the "surround and watch" movement. The farmers, with less access to the Internet, are outside of the crowd that surround and watch. The middle-aged and middle-class populations tend to watch TV and read newspapers for news, rather than going online. This digital divide actually limits the impact of Internet public opinion. Without the participation of the middle class and general masses, Internet protests hardly extend to offline lives. The positive note is that a more thorough counter-hegemony established among the youth may affect the future generations of China.

So far, Internet protests are concerned with individual and isolated events. These are the sudden and sensational events that can increase watching rates and sales. These isolated and random incidents do not form a sustained and continuous social movement. In every microblog mass incident, the focal point of "surround and watch" is how the incident concludes. All the incidents are "problem-solving" incidents: each experiences cycles of concern > excitement > calming down > forgetting. When netizens surround and watch, most of them are watching a movie. They are excited about the drama in it. If they are watching with the attitude of watching for excitement, they are unable to form any common interests and demands for structural change.

Large-scale Internet protests have accomplished a great deal with regard to generating public opinion pressure and supervising government behavior. Some scholars believe that the Internet community is a new type of civil society. Yet, this is a civil society without much order and civility. The majority of netizens are more interested in venting their frustration than the pursuit of social justice. Language violence is the common feature in these protests. Rumors travel far.

However, because of the anonymous nature of the Internet, Internet users feel relatively safer to issue radical or irresponsible statements. The resonation effect radicalizes or sensationalizes the discussion. As a result, Internet public opinion tends to be intolerant. For example, during the Tonggang incident mentioned in a previous chapter, when the general manager appointed by the private company was beaten to death by workers, almost all the online comments cheered, commenting that the "working class is the greatest!" and "so what if a couple of capitalists were killed?"[54]

The intolerance also spills over into the real world. The worst consequence of Internet mass incidents is the so-called "human flesh search." The virtual mobs identify the "offenders," publicize their personal information and call for their harassment. For example, a woman, in 2007, claimed in her blog that her husband had had an extramarital affair and she wanted to commit suicide. Two months later she jumped from the window on the 24th floor. Not only had her message received tens of thousands of supporting responses, but the "moral mobs" also searched for the true identity of her husband and harassed him.[55] At the height of the pre-Olympics nationalistic sentiment in the spring of 2008, when the news of a Chinese student at Duke University supporting Tibetan independence broke out, her identity was disclosed and her family was harassed.[56] These are just two of the millions of such incidences that demonstrate the strong moral orientation of popular judgment.

Conclusion

With access to the Internet eased and the improvement of online communication, the Internet has increasingly become a space for ordinary people to voice their concerns and wage protest against perceived injustice. The government has taken an appeasement approach to Internet mass incidents and protests have had significant successes.

However, we should be cautious on the prospects of technological innovation bringing dramatic political change. As we pointed out earlier, there are limits to Internet protest. The participants are primarily students, not the middle class or middle aged. The interests of the young people are short lived. The motivation is solely on moral appeal. Moreover, when people can participate in protests at home alone, they may not be interested enough to go out into the street.

Larry Diamond admits that when the social and political structure is not ripe for profound change, technology may not lead to democracy. Instead, he argues, we may find the Internet to be a kind of accountability technology, in which Internet public opinion forces government to be more accountable.[57] His argument is primarily based on the Chinese experience and is a valid observation. The Chinese government seems to be more susceptible to public opinion pressure than many other authoritarian regimes. Most of the major Internet protests ended with punitive actions against related government officials.[58] Have these protests made the government more accountable? In individual cases, the answer is yes, but on a systematic basis, no. Following the trend of the term "micro revolution," we would term these concessions "micro changes" or "micro accountability." The problem is that more government micro accountability might reduce the pressure for more democratic change. If the incidents are resolved more or less according to what the netizens hope for, they feel satisfied afterward. If you can have justice served sitting at home in front of the computer, there is no pressing reason to go out into the street and risk your life.[59]

Notes

1 Larry Diamond, "Liberation Technology," *Journal of Democracy* Vol. 21, No. 3 (July 2010): 69–83.

2 For a detailed discussion of the "Sun Zhigang incident," please see Zheng Yongnian, *Technological Empowerment: The Internet, State, and Society in China* (CA: Stanford University Press, 2007).
3 collection.sina.com.cn/cjrw/20110113/161912122.shtml.
4 news.sohu.com/s2009/diaoyuzhifa/.
5 news.xinhuanet.com/politics/2009-10/10/content_12207171.htm.
6 politics.people.com.cn/GB/14562/11633652.html.
7 china.huanqiu.com/roll/2010-11/1294495.html.
8 www.safea.gov.cn/content.php?id=12744331.
9 news.ifeng.com/mainland/200906/0623_17_1216177.shtml.
10 news.sina.com.cn/c/2010-12-30/110321734006.shtml.
11 news.hsw.cn/system/2009/11/23/050368057_01.shtml.
12 cn.reuters.com/article/wtNews/idCNChina-4607220090527.
13 news.xinhuanet.com/fortune/2008-04/06/content_7927258.htm.
14 Sina Corporation, "White Paper on Year One of China's Microblog Market," wenku.baidu.com/view/a63536cea1c7aa00b52acb49.html.
15 Registration for a microblog account does not require a real name. People can register with pseudonyms. However, for celebrities, use of their real name will attract more followers.
16 李开复 & Lee Kai-fu], {#12298;微博改变一切》 [Microblog Changes Everything] (上海财经大学出版社 [Shanghai University of Finance and Economics Press, 2011]).
17 Ibid., 26.
18 Joseph Fewsmith, China since Tiananmeu, Cambridge University Press, 2001.
19 weibo.com/lichengpeng.
20 www.weibo.com/zhyj?topnav=1&wvr=3.6&topsug=1.
21 This is a pseudonym for someone who portrayed herself as female, but occasionally (with questionable sincerity) indicates that they are a team: weibo.com/followher.
22 weibo.com/simanan.
23 In an interview, a local Public Security Bureau official in charge of Internet security admitted that the government has Internet commentators, but said that there is no practice of paying 50 cents per comment.
24 *New Weekly* [《新周刊》], No. 315 (January 15, 2010).
25 *Time-Weekly*, "微博意见领袖'围观'中国" [Microblog Opinion Leaders "Surround and Watch" China], November 25, 2010, news.time-weekly.com/story/2010-11-25/421.html.
26 There is no fixed pagination of a particular microblog. The latest post will always be on page one. You may put in a particular date or key words to search for relevant comments.
27 twitter.com/#!/fzhenghu.
28 weibo.com/limengmeng.
29 weibo.com/liangcha.
30 Phoenix TV station is based in Hong Kong with some official representation in China. Its liberal leaning is quite strong when reporting inside China.
31 weibo.com/1645565044.
32 weibo.com/hawking.
33 weibo.com/1642326133.
34 news.xinhuanet.com/politics/2010-10/11/c_13551348.htm.
35 news.ifeng.com/mainland/detail_2010_12/27/3710038_0.shtml.
36 weibo.com/1700757973.
37 weibo.com/tulipfx.
38 In China, there is a general distrust of the official media, such as the *People's Daily*. However, there is significantly more public trust in the liberal-leaning media, such as the Southern Media Group. In this case, we are referring to the liberal-leaning media.

39 In Chinese, "tour" is translated in short as 旅, with the same pronunciation as "donkey" 驴. On the Internet, netizens usually jokingly call travel/tour partners "donkey partners." In this incident the usage is obviously derogatory.
40 weibo.com/1414188093.
41 "Human flesh search" is the voluntary effort of netizens to hunt down the identity of the person in the real world. For some other similar cases, see Tom Downey, "China's Cyberposse," *The New York Times Magazine*, March 3, 2010.
42 weibo.com/yujianrong.
43 weibo.com/danhon.
44 weibo.com/xiaoshushiping.
45 news.sina.com.cn/c/2011-01-07/020321773074.shtml.
46 weibo.com/1768792847.
47 Cass Sunstein, *Republic.com 2.0* (Princeton University Press, 2007).
48 Daniel Lynch, *After the Propaganda State: Media, Politics, and "Thought Work" in Reformed China* (CA: Stanford University Press, 1999); Sherman So and Westland Christopher, *Red Wired: China's Internet Revolution* (London: Marshall Cavendish International, 2010); Guobin Yang, *The Power of the Internet in China: Citizen Activism Online* (New York: Columbia University Press, 2009), 119–20; Daniela Stockmann, "Race to the Bottom: Media Marketization and Increasing Negativity toward the United States in China," *Political Communication* Vol. 28, No. 3 (2011): 268–90.
49 According to our personal interviews, the Chinese media now recruits reporters on a contractual basis. If reporters have interesting stories and get published, they get paid. If their reports cross the official limit and get pulled by the editors, they do not get paid.
50 www.boxunblog.com/2011/02/227.html.
51 Raymond Li, "Web Campaign Mixes Fact and Fiction to End Petitioner's 14 Years in Detention," *South China Morning Post*, January 13, 2011.
52 Pippa Norris, *Digital Divide: Civic Engagement, Information Poverty, and the Internet Worldwide* (Cambridge: Cambridge University Press, 2001).
53 DCCI (Data Center of China Internet), *The Internet Microblog and Community*, 2010, wenku.baidu.com/view/64b9a12f0066f5335a812164.html.
54 www.infzm.com/content/32048.
55 news.21cn.com/social/shixiang/2008/01/14/4159718.shtml (accessed June 4, 2009); cache.tianya.cn/pub/c/free/1/1201141.132.shtml (accessed June 4, 2009).
56 cache.tianya.cn/publicforum/content/sport/1/104516.shtml (accessed June 4, 2009); www.chexing.net/simple/t58147.html (accessed June 4, 2009).
57 Diamond, "Liberation Technology," ibid., 69–83.
58 Yanqi Tong and Shaohua Lei, "Creating Public Opinion Pressure in China: Large-scale Internet Protests," *EAI Background Brief*, No. 534 (2010).
59 Michael Margolis, "E-Government and Democracy," in Russell Dalton and Hans-Dieter Klingemann (eds) *The Oxford Handbook of Political Behavior* (Oxford University Press, 2009), 765–82.

8 Government responses and regime resilience

In this chapter we will discuss the government responses to social protests. We will first discuss our conceptual model of "multilevel responsibility structure" to explain the government responses to social protests and the reason why the regime has been resilient. We then will elaborate on the state responses with the framework of multilevel responsibility structure.

Multilevel responsibility structure

In his article "Power Structure and Regime Resilience," Yongshun Cai pointed out that the state response to social protest is shaped by the political arrangement. In China the political arrangement is a divided state power structure. Unlike the situation where there is only a single authority, Cai argues, the existence of multiple authorities implies that the state's policies toward protesters are inconsistent when the interests of those state authorities differ.[1] Local governments have gained more autonomy during the reform era and developed different interests, which may reflect in their handling of local social protests.

However, we would like to propose a different perspective—multilevel responsibility structure—to analyze the state responses to social protests. The difference is "responsibility" instead of "power." After all, China remains an authoritarian system. No matter how much financial autonomy the local governments have obtained, they have never gained crucial control over personnel appointment, which is retained by the center. Therefore, the concept of "divided power structure" or "multilevel power structure" is not accurate to reflect the nature of the local autonomy. We need to analyze China's political institutional arrangement through the lens of responsibility, not power.

In contemporary public administration, Kent Weaver argues, successful government policies always strike a balance between "credit claiming" and "blame avoiding."[2] According to Weaver, authoritarian states are less able to avoid blame because of the concentration of power in the hands of the government, which also means the concentration of responsibility and blame.[3] In general, the multilevel governance system tends to blur the lines of responsibility and blame. If policy responsibility is shared between different levels of authorities, individuals may not know which level of government is more responsible for a particular outcome.⁴ Complexity allows governments to claim credit for successful policies and shirk blame for undesirable outcomes.

According to the classification by Herbert Hart, there are two types of responsibility. One is functional responsibility, which refers to the role and tasks for which the government is responsible, that is the areas over which it has policy-making duties. The other is causal responsibility, which refers to the influence an actor has on bringing about a specific outcome. Perceptions of causal responsibility can lead to attributions of credit for positive outcomes and blame for negative results.⁵ In the context of our analysis, the concept of responsibility refers to what Hart has defined as casual responsibility, which is credit/blame for certain outcomes.

At the beginning of the reform, under the influence of the traditional benevolent governance, the government had been pursuing credit claiming, and put blame avoidance as a secondary consideration. With the deepening of the reform and rapid economic growth, alongside the rising living standard of the people, came the uneven distribution of wealth between different regions and different social groups. Those gaps violated the benevolent governance principles. Various social grievances emerged. People blame the government much more than they praise it. In a transitional society, individuals are more sensitive to their losses than their gains. While individual gains usually do not automatically translate into government credit, individual losses would immediately become government responsibility. As the Chinese government is going after credit claiming, people continue to blame the government based on their own calculation of personal losses. Within such a context, there emerged the demands for democracy (which people hope could solve all the social and political problems) and reverse racism (that is, whatever China does is bad).⁶

During the reforms of the 1980s, the central government delegated more power to the local government for economic development, and tied the economic performance to the promotion of local leaders. While the local governments obtained more financial autonomy, they also have to shoulder more responsibility for maintaining local political and social stability. Therefore, we have observed the development of a structure of multilevel responsibility. The layer of local government in the political structure has been significantly strengthened. Consequently, the reform made local government an ideal entity to take responsibility for the center.

The multilevel responsibility structure subsequently led to changes in state-society relations in China. Local government emerged as a distinctive layer in the structure, which replaced work units and collectives as the buffer zone between society and the central government. Local government became the target of all the interest conflict because of its economic responsibility. During social protests, local government has to serve as the cushion for the upper-level government.

Even when some of the social instability was caused by central government policy, it was the local government that had to take the blame. For example, the 1998 state-owned enterprise (SOE) reform has led to large-scale workers' protests. The reform was the central policy. Yet, the local governments in Northeast China had to face the brunt of the workers' protests. Therefore, it is a multilevel responsibility structure, not a simple divided power structure or multilevel power structure.

The previous structure, in fact, was one of chain gangs. In other words, the central government and local government were chained together, sharing both glories and failures. Multilevel responsibility structure is a structure of passing the buck. It localizes and stratifies social protests. The central government would stay away from social protests. The shock waves of the social protests would be absorbed by levels of local government, therefore reducing the shock to the center. Except for the Falun Gong protest in 1999, there has been no large-scale mass protest targeting the central government since 1989.

The multilevel responsibility structure also fits well with the Chinese political tradition. People trust the central government and distrust the local government. One of the characteristics of the Chinese benevolent government is that people oppose the corrupt officials, but never the emperor. This is the core belief of the peasant uprisings in the past and large-scale social protests today. In contemporary contentious politics, paying a visit to upper-level government has been one of the major means for redressing grievances. In the eyes of the ordinary people, only the central government can solve their problems. One could observe crowds of such visitors every day in front of all the major institutions of central government, such as the Supreme Court, Ministry of Justice and State Council.

During our interviews with local officials, from provincial level down to village level, without exception, all of them were unhappy about the active blame avoidance by the central government. For instance, a vice-provincial-level official put it bluntly: "the central government gets all the money and leaves all the blame to the local government."[7] A city mayor complained: "maintaining stability generates a lot of stress in daily work, yet in the end, we have to be the bad guys."[8]

Complaints from the local government do not necessarily indicate divisions inside the power structure. With the central government controlling the personnel appointments, the promotion mechanisms for local cadres have allowed the Chinese Communist Party (CCP) to reward officials for the development of their localities without weakening political control.[9] Within the multilevel responsibility structure, the central and local governments, in fact, play the roles of good cop and bad cop.[10] In essence, both are cops. The good cop/bad cop method provides institutional flexibility for the government in dealing with large-scale social protests.

Strategies of blame avoidance under the multilevel responsibility structure

Kent Weaver, in his *Politics of Blame Avoidance*, summarized eight blame-avoiding strategies in Western democratic systems.[11] Borrowing from his scheme, we have developed four strategies of blame avoidance in China's multilevel responsibility structure: 1 establishing a responsibility system; 2 playing good cop/bad cop; 3 throwing good money after bad; and 4 passing the blame to the lower levels.

Establishing a responsibility system

Since 1992, the Chinese Academy of Social Sciences (CASS) has been publishing the annual bluebook series on the state of Chinese society. One of the most notable changes was that since 2003, the bluebook has included summaries and predictions of "mass incidents." The fact that mass incidents have become a regular item in the reports of the largest think tank in China indicates that the Chinese government has accepted contentious politics as one of the normal ways of social life.

After the Shishou incident in July 2009, the central government enacted a "responsibility system" for officials above the county level of government, including the central government. It stipulates that if the misconduct of officials leads to the outburst of social protest or the officials mishandle social protest, they will be held accountable. Depending on the seriousness of the incident, the officials will either have to make public apologies, or resign or be dismissed.[12]

This is the first effort to link the handling of social protest to the evaluation of official performance. While on paper central and provincial government officials would be subject to the same responsibility system, in reality it only applied to county-level cities and below. So far we have not seen any provincial-level officials being held responsible for mass protests. For example, Guangdong has the most mass incidents in China, but none of its provincial officials have been held responsible.

Before 2009, the evaluation of county-level officials was primarily based on their ability to attract foreign investment and gross domestic product (GDP) growth. After 2009, the "social security comprehensive index" became the primary measurement in the country. For example, in Jiangxi Province, the standards for the township governance evaluation are, in descending order: 1 zero petition visits to Beijing; 2 zero mass incidents; 3 family planning; 4 environmental protection; and 5 solicitation of outside investment.[13] The meeting of the first two measurements is crucial, as the failure of these will cancel out or negate any achievement in the other categories. Other provinces have also set comparable criteria.[14]

Shaanxi Province even enacted a stricter evaluation system. Within each prefecture, if one county is listed as last in the evaluations for two consecutive years, the mayor would be dismissed. Among the measurements, "social security comprehensive index" is vital. That is, if there were a large-scale social protest, major leading officials would fail the evaluation.[15]

This kind of responsibility system guaranteed the authority of the central government to stay far away from the blame trap. The lower the administrative level, the more responsibility it bears. Officials at the township level shoulder the most burden of maintaining stability. Whenever there is a crucial date, be it June 4, the National Day, or some important state ceremony (such as the Olympic Games), township officials are on duty for 24 hours, being highly alert for any potential social protest or petition visit to upper-level government.

During our fieldwork in Jiangxi Province in the summer of 2008, Yongxiu County government ordered the township government to suspend all the daily work and go all in to ensure social stability during the Beijing Olympics. If any petition visit to Beijing occurred, the head of the township government would be dismissed. In order to prevent such an event from happening, township officials had to invite those visitation regulars to dinner all the time. During the day, the wives of the officials had to sit at these households and chat. The bus companies were warned not to sell tickets to these regulars. One visitation regular slipped through the prevention net and managed to go to Beijing. He was met by the township officials outside Beijing train station. The officials begged him to return home and promised to meet all his demands. Finally he agreed to return home on the condition that the township government paid to fly him back.[16] This responsibility and evaluation system provides direct incentives to the local government to eliminate potential social protests, as their political career is closely tied to local stability. The higher the level of government, the less blame they would take.

Playing good cop/bad cop

In China's multilevel responsibility structure, the central government strategy also includes a mixture of scapegoating or jumping on the bandwagon. After the eruption of a protest incident, the upper-level government would support the protesters if they had become politically popular and deflect responsibility by blaming lower-level government.[17] Lower-level government officials would receive disciplinary measures and take the responsibility for the upper-level government. This is an advantageous position for the central government in a multilevel responsibility structure.

Reforms inevitably incur redistribution of interests among individuals and social groups. The losses are not necessarily the consequence of local policies. For example, the SOE reforms are macropolicies designed by the central government. The SOE reform that started in 1998 affected Northeast China—the traditional industrial base—the most. The period of 1999 to 2002 was the hardest for workers. Some laid-off female workers had to engage in prostitution to maintain a minimum living standard.[18] Because of the multilevel responsibility structure, the central government played the role of good cop, while the local government played bad cop. The central leaders would pay visits to the workers and show their people-friendly attitudes by listening to the complaints. The workers, thus, kept their high expectations for the central government and would not engage in more desperate protests. This is the typical performance by a benevolent government.

Once there is a vicious riot, central government tends to dispatch a "central work group" to the location. The work group most of the time would jump on the bandwagon with the protesters and discipline the local officials. This strategy would pacify the social anxiety and gain more credit for the central government. The dismissed local officials, after a period of "freezing," would be quietly transferred to another place at the same level. This practice is the most criticized element in benevolent governance: "officials protecting officials (官官相护)." In addition to the reinstatement of local officials, the central government would also compensate the local government by allocating more financial resources after the incident. Carrot and stick is the most effective means to ensure that local government continues to play the role of bad cop.

Throwing good money after bad

Throwing good money after bad refers to the provision of resources to help out constituencies to prevent or delay blame after a bad policy.[19] In a multi-level responsibility structure, the upper-level government cannot pass the blame to lower-level governments indefinitely. When the lower-level governments face ever-increasing social pressures, the upper-level government has to find ways to alleviate such pressures. Since the local government does not have any ideological or political responsibilities, the social pressures are primarily from the redistribution of material wealth and administrative misconduct.

In order to lower the pressure from social protest, local governments usually adopt two approaches. One is to improve the style of administration, especially law enforcement. The other is compensation for interest losses. Brutal law enforcement often triggers social protest. Upper-level government could use a responsibility system to force lower-level officials to behave themselves in order to prevent such outbursts. For a social protest triggered by loss of interest, upper-level government could distribute more resources to weaken the cause of the social protest. After the taxation reform, the central government collected increasing revenue income. It is able to compensate those who were affected by the reform. The center would both gain credit and avoid blame.

The SOE reforms of the 1990s have affected the traditional industrial base. The reform separated the hospitals, schools, kindergartens and shops from the enterprises and shifted the welfare responsibility for the workers to the local government. Sometimes the enterprise would go bankrupt, the work unit would collapse, and gone were all their welfare responsibilities. The marketization schemes for education, medical care and housing have created huge dislocation pains for SOE workers, especially those who lost their jobs. Local governments had to take on the reform cost more than the central government.

As a way of throwing good money after the bad, the central government distributed a large amount of money to improve the living standard of workers in Northeast China. The most typical case was the renovation of shelter districts in 2005. The central government picked up the largest portion of the renovation costs, with local government and individuals sharing the smaller portion. Within three years, the program solved the housing problem for middle- and low-income families.

Passing the blame to lower levels

Goldstone and Tilly argue that authoritarian governments may face serious uncertainties in dealing with popular protests. Making concessions tends to trigger more protests or even the collapse of the regime, but reliance on repression damages the regime's legitimacy and makes it less sensitive to popular demands.[20]

It is common practice to use police forces to maintain social order and to suppress unauthorized protests in Western societies. Yet, different political traditions lead to a different environment for law enforcement. According to Chinese tradition, police brutality and repression of social protest is considered a violation of the principles of benevolence. The most criticized element of the government handling of the Tiananmen incident was its use of force. This is considered a loss of government virtue.

Having learned the lessons that the military should not be employed to suppress social protests, the central government has established the armed police forces since 1989 to deal with social unrest and activities that may endanger social stability. The central government is learning how to stop violent social protests while at the same time not to be blamed for losing virtue. In June 2008, Minister of Public Security Meng Jianzhu promoted three principles to deal with emergency incidents: "use police forces with caution, use weapons with caution, and use coercive measures with caution."[21] The phrase "with caution" does not mean that you cannot use it. Therefore, the decision to use force is delegated to the local government. The preconditions for using force are: police are attacked when maintaining public order; there are violent activities, such as killing, looting and burning; and social protest with political agendas.[22]

If the local government decides not to repress with force, it has to take responsibility for all the consequences when the incident endures and expands. If the local government decides to use force, then it has to shoulder the accusation of losing virtue. The central government could later come in and use the local government as the scapegoat, discipline the local officials and issue huge compensation to the victims to alleviate social pressures. In either case, the local government is the responsibility bearer.

In July 5, 2009, Urumqi City had a vicious ethnic conflict between Uyghur and Han. Since the local government did not dispatch police forces in time to prevent the killing from going further, the police chief of Xinjiang

Autonomous Region and the Party secretary of Urumqi City were dismissed by the central government. Many police officers were upset about the dismissal. An anonymous senior police officer commented, "without the order from the central government, who dared to repress the minority group?"[23] Because of the complexity of the minority issues, local governments usually are hesitant to suppress minority protest. This is the consequence of the rigid minority policy-making system and the central government should take the responsibility. However, the responsibility was transferred to local government through a multilevel responsibility structure.

In contrast, during the Shishou incident in Hubei in 2009, the local government deployed police forces excessively. While the local government managed to maintain social stability, it violated the benevolence principles. The central government was under tremendous pressure to discipline the officials responsible for making the decision to use excessive force. The Party secretary and mayor of Shishou City were consequently disciplined.

The multilevel responsibility structure effectively solved Goldstone and Tilly's dilemma which argues that if the authoritarian regime represses social protest with force, it will damage the regime legitimacy and makes it less sensitive to popular demands. In such an arrangement, repression would stop the spread of social protest, local government would take the responsibility of repression, and the central government would take credit for solving the crisis, hence, increasing its legitimacy.

The institutionalization of social protest

The multilevel responsibility structure provides a cushion to lessen the shock of social protest to the authoritarian regime. At the same time, it also provides time and space for Chinese government at all levels to learn to deal with the increasing occurrence of protest events. Society is also learning to use protest to the best of its interests. This is a process through which contentious politics reaches a dynamic equilibrium. In other words, this is the process of institutionalizing social protest.

Primary stage: repression and lack of compromise

Social protests during Mao's era were usually solved through the work units and grassroots collectives. The news media was strictly in the hands of the Party. Therefore, the protests were limited to the smallest possible spaces. After the reform, with the layer of work units and collectives wearing thin, social protests posed new challenges to the central government and its approaches to society management. Governments at all levels were inexperienced and lacked preparation.

For individuals or social groups, protest is an extreme expression of political and economic interests and the ultimate way to protect personal interests by the groups that are lacking resources. Social protest in the beginning of the reform era was still holding onto the Maoist teaching that "it is innocent to join the revolution and it is reasonable to revolt [革命无罪，造反有理]." Together with the anticorruption tradition as part of the benevolent heritage, society firmly believed that the central government would support mass movement and social protest.

For the government, it inclined to hold that social protest was part of the class struggle and counterrevolutionary activities and, therefore, intolerable. The consequence of these misperceptions was the final outcome of the Tiananmen incident. The central government designated the student movement a "counterrevolutionary" riot, and the protesters believed that the People's Liberation Army (PLA) would not open fire on the people. The regime underestimated the cost of repression, and the protesters overestimated the benefit of prolonged protest. Without enough information and communication, the protest became a "game of chicken," and ended in bloodshed.

After the Tiananmen incident in 1989, the state and society developed new perceptions for contentious politics. The regime understands that the cost of repression is too high, especially to put PLA field troops on the frontline of repression, which destroyed the army's long-established reputation of a "people's army for the people." The central government reclarified that the function of the military is to defend the country from outside threat. The regime quickly established the armed police forces to be used in maintaining domestic order and suppressing social unrest. It was not until the 1998 flood disaster, during which the PLA served as the main force to battle the natural disaster and the disaster relief efforts by the benevolent government, that the reputation of the PLA was restored.

Individuals and social groups started to realize that uncompromising political protest movements would lead to regime violence. The hot heads cooled down. The entire society was going after material betterment. Travel fever and money worship have become the mainstream lifestyles among the youth. The chaotic social and economic situation in Russia and other Eastern European countries also made the Chinese realize that they need to learn to compromise with the regime in their negotiation with the state.

Secondary stage: tolerance and compromise

In the 1990s, China entered into a stage of comprehensive reform. Work units and grassroots collectives totally collapsed. Local government assumed the function of intermediate-layer organizations and became the front line facing society. Yet, this lacks the inclusive characteristics of the work units and collectives and would never provide a sense of identity. In other words, it lacks the soft power to handle the protests. At the same time, reform has empowered society with more freedom and resources. The conflict, therefore, hardened into direct confrontation.

The nature of contemporary Chinese social protest is the pursuit of material interests. These interests include salaries, pensions, land use compensation, as well as the desire for a more equal distribution of wealth and a sense of social justice. In contrast to social protest in Western societies, such as the gay rights movement, which are protesting against state interference in private matters, Chinese social protests demand state intervention.

The state has adopted a tolerant position toward social protests that have no political agenda, with specific grievances, and are peaceful. Perry argues that "instead of beating and arresting protesters as they might have some years ago, officials seem more willing these days to accommodate, negotiate or simply pay them off. As long as demonstrators don't make personal attacks against top leaders or demand political change, they are often free to vent their anger."[24]

Society has also learned to compromise, to avoid attacking the central government and leaders and raising political demands. The protest organizers also learned to use the Internet and media to generate public opinion pressure, and to seek broad social support. In this interactive process of tolerance and compromise, the state and society learned each other's bottom lines. The state's attitude toward social protest depends on the measures taken by the social protest. The state would tolerate localized, nonpolitical and peaceful protest and use limited repression on violent protests. At the same time, in order to pacify public opinion pressure, it would discipline some officials.

The multilevel responsibility structure has a strong learning capability. After the 2008 Weng'an incident, since contentious politics had become a major component in the political life of the country, the central government organized a study session in Beijing for all the county-level Party secretaries (more than 2,000) nationwide to learn to deal with emergency incidents.[25] Then each county would organize the same workshops for lower-level government officials. This also sends out a signal that it is the responsibility of the county government to deal with social protest, not the central government. In February 2009, the Ministry of Public Security called more than 3,000 county police chiefs to Beijing to study. After any vicious riots, all government officials were required to discuss lessons from these incidents in order to avoid them from happening in the future.[26]

Some individual government officials have come out of the shadows of fearing contentious politics, and have held direct dialogue with protesters, which has enhanced the government ability of crisis management in contentious politics. For example, there was a taxi drivers' strike in Chongqing in 2008. The then Party secretary of Chongqing, Bo Xilai, invited the representatives of the striking taxi drivers and listened to their complaints. The entire process was broadcast live on TV. Bo promised to meet the demands of the taxi drivers. The strike ended peacefully.

The protesters have adapted to the government positions toward social protest, and have learned to use approaches that would be tolerated by the government. Nobody wants to go to jail. What they want is to have their demands met through uncontentious politics. They use peaceful means and have clearly defined targets that are nonpolitical. Organizers choose the location of protest carefully to avoid politically sensitive spots. They have also learned to use the Internet and media to search for social support and government sympathy. For example, there were waves of strikes in the Yangzi River Delta and Pearl River Delta in 2010. The locations of most of the protests were inside the factory walls, not on the street. The target of the strikes was clearly defined: an increased salary and improved working conditions. The strikers used the Internet to report the new developments of the strikes. These measures gained social support and government attention. With the coordination of the local labor department, workers had most of their demands met.

In 2006, citizens in Beijing protested against the administrative order to kill dogs. Protesters chose the location of Beijing Zoo, eschewing government buildings or sensitive political symbols. The protest was peaceful and with a clearly framed purpose. In 2010, employees of state-owned banks who were bought out gathered in Beijing to protest. They chose to protest in front of the All China Trade Unions (ACTU). The location is close to Tiananmen Square. The protesters initiated fundraising for the earthquake victims in front of the ACTU, a tactic that made the protest seemed less self-serving. Such a flexible measure thus prevented the government from repressing the protest.

Organized protest guarantees the control of the protest. Unorganized contentious politics tend to evolve into riots. The government has learned to institutionalize social protest. In 2010, some students in Beijing applied to protest in front of the Japanese Embassy. The Beijing Bureau of Public Security approved this application, with the condition that the protesters had to come in limited groups and at different time slots. The organizers accepted the condition. Therefore, protesters were organized into smaller groups and went to the Japanese Embassy at different times. In this way, the Beijing government could meet the demands of the protesters and reduce the damage in which an orderless protest could result.

Government responses under the multilevel responsibility structure

Different political systems respond to social protests differently. In Western democratic countries, especially in the United States, contentious politics has been institutionalized. Social protests are restricted within the confines of existing legal frameworks. Demonstration organizers need to file an application for permission from the police. Local authorities usually approve such applications on the grounds of freedom of speech. However, there would be restrictions on the place, time and size of the demonstration. Most social protests proceed peacefully within this legal framework. Any protests that exceed the boundary of peaceful protests or protests that are not approved would be met with ruthless repression. There is wide public consensus on these legal parameters. Legally endorsed repression does little damage to the political system. Therefore, the institutional arrangement transforms repression into legal issues and minimizes the linkage between social protests and regime legitimacy.

In China, adherence to strict legal procedures has never received any weight in the benevolent political tradition. Social protests were perceived as a demand for government to fulfill its moral responsibility. Therefore, the government is extremely sensitive to contentious politics. The government cannot turn contentious politics into a legal issue as democratic governments do. If the government were to use repression, it would seriously damage the legitimacy of the regime. The regime has to seek a balance between concession and repression, calculating rationally the costs and benefits of these. Since the cost of repression is very high, unless the protests intend to overthrow the central government or involve violence, the regime rarely takes this step.

"Maintaining stability" is the foundation policy of the Chinese government. In order to avoid central government being the target of protests, the strategy of the central government is to limit social protest to local levels. The multi-level responsibility structure serves this purpose well. In reality, there has not been any large-scale social protest that challenged the central government since the 1989 Tiananmen incident and 1999 Falun Gong movement. The responsibility of dealing with social protests is delegated to local governments and the central government has stayed away from the focus of public opinion over the protests.

The government response is not a dichotomy of either concession or repression. Instead, it is a graded or mixed response depending on the nature of the particular protest. Based on the data we have for 2003–10, we have summarized four types of government response to social protests. Local government primarily used a mixture of three types of response to social protests: 1 tolerance; 2 concession; and 3 repression.[27] When the central government intervened, it added another approach: disciplinary measures against the local officials responsible for the outburst of the protest. Table 8.1 shows the distribution of various types of government responses.

The government tolerated the majority of the protests (65.7 percent) and made concessions or compensation to the protesters for 29 percent of the cases. Repression is minimal. The 29 percent compensation rate plus minimal repression are two of the reasons why social protest is on the rise. This

Table 8.1 Government responses to large-sale social protests

Government response type	Total	Percentage
Tolerance	360	65.7%
Concession	159	29.0%
Repression	19	3.5%
Discipline	37	6.8%

Source: (Authors' data)
Note: In some cases, the government used more than one method. Therefore, the summation of different methods is slightly larger than the total number of cases.

Table 8.2 Government responses to social protests

	State		Private		Land		Riot		Others		Total	
Tolerance	23%	83	27%	98	14%	52	11%	40	24%	87	100%	360
Concession	62%	99	8%	12	19%	30	6%	9	6%	9	100%	159
Repression	0%	0	11%	2	32%	6	26%	5	32%	6	100%	19
Discipline	5%	2	3%	1	32%	12	43%	16	16%	6	100%	37

Source: (Authors' data)
Note: In some cases, the government used more than one method. Therefore, the summation of different methods is slightly larger than the total number of cases.

partially confirms Goldstone and Tilly's argument that concession would encourage more social protest. In the following sections, we will discuss these types of responses in more details. Table 8.2 shows the government responses to different types of social protests.

Tolerance

This is the most popular response the government uses. By tolerance, it means that the government would monitor the development of the protest closely, but refrain from using force. The government would tolerate slight confrontation and property damage. The police may detain a couple of activists, but would release them after the protest is over and would not file legal charges against them. Occasionally, the police would arrest the organizers afterward and give them prison terms in order to intimidate future protesters.

The protests that were tolerated mostly have the following features: no political appeal, short-term material requests, no target of central government, and the protests are not held in front of government buildings, are peaceful and with no or only slight damage to property. The typical cases are the labor protests in the nonstate sector, anti-Japanese demonstrations and student protests against school administrations. Local government usually takes a neutral stand on capital-labor disputes in the nonstate sector. Sometimes it only involves arbitration and lets the enterprise settle the disputes itself. Figure 8.1 shows that all the types of protests are more or less evenly distributed by this approach, especially labor protests in the nonstate sector.

Some protests are against particular local policies. These types of policies only affect limited interests, be it material interests or cultural interests. For example, protests to defend the Cantonese dialect and the protest against the killing of dogs only reflected the interests of a minority in society and rarely received popular sympathy. The government may continue, or quietly cease, or change its policies, but would not take any punitive action against protesters. The central government would stay away from these protests and would not punish local officials for such protests.

Government responses and regime resilience 187

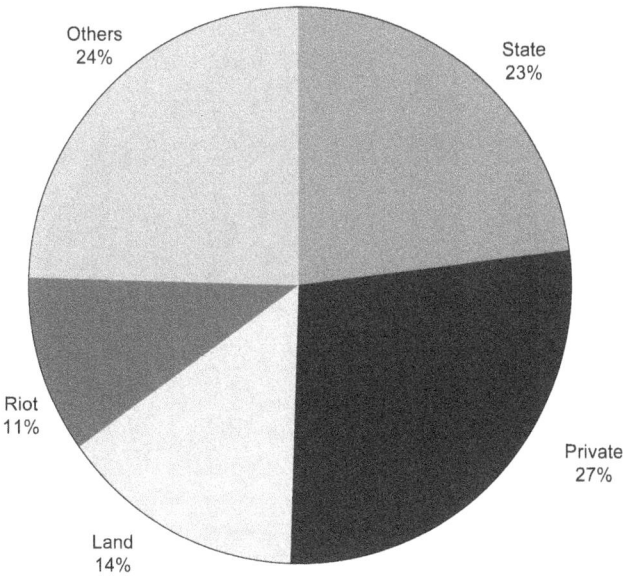

Figure 8.1 Distribution of types of social protest tolerated by the government

Concession

This is the settlement of protests with substantive government compensation, which is 30.2 percent of the total cases. Most of the cases in this category are the protests caused by: 1 unemployment, delayed pension, health care issues caused by the SOE reforms; 2 housing demolition, relocation, land requisition and environmental pollution caused by local government development policies; 3 poor welfare packages in SOEs; and 4 private enterprise owners owing back salaries and the government picking up the bill to pacify the restless workers. In general, they all fall into the sphere of state moral responsibilities.

Figure 8.2 shows that protests in the state sector receive the most government concessions. This may be explained by the state moral responsibility to its employees. The cases of government compensation to labor protests in the nonstate sector are small. Yet, it is amazing that there is even 8 percent (12 cases) that the government paid of its own money to compensate the workers in the private sector when the government was not at fault. In fact, there were also many cases where the government exerted pressure on the private owners to compensate workers' demands.

Government picking up the bill for foreign investors is not a common practice in any government response to social protests. Yet, it is quite in line with the tradition of benevolent governance. As we discussed in Chapter 4, the government of Zhangmutou Township in Guangdong Province paid back salaries owed by foreign investors who disappeared after the financial crisis in October 2008. A similar case was found in Xixiang Township, Shenzhen,

188 *Government responses and regime resilience*

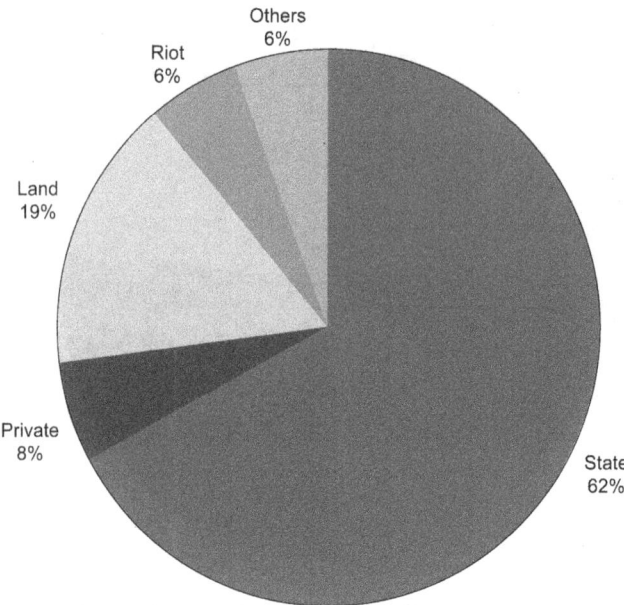

Figure 8.2 Distribution of the types of social protests where the government makes concessions

Guangdong Province, where workers from the bankrupt enterprises protested in front of the local government building. In the end, the township government paid 300 RMB for each worker as a provisional stipend. These types of protest were caused by the capital-labor disputes and the government is the third party. However, in order to maintain social stability, the government paid the dues for the owners. There are 12 such cases in our data set of large-scale social protests from 2003 to 2010. One cautious note is that this kind of resolution only occurs in developed areas. Poorer areas do not have the financial capability to do this.

If a protest was not violent, the central government stayed away. Some protests were compensated, some were not. The amount of compensation varies and was subject to negotiation. The local government would rarely meet the workers' demands fully. Even in those protests that did not receive compensation, neither were they repressed. Local governments also tried all means to raise funds and create job opportunities to ease the pain for laid-off workers. This is a long-term effort and will not produce immediate returns.

The most sensitive issue is the protest by ex-servicemen. The local government has been very prompt in resolving this kind of protest. All eight veterans' protests received compensation. The quick settlement of these protests is because the welfare issue for ex-servicemen is sensitive for the regime, relating to the stability of the current military forces in service and the success of future conscription. Since it relates to state security, settlement for ex-servicemen and taking good care of the military families are important indicators for governance evaluation. It would directly affect the future political career of the top leaders. The local government, therefore, is willing to make compromises and give compensation.

During rapid economic growth, the need for land increased dramatically. Land requisition also generated other social grievances related to demolition and relocation. Together they became one of the major causes of social protest from 2003 to 2010. Some of the land-related protests led to bloody conflict. The core issue in the land-related protests is compensation. In most land-related protests, local governments would raise the compensation package to appease the peasant. Again, the amount was subject to negotiation. As long as the demand for more compensation was satisfied, such protests would be settled.

Repression

Repression is the government reaction to serious violent conflict. Only 3.5 percent of the total cases belong to this type. Repression here refers to the fact that government uses police force during the process of the protest to arrest protesters and formally presses charges. It does not include the arrest of some organizers after the protest is over or the arrest of some protesters, who are released later without prosecution. Since ongoing social protest attracts the most public attention, the government would meet great pressure if it used force. After a protest is over, when the reasons and causes of the protest are revealed, public opinion would calm down and repressive government activities would not be too greatly blamed.

Some 19 out of all 548 large-scale social protests met with repression. Most cases involved violent attacks on the police force maintaining public order, vicious ethnic conflict and killings, and clan feuds. Examples include the 3.14 incident in Tibet, the 7.5 incident in Urumqi, Hui–Han ethnic conflict in Henan, and the Dongzhou Village land protest in Guangdong. We have discussed these protests in Chapters 4 and 6 and will not elaborate here.

Riots are by nature violent, as they often involve burning, looting and beating. It is understandable that a riot is more likely to be suppressed by force. Land-related protests tend to be violent as well and repressive measures were adopted. The reason why the "other" category has a higher percentage of repression is because we put ethnic conflict into this group. Four out of the total five cases of repression in this group are ethnic conflicts. As ethnic conflict also tends to be violent, it is often suppressed with force. There was no repression of labor protests in the state sector.

After the Dongzhou incident, as the firing was under circumstances when the life of the policeman was in danger, public opinion was not enraged. No governments, either central or local, were blamed. Even though this was the first case of opening fire on protesters, the multilevel responsibility structure was able to limit the political pressure on the response to the very minimum and absorbed the shock waves. The central government stayed away from the

190 *Government responses and regime resilience*

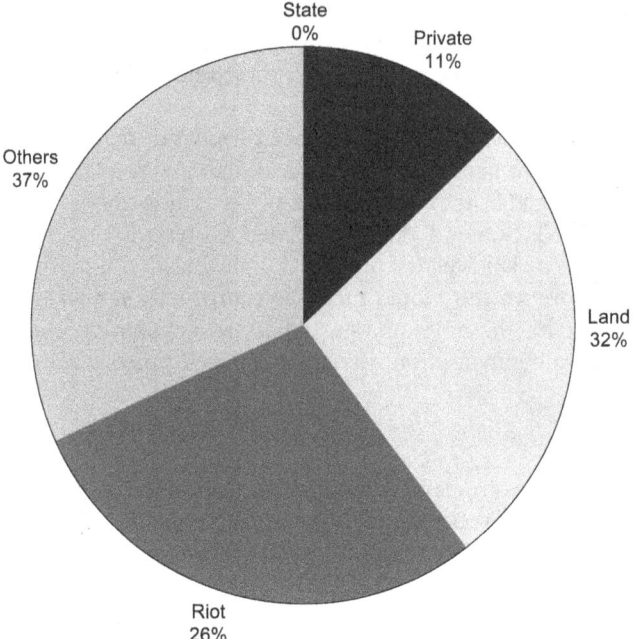

Figure 8.3 Distribution of the types of social protests suppressed by the government

whirlpool of blame. The Dongzhou incident sent out a clear signal that under the multilevel responsibility structure, the state could suppress uncompromising social protest with force. It also demonstrated that the use of force would not necessarily affect the authority of the central government and would be limited in its challenge to the legitimacy of the regime.

Discipline

Disciplining government officials is one of the solutions to social protest, especially riots, which consist of 6.8 percent of the total cases. This is a measure that can only be administered by the central government. The disciplinary measures includes dismissal or forced resignation. This is to assuage public anger and warn other officials. For example, in the Zhengzhou incident, Guangxi Bobai incident, Sichaun Dazhu incident, Hubei Shishou incident and Guizhou Wong'an incident, local head officials were all disciplined. The public is very sensitive to police brutality, as it directly damages the image of a benevolent government. In general these riots were triggered by the misconduct of government officials, and there were neither material demands nor political appeals. There was no party with which to negotiate. Usually, with the discipline of government officials and short-term social disorder, such events die down and are forgotten.

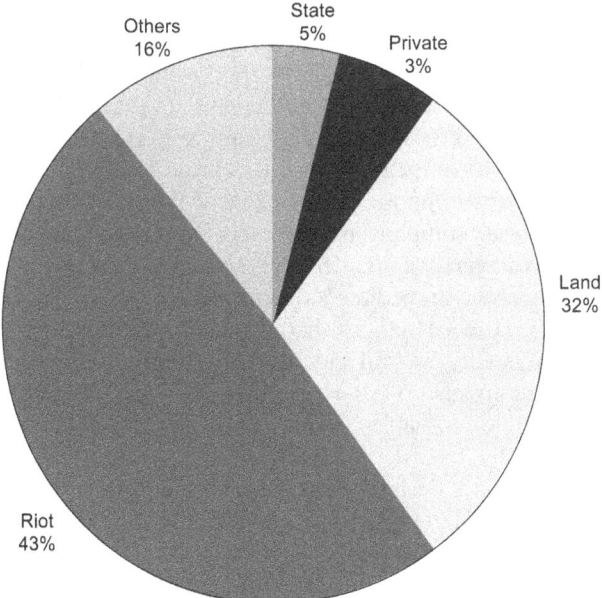

Figure 8.4 Distribution of the types of social protests ended with disciplinary measures against officials

As Figure 8.4 suggests, government officials are often held responsible for social disturbances. This is because such incidents tend to incur the most damage to property and lives. Officials are much less responsible for labor protests in nonstate sectors. Mishandling of violent land-related protests may also lead to disciplinary measures against officials. Corruption accusations that are common in labor protests in the state sector seem not to produce much consequence.

There are a few other cases that might result in the disciplining of officials. Here is an example. On April 13, 2010, thousands of villagers protested in front of the Zhuanghe City government building in Liaoning Province, demanding the investigation of corruption in local land requisition. Villagers asked the mayor to come out and receive their petitions. The mayor did not come out. Then most of the villagers knelt down in front of the government building, claiming that they would not stand up if the mayor did not come out. However, the mayor remained absent. Photos of villagers kneeling down were circulated on the Internet and caught public attention nationwide. Kneeling down is a political tradition when people beg the government for help. If the major local leaders remain absent from the scene, this seriously damages the legitimacy of the regime. The mayor of Zhuanghe City was forced to resign because he was considered to have violated benevolent conduct.

In a country with a benevolent tradition, the least tolerated action is a government official organizing or participating in social protest. Once discovered, the official would be expelled from the Party, dismissed from their position, even given a prison sentence. We discussed the 2004 Hanyuan incident in Sichuan Province in Chapter 4. Following that incident the State Council dispatched a work group to investigate. It found out that the Party secretary of Hanyuan City was behind the protest. He believed that the city did not receive enough compensation for this project, and therefore attempted to incite the villagers to oppose the building of the power station so that he could force the power company to pay more compensation. However, once the anger of the villagers was ignited, the situation went out of his control. The Party secretary was immediately dismissed.[28]

In August 2005, Hubei Huangshi had a protest organized by local government officials. Daye City was an independent county and became a county-level city under the jurisdiction of Huangshi City. Daye has abundant mining resources and, therefore, sizable revenue. Daye never identified with the jurisdiction of Huangshi. In order to unify the finance and control the mining resources, Huangshi City declared that Daye would cease to be a county-level city and be a district of Huangshi instead. Since the decision cost tremendous loss of political power and economic interests, the vice-Party secretary and deputy mayor of Daye opposed the decision. The People's Congress of Daye also drafted an opinion paper, collected signatures and sent it to the provincial and central governments. They also organized retired officials to visit Wuhan and Beijing to lodge complaints.

On August 1, many retired officials organized a signature movement. On August 4, when nearly 100 retired officials went to the Huangshi City government, they were attacked by police dogs. Then the owner of the copper mines organized several hundred workers to support the retired officials. On August 6, tens of thousands of Daye citizens demonstrated in Huangshi City. The Huangshi police fired tear gas into the crowd and control of the situation was lost. Mobs attacked the city government buildings, destroyed the windows, vehicles and other facilities. Other protesters blocked the Wuhan–Huangshi highway for two hours.

Hubei provincial government sent out a work group to investigate the incident, especially the sources of financial support for the protest. The work group defined the incident as "an illegal incident, out of discontent with the abolition of the city into the district, planned by some leaders of Daye City, organized and initiated by some leaders and retired officials, funded by some owners of mines, participated in by the floating population."[29] Those who had destroyed the government buildings were arrested and sentenced. Seven major leaders of Daye City were expelled from the Party and dismissed from their positions.

The Hanyuan and Huangshi incidents were organized by government officials who felt that their local interests were undermined. This is intolerable in the existing Chinese political system. The punishment was severe. Compared to the Hubei Shishou riot, which involved the largest number of participants since the Tiananmen incident, in which the city leaders were only removed from their position and later assigned to another place without suffering any downgrading, the harsh punishment for officials instigating mass incidents is meant to ensure the unity of the ruling elite and to maintain the stability of the entire regime.

Government responses and types of protests

In this section, we would like to present a slightly different perspective on government reactions to different types of social protests. Let us first present the table and charts of the government responses by types of social protests.

For labor protests in the state sector, the government either tolerated or made concessions 99 percent of the time. In fact, the government had the highest compensation rate for protests in the state sector. Repression was zero. In comparison, labor protests in nonstate sectors were tolerated the most (88 percent). Land-related protests are the type of protest that received the second most compensation, at 34 percent. This is why we argue that most of the land disputes have to be settled with compromises on moral grounds. About 66 percent of the disturbances are tolerated despite the disruptive nature of such incidents. While disturbances received the highest repression rate, it was only 8 percent of the total of such incidents. Tolerance was high for "other" types of protest. Overall, one could argue that the regime has been much less repressive toward social protest than many expected from an authoritarian regime. The state is most accommodating to labor protests in the state sector.

Appeasement

In addition to the four government approaches to social protest discussed above, we would like to propose one more category of government reaction to social protest: appeasement. This is mainly the government reaction to Internet protest. As the Internet protest occurs in the virtual space, not the real space, the challenge such protest poses to the government is public opinion pressure. The government takes an appeasement approach to most Internet protests. Compared to other governments, the Chinese government has been

Table 8.3 Government responses by type of protests

	Tolerance		Concession		Discipline		Repression		Total
State	45%	83	54%	99	2%	2	0%	0	183
Private	88%	98	11%	12	1%	1	2%	2	112
Land	59%	52	34%	30	14%	12	7%	6	88
Riot	66%	40	15%	9	26%	16	8%	5	61
Others	84%	87	9%	9	6%	6	6%	6	104

Source: (Authors' data)
Note: In some cases, the government used more than one method. Therefore, the summation of different methods is slightly larger than the total number of cases.

194 *Government responses and regime resilience*

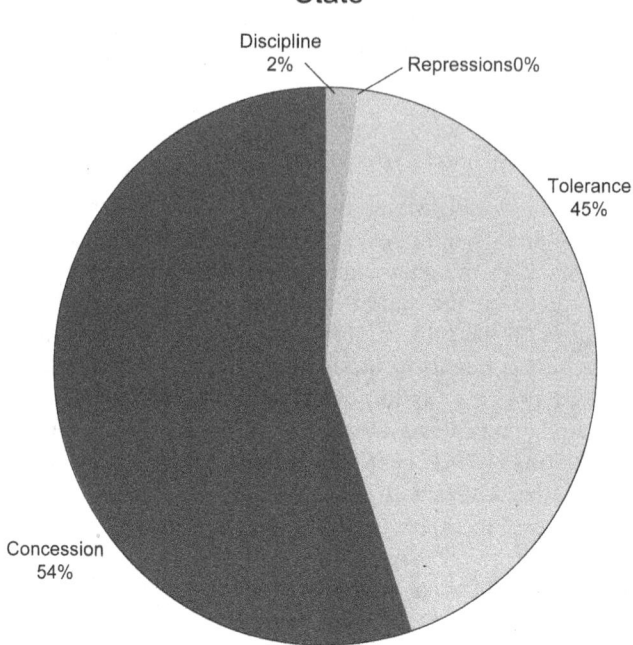

Figure 8.5.1 Government responses by type of protest

much more sensitive to Internet public opinion pressure, even willing to yield to public opinion interference in judicial procedure. Although the Chinese government imposes strong censorship on Internet discussions, it is becoming more and more difficult to censor and control online information with the explosion of the Internet population and the development of microblogs. The government is unable to prevent or control Internet protest over randomly erupting incidents.

As we discussed in Chapter 7, the government struggled to deal with the explosion of Internet public opinion over particular incidents. In general, government reaction to Internet protest is twofold. On the one hand, the government would take an appeasement approach, either reverse some administrative decision or discipline the exposed corrupt official. On the other hand, the government would quickly set up firewalls to block unwanted websites, such as Facebook and Twitter. It also actively collects public opinion information to monitor the pulse of society.

We need to point out that the appeasement is limited. It does not include the change of institutions or laws, except for the Sun Zhigang case. The government only attempts to pacify public anger for the moment. If sensitive political issues are involved, the government will tighten censorship and close down certain forums and some microblogs, even to the extent of arrest. For

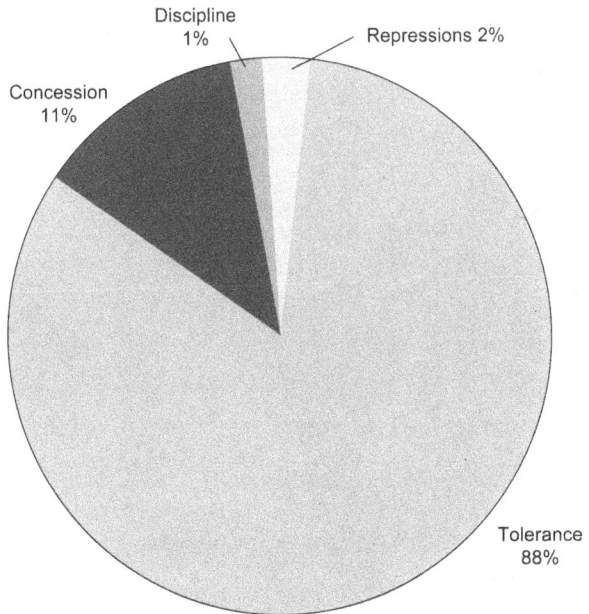

Figure 8.5.2 Government responses by type of protest

example, in March 2012, when the Politburo decided to sack Bo Xilai, a political heavyweight in the high power circle, some forums and microblogs that were supporting Bo were closed down. The police chief of Beijing had warned that web users who "attacked" leaders of the CCP and the country or the current system would be severely punished.[30]

Changing government responses

Under the multilevel responsibility structure, the government response is much more nuanced with a mixture of different methods. In general, there are three phases of reaction when facing a particular large-scale social protest. In the initial phase, the local public security agency will decide how to maintain public order, depending on the method the protesters use. In the second stage, depending on the nature of the protest, the local government will decide on how to react to the demands of the protest. It will either tolerate or persuade the protesters to give up, or promise compensation. The third phase is the aftermath of the protest, when depending on the political implications and public attention, the government will take remedial measures such as disciplining officials, making compensation or arresting protest organizers.

Under the benevolent governance framework, public attention is focused on the initial phase, which is the response of the public security agency. The

196 Government responses and regime resilience

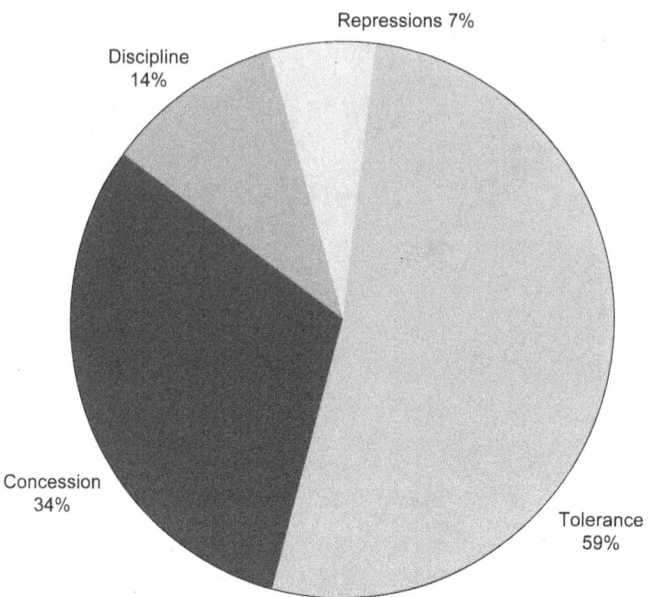

Figure 8.5.3 Government responses by type of protest

modern police system is naturally the antithesis of a benevolent government. The benevolent tradition puts moral constraints on state violence against protests, while the nature of the police force is the instrument of coercive deterrence. Under the multilevel responsibility structure, local governments shoulder the consequences of police action.

According to an analysis by the public security agencies in 2003, only about 3 percent of social protests adopted radical approaches such as blocking traffic, attacking government buildings, burning, looting and so on.[31] Our data set from 2003 to 2010 shows that social protests with radical tactics have significantly increased, yet the government reaction has changed from repression to more accommodation. The moderate government reaction is the result of the development of the Internet and the new Hu-Wen administration.

From the mid-1990s to the early twenty-first century, the main body of large-scale social protests was peasants' antitaxation protests and state workers' resistance to SOE reforms. Most of the scholarship on social protests focused on this period. Before the Internet reached every corner of society, the public had to rely on newspapers and TVs to obtain information. Since the government has firm control over the traditional media, the public was unable to learn much about social protest and form public opinion pressure on the government. For example, a 2004 book titled *An Investigation of Rural China*, which described rural protests, was soon censored by the

Government responses and regime resilience 197

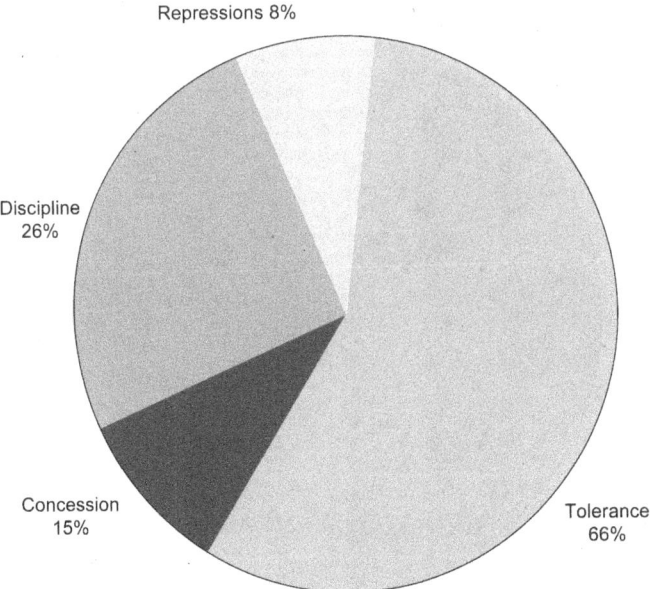

Figure 8.5.4 Government responses by type of protest

government.[32] One has to purchase the book from Hong Kong bookstores or obtain an illegal, pirated copy.

Since the local government could control the news media and cover up local protests, protests usually would not generate effective pressure on the government. Local government also was free to use excessive coercive force, which often led to vicious incidents. For example, in Fengcheng county of Jiangxi Province, the peasants protested against excessive taxation in 1999. The government used force to repress the protest, which led to large-scale uprisings. Several tens of thousands of peasants smashed a township government and buried two top leaders of the township government alive.[33] There has never been any report of this incident in any official media. There is not even a detailed report on the Internet.

In 2003, the new Hu-Wen government promoted a "people-oriented" governing principle. It was also the year of Severe Acute Respiratory Syndrome (SARS) and the first Internet protest over the Sun Zhigang incident. The Internet has released unprecedented political energy in China's political life. It has created tremendous public opinion pressure on all levels of government. Chinese government may be the most sensitive to Internet pressure, and Chinese netizens may be the most active in utilizing the Internet to supervise the government. The Internet has broken through official censorship. Even a

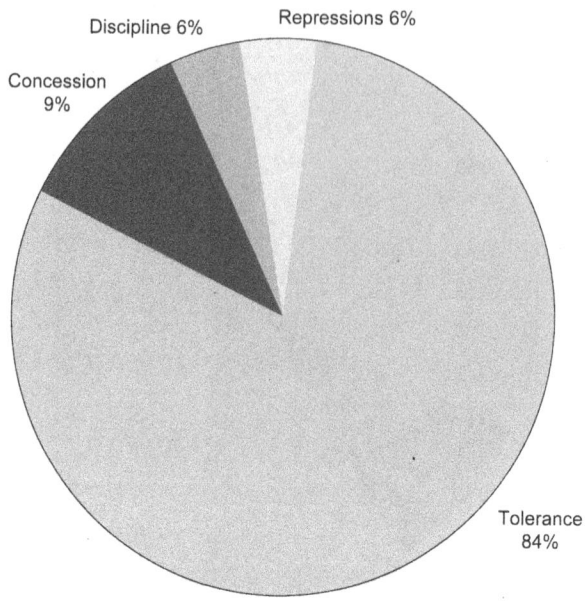

Figure 8.5.5 Government responses by type of protest

minor incident may trigger a public uproar online. The emergence of microblogging has also enabled ordinary citizens to broadcast some incidents live.

However, because of the multilevel responsibility structure, Internet public opinion has created great pressure on local government leaders. It forces the government to be extremely cautious when reacting to social protest in the first phase, especially in dispatching police. Any further incident triggered by the use of coercive power would generate greater Internet opinion pressure and the local government leaders would be disciplined or even end see an end to their political careers.

Elizabeth Perry once argued that as long as protests are localized and do not challenge central authority, the state is more willing to tolerate them. Only when such protests spill over state-sanctioned boundaries are they certain to draw swift and strong state suppression.[34] Yet, it is up to the local government to determine where the state-sanctioned boundaries are. In general, the government would not tolerate large-scale protests that are across regions. For example, in the spring of 2002, when more than a dozen factories in Liaoyang went out on strike simultaneously, the protest was suppressed swiftly.[35]

Now the government has become more sympathetic toward SOE workers' protests. It usually tolerates or compensates these. For labor protests in the nonstate sector, the regime will take an active role in mediating and push for a settlement acceptable to both sides. For example, during the strike waves in Guangdong and Liaoning in 2010, when the local government was hesitant over whether or not to deploy the police force, many government agencies advised that the timing was not right and the government needed to "be cautious."[36] There were also several cross-regional large-scale protests by bank employees and veterans. In the past, the cross-regional protests would not be tolerated by the regime, but these protests were neither suppressed nor investigated. In contrast, the governments showed a great deal of sympathy toward the protesters and accommodated their demands. All these changes come from the learning process of the government to adapt to social protests, the development of the Internet with the multilevel responsibility structure, and the increased financial resources of the central government.

The Wukan incident: a case study

The Wukan incident is a social protest that occurred from September 2011 to March 2012. Technically speaking, this incident does not belong in our range of study, which covers the large-scale social protests from 2003 to 2010. However, this incident contains all the characteristics of social protest in China today: land dispute, anticorruption, interest compensation, political demand, organization, violent conflict, peaceful protest, death, international media coverage, government (both central and local) involvement, and grassroots democratization. It is a typical case to study contemporary social protest under the multilevel responsibility structure in China.

The story

Wukan Village is located in Donghai Township, Lufeng City, Shanwei City of Guangdong Province. Figure 8.6 demonstrates the multilevel responsibility of the administrative structure involving Wukan Village.

On September 21, 2011, about 4,000 villagers from Wukan went to the city government of Lufeng to protest about disputes over land compensation, corruption and election. At the same time, other protesters smashed the village committee building and public security station in the village. The next day Lufeng City dispatched police to maintain order. The police were blocked by the villagers, who also burned police vehicles. Then Shanwei City government sent out a work group to the village and tried to coordinate the solution to this protest. The village then held an election and formed a "Provisional Board of Villagers' Representatives" to replace the administrative function of the village committee. In November, Donghai Township government dismissed the Party secretary and the head of the village and started to investigate their corruption cases.

In mid-November, unsatisfied with the mediation by the Lufeng City work group, the Provisional Board started to post on the Internet and claimed to

200 *Government responses and regime resilience*

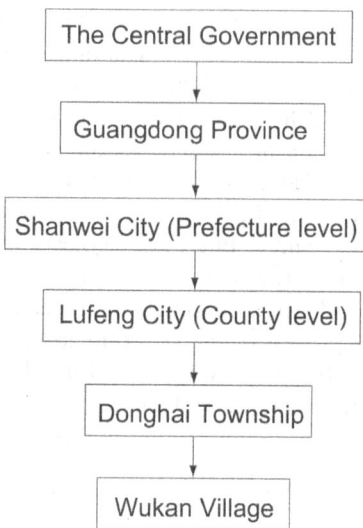

Figure 8.6 Multilevel responsibility of the administrative structure involving Wukan village

initiate another collective action. On November 21, the Provisional Board organized 400 villagers to go to the city government of Lufeng to protest. After mediation by both the township and city governments, the protest was temporarily suspended.

On December 9, the Public Security Bureau of Lufeng City announced that the "Provisional Board of Villagers' Representatives" and the "Women's Association" of Wukan Village were illegal organizations. At the same time, it arrested six villagers, including the Vice-Chairman of the Provisional Board Xue Jinbo, on the charge of physically attacking the police. On December 10, the villagers held another protest. The villagers used the Internet and microblogs to broadcast the process of the protest. They also posted photos of their protest slogan posters, such as "oppose dictatorship," "return our human rights," "open up national elections," and "return our farm land." Shanwei City once again dispatched a large number of armed police to Wukan Village, and met with another violent confrontation by the villagers. Tens of thousands of villagers set up roadblocks and only allowed foreign and Hong Kong journalists to get into the village.

On December 11, Lufeng City government announced that Xue Jinbo had died of a heart attack while in custody. This immediately radicalized the protest. Villagers set up a mourning hall for Xue, claiming that they would never trust any government official from Guangdong, and demanding that the central government intervene.

On December 18, villagers disseminated information on the Internet, claiming that the police had blocked the village and turned off the supply of water, electricity and food. They also claimed that more PLA field troops were mobilized to encircle Wukan. News media in Hong Kong first picked up this information and it attracted media attention worldwide. Then the villagers changed the slogans to "pleading for the central government to save the people of Wukan" and "supporting the Party Central Committee." On December 20, the Shanwei City government representatives entered the village to negotiate with the Provisional Board. The same night, Guangdong cable TV broadcast the speech by Vice-Party Secretary of Guangdong Zhu Mingguo. Zhu declared that the villagers' demands were reasonable and some of the extreme behaviors were understandable and forgivable. He promised that if the villagers stopped the organizational confrontation with the government, the police would not make any arrests. If the protest organizers would turn themselves in, they would not be punished.[37]

The Provisional Board immediately issued a positive response on the Internet: "We only protested over land issues. We are Party members and Youth League members, please do not exaggerate the nature of our protest." "We trust the Party Central Committee. We trust the leadership of the Provincial Government." Zhu Mingguo then paid a visit to Wukan on December 21. Villagers removed all protest slogans and put up new slogans such as "thankful to the Party Central Committee, thankful to Chairman Hu." All villagers stood along the street waving national flags to welcome Zhu Mingguo. Zhu returned the body of Xue Jinbo and agreed to let international media observe the autopsy procedure. Zhu also acknowledged the legitimacy of the Provisional Board. The Public Security Bureau then released all the detainees on the grounds that "they had shown repentance and participated in the investigation, therefore are released on bail."

From January to February 2012, Shanwei City and Wukan village reached an agreement over land compensation and village election. The local government would pay 900,000 RMB to Xue Jinbo's family. The village set up a new Party branch. In March 2012, Wukan held an election for a new village committee. The former chairman of the provisional board was elected. The government acknowledged the result legitimate. The newly elected head of the village emphasized that "villagers were demanding real democracy and felt there was no contradiction between those goals and supporting the Party."[38] Hence, the Wukan protest ended.

Interpreting the Wukan incident from the perspective of the multilevel responsibility structure

First, from the beginning to the end, the Wukan protest was never targeted at the central government, despite the political demand for democratic elections. The protest organizers paid special attention to support the authority of the central government in order to gain sympathy from above. The protest only targeted the governments below the provincial level.

Second, the decision to use police depends on the degree of confrontation. At the beginning, there were two groups of protesters. One group went to the city government and protested peacefully. The other group smashed the village committee and public security station. The local government did not arrest the peaceful protesters, but arrested those who committed violent activities. When all the protesters returned home, the police did not go into the village but stayed outside of the village.

Third, the handling of the incident was strictly following the multilevel responsibility structure from bottom up. Upper-level governments could adjust their policies depending on the evolution of the event. In the Wukan incident, the farmers had consistently focused their protest on the city government of Lufeng and below. Therefore, the upper-level government—Shanwei City—was able to maneuver. For both sides there were ways to get out of a dead corner and they did not have to worsen the situation. The government of Guangdong Province could also take the proper time and manner to intervene as mediator and arbitrator. The central government was watching the entire incident closely but did not make any public appearance.

Fourth, one of the characteristics of the Wukan protest is its effective organization. Organized protest would overcome the dilemma of collective action—the problem of the free rider. The protesters not only set up the Provisional Board to be the leading core of the protest, but also established the Women's Association to mobilize women and children to participate in the protest. These organizations effectively established a triple layer of blockade to defend the village: children in the outer layer, women in the middle and the adult males in the rear. The police were unable to do anything to break these layers of protest.

This kind of mobilization structure has restored the collective function under the Mao era. The villagers would follow the arrangement by the organizers. The organizers would adjust their strategies over time. For example, the change of slogans from opposing dictatorship to thankful to the Party, and villagers holding out national flags to welcome the vice-Party secretary of the provincial government, all reflected the strategic adjustment of the organizers. The highly organized protest had made the protest more rational and minimized the cost of protest. In the meantime, organization had also created opportunities to communicate with the government. This facilitated the eventual compromise between the villagers and the government.

Finally, the protesters had learned to use the news media. They understood that only with the involvement of the international media would the central government pay attention to their case. In the beginning, the organizers used the slogans of opposing dictatorship and returning our human rights to attract the attention of the foreign media. This was not what the farmers wanted, but was a way of making noise. They also created the story of being blockaded by the armed police and the entire village being without water, electricity and food to win international sympathy. Their methods successfully got the international media involved.

Once the media effect was achieved, the organizers immediately switched their position, changing slogans from opposing dictatorship and opening up elections, to supporting the Party. This was intended to persuade the central government to put pressure on the local government to resolve the incident. One Hong Kong journalist later commented that "we are all used by the villagers."[39]

The Wukan incident is a win-win case under the multilevel responsibility structure. The protesters won their material demands. The government, through the multilevel structure, claimed credit for being able to handle the social protest successfully. During the annual meeting of the National People's Congress, the Party secretary of Guangdong cited the Wukan incident as one of the province's achievements in governing.[40] The news media also used "progressive" and "enlightened" to describe the way the incident was resolved.[41]

Conclusion

The collapse of work units and collectives and the emergence of local governments during the reform era provided the structural background of contemporary social protest in China. The multilevel responsibility structure has broken through the dilemmas of concession-repression under an authoritarian regime formulated by Goldstone and Tilly. Through such a structure, the central government is able to push the blame level by level down to the local governments. With the center staying away from the focus of blame, it not only maintains its authority, reducing the shock of contentious politics to its claim to legitimacy, but also gives more flexibility to the central and local governments to deal with contentious politics. Therefore, it creates a dynamic equilibrium during the process of interaction between the state and society.

The government reactions to social protests during the period of 2003 to 2010 were moderate. The government tolerated or compensated more than 90 percent of the incidents. Repression was extremely low, in only 2.8 percent of the cases. Labor protests in the state sector touched a soft spot of the regime and received the most compensation. Land-related protests received the second most compensation, as the peasants have a rightful claim to the state subsistence responsibility. Even violent riots were not all forcefully suppressed. The moderate government reaction during this period was the result of the congruence of several factors: the learning ability of the regime; the new Hu-Wen administration's mild approach to governance; the development of the Internet in creating public opinion pressure; and the increasingly large purse of central government.

The multilevel responsibility structure cannot guarantee the absolute stability of the authoritarian regime in China. The multilevel responsibility structure would work well in dealing with contentious politics driven by material demands. However, such a structure may not work well in dealing with politically contentious politics, such as the Xinjiang 7.5 incident and protests over ideological causes. Even though the local government becomes the buffer zone between the central state and society, it cannot solve the fundamental friction between the state (as a whole) and society. Without an effective intermediate organizational layer between the state and society, society easily becomes a mass society, and leads to the popularity of populism.

Notes

1 Yongshun Cai, "Power Structure and Regime Resilience," *British Journal of Political Science* No. 34 (2008): 414.
2 Kent Weaver, "The Politics of Blame Avoidance," *Journal of Public Policy* Vol. 6, No. 4 (1986): 317–98.
3 Ibid., 373.
4 Kevin Arceneaux and Robert Stein, "Who is Held Responsible when Disaster Strikes? The Attribution of Responsibility for a Natural Disaster in an Urban Election," *Journal of Urban Affairs* Vol. 28, No. 1 (2006): 43–53.
5 L.A. Hart, *Punishment and Responsibility: Essays in the Philosophy of Law* (Oxford University Press, 1968), 214.
6 The concept of "reverse racism" was originally raised in opposition to Affirmative Action in the United States. Chinese scholar Wang Xiaodong introduced the concept to China and argued that some Chinese have suffered a "reverse racism" syndrome, which is that these people believe that whatever is related to China is inferior. See Wong Xiaodong, 《中国不高兴》 [China is Unhappy] (江苏人民出版, 2009 [Jiangsu People's Press, 2009]).
7 Personal interview.
8 Personal interview.
9 Pierre Landry, *Decentralized Authoritarianism in China* (Cambridge Press, 2008), i.
10 Good cop/bad cop, also called joint questioning and friend and foe, is a psychological tactic used for interrogation. "Good cop/bad cop" tactics involves a team of two interrogators who take apparently opposing approaches to the subject. The interrogators may interview the subject alternately or may confront the subject at the same time. The "bad cop" takes an aggressive, negative stance toward the subject, making blatant accusations, derogatory comments, threats, and in general creating antipathy between the subject and himself. This sets the stage for the "good cop" to act sympathetically, appearing supportive, understanding, in general showing sympathy for the subject. The good cop will also defend the subject from the bad cop. The subject may feel he can cooperate with the good cop out of trust or fear of the bad cop. He may then seek protection by and trust the good cop and provide the information the interrogators are seeking. *CIA Human Resource Exploitation Training Manual* (1983), 26–27.
11 These are: 1 agenda limitation; 2 redefine the issue; 3 throw good money after bad; 4 pass the buck; 5 find a scapegoat; 6 jump on the bandwagon; 7 circle the wagons; and 8 stop me before I kill again. See Weaver, "The Politics of Blame Avoidance," 385.
12 中共中央，国务院 [Central Committee of the CCP and the State Council], 关于实行党政领导干部问责的暂行规定 [Provisional Procedures on the Responsibility System of Leading Party and Government Officials] (2009年7月12日 [July 12, 2009]).
13 Personal fieldwork.
14 Personal fieldwork
15 Personal interview with a county Party secretary in Shaanxi.
16 Personal interview with a township head in Yongxiu.
17 Weaver, "The Politics of Blame Avoidance," ibid., 385.
18 潘绥铭 [Pan Suiming], 《小姐：劳动的权利》 [Misses: The Right to Work] (香港：大道出版社，2005 [Hong Kong: Dadao Press, 2005]).

19 Weaver, "The Politics of Blame Avoidance," ibid., 386.
20 Jack Goldstone and Charles Tilly, "Threat (and Opportunity): Popular Action and State Response in the Dynamics of Contentious Action," in Ronald R. Aminzade *et al.* (eds) *Silence and Voice in the Study of Contentious Politics* (New York: Cambridge University Press, 2001), 179–94.
21 孟建柱 [Meng Jianzhu], "深入学习科学发展观，做党的忠诚卫士和人民群众的贴心人" [Study the Concept of Scientific Development, Be the Loyal Guards of the Party and Close Friends of the People], 《求是》, 2008年第21期 [*Qiushi* No. 21 (2008)].
22 Personal interview with a county vice-mayor in Jiangxi.
23 Personal interview with an onsite reporter from CCTV.
24 Elizabeth Perry and Mark Selden (eds), *Chinese Society: Change, Conflict and Resistance* (London: Routledge, 2000, 2nd edn), 19.
25 《中国新闻周刊》, 第45期, 2008年12月8日 [*China News Weekly* Vol. 339, No. 45 (December 8, 2008)].
26 For example, "Deliver and Study the Conclusions of the Central Committee, Unify Thoughts, and Further our Ability to Handle Mass Incident," study document of a county government in Shaanxi Province [原标题，"《传达和学习中央处理意见，统一思想，进一步学习提高处理和应对群体性事件的能力"》].
27 This typology has borrowed heavily from Cai's "Power Structure and Regime Resilience," ibid.
28 The Hanyuan incident was frequently cited by social protest scholars, but all the research was based on secondhand information and inaccuracies. This writing is the first to disclose the fact that the Party secretary of Hanyuan was the instigator of the protest. This is based on our fieldwork in Hanyuan and interviews with a member of the investigation group.
29 《中国青年报》, 2006年2月26日 [*China Youth News*, February 26, 2006].
30 "Beijing Police Launch Internet Restrictions," *Global Times*, July 26, 2012, www.globaltimes.cn/content/723383.shtml.
31 《工人集体行动十一年:基于553个个案的分析》 [Eleven Years of Workers Collective Action: Analysis of 553 Cases] (香港：中国劳工通讯，2011年12月 [Hong Kong: China Labor Newsletters, December 2011]).
32 春桃、陈桂棣 [Chun Tao and Chen Guidi], 《中国农村调查》 [An Investigation of Rural China] (北京：人民文学出版社，2004 [Beijing: Renmin Wenxue Press, 2004]).
33 Personal fieldwork in Fengcheng, 2008.
34 Elizabeth Perry, *Challenging the Mandate of Heaven: Social Protest and State Authority in China* (Armonk, NY: M.E. Sharpe, 2001), 20.
35 Ibid.
36 "工会的新机会" [New Opportunities for the Trade Unions], 《中国新闻周刊》, 2010第23期, 18–23 [*China News Weekly* No. 23 (2010)].
37 Personal interview with the onsite reporter from CCTV.
38 "Beijing Appoints Wukan Protest Leader as Official," *Financial Times*, January 16, 2012.
39 Personal interview with the onsite reporter from CCTV.
40 finance.jrj.com.cn/2012/03/06030712410678.shtml.
41 news.xinhuanet.com/politics/2012-08/01/c_123505772.htm.

9 Conclusion

Some readers may be surprised at there being only 548 large-scale social protests from 2003 to 2010 in China. With media coverage of social unrest all over China in recent years, the number of large-scale social protests was expected to be significantly higher. The sensationalist media coverage of selected cases gives the public the impression that there are protests everywhere, all the time, hence the conclusion that China is sitting on the mouth of a social volcano. Our research shows, first, that large-scale social protests are not as frequent as some pundits tend to believe. Second, as far as the regime is able to be responsible for the subsistence of people, there is no active social volcano in sight. In this concluding chapter, we would like to extend our discussion a little further to the scenarios of future social protests, the prospects of democracy and the implications for regime legitimacy.

Continued transitional pains or the passing of economic distress?

This book has portrayed a comprehensive picture of the social costs and pains of a society in transition. Various types of protest pinpoint the places where structural displacements occur. Labor protests in the state sector exemplify the social resistance to privatization, while large-scale social disturbances reveal the public frustration over bad local governance. We have also witnessed the coming and going of certain types of social protest. For example, antitaxation protests disappeared after the abolition of the agricultural tax. Student political protests that were common in the 1980s turned into anti-Japanese nationalistic demonstrations in the 2000s. The steady increase of labor protests in nonstate sectors indicated that the labor cost is on the rise and probably China is no longer a manufacturing paradise for foreign-invested enterprises (FIEs).

Now we would like to conclude the discussion of social protest in contemporary China with several future scenarios. The premise of our discussion is that China is in the process of socioeconomic transformation. The causes of certain grievances that have arisen during the process will also disappear as the process evolves. In other words, many forms of grievance are developmental, and they will be solved by further development.

Some of the current causes of large-scale social protest may be passing on soon. The most frequent large-scale mass incidents during 2003–10 were labor protests in state-owned enterprises (SOEs). Labor protests in SOEs are the typical reaction to the structural changes caused by SOE reforms, the core of which is privatization. As ownership was transferred to private hands, gone were all the state moral responsibilities for the welfare of the workers. Workers, who had developed a sense of belonging to the SOEs, were reluctant to give up their entitlement and continue to hold the state responsible for their subsistence living. This is the cause of labor protests in SOEs.

However, structural changes to the SOEs may have passed their most difficult stage. With the near completion of the SOE reforms, there will be fewer large-scale lay-offs, hence less subsistence grievance from SOE workers. Moreover, in today's China, the SOEs have become the equivalent of the rich with a huge surplus in savings. They are able to settle financial disputes with their employees more easily than before. Other social security mechanisms have also matured over time and are likely to reduce the number of large-scale social protests. The dying pains will die out.

The type of social protest that is likely to continue is labor disputes in the nonstate sector. New generations of workers volunteered to join the newly developed private sector on a contractual basis. They have lower expectations of government responsibility for their welfare and are taking matters into their own hands to fight for better working environments and better pay. The diminishing labor supply has enhanced the bargaining power of the workers. Since labor disputes with foreign or private investors do not directly involve the government, these kinds of social protests do not threaten regime stability. Sometimes the government has to step in to be the mediator between the workers and the investors. At other times, the government even has to provide financial assistance to calm down the angry workers. This would only further strengthen the legitimacy of the government. With the upgrade of China's low-end industry coming of age, the growing pains will continue to grow.

Land disputes are the consequence of the process of urbanization. As more and more farmers are engaging in nonagricultural professions and becoming urban residents, city expansion is unavoidable, as are land disputes. Land disputes usually occur between peasants and developers or businesses. However, as developers or businesses are typically backed by the local government, these land disputes often evolve into a confrontation between the peasants and the government. The central issue in the disputes was the amount of compensation. The vague collective ownership of land leads to many procedural loopholes in land deals. In some cases, the compensation money was embezzled by grassroots cadres. In other cases, the farmers retracted their previously agreed prices and demanded more. Some of the peasant resistance was fierce. However, land disputes only occur in certain areas. While we foresee the continued land-related protests in the future, they are not system threatening. If it is a matter of economic compensation, it is not difficult for the government to settle the dispute.

The other type of social protest that is more likely to increase is environmental pollution protests. However, because of the worldwide consensus (the Chinese government included) on environmental protection, the political opportunity for such protests is relatively larger than with other protests. Prolonged economic growth inevitably brings more pollution. As Chinese society moves into a higher developmental stage, public environmental awareness is going to rise. More importantly, the number of pollution victims is much larger than in other cases of economic grievance. Low air or water quality affects a big portion of the population. Unlike laying off workers which only touches several thousand households, bad air quality victimizes an entire city. Therefore, it is easier to create protest identities and mobilize large-scale pollution protests. Moreover, because of the worldwide consensus on environmental protection, environmental international nongovernmental organizations (INGOs) can play a more active role in promoting such protests, hence producing more international linkages inside China.

Ethnic conflicts are caused by different rationales. They are based on irreconcilable ethnic identities. The uncertainties created by transition would strengthen the cohesiveness of ethnic groups, if the group members perceive that they are left out as a group. Economic distress, such as income disparities, has compounded ethnic conflicts. We expect that the continued economic prosperity will ease, but not solve, certain ethnic frictions. Although conflicts of different ethnic identities are hard to reconcile, they are mainly confined to minority areas. By fighting against separatist movements, the communist regime would win more legitimacy among Han people, who account for 91 percent of the population. It would be a serious blow to the regime legitimacy if it were to lose minority areas to separatist movements, which is extremely unlikely to happen.

The most system-threatening social protest is disturbances and riots with no specific economic demands. The outburst of disturbances is often the product of broad and diffused social grievances over a variety of issues ranging from inequality, corruption and social injustice, to increased drug addiction. Disturbance is often triggered by the violation of benevolent governance, especially the misconduct of city management staff (*chengguan* 城管) or the police. In these cases, social anger, not economic demands, is directed at the authorities. These incidents could be system threatening because they are challenging rather than endorsing regime legitimacy. The reduction of disturbances requires the improvement of local governance and crisis management skills. This is not impossible to achieve. It seems that the frequency of riots has slowed down, which reflected the learning capabilities of the regime.

Internet protests will definitely continue in the future. With access to the Internet eased and the improvement of Internet communications, the Internet has increasingly become a space for ordinary people to voice their concerns and wage protest against perceived injustice. The government has been taking an appeasement approach to Internet mass incidents. The Internet protests have accomplished a lot by addressing social injustice and exposing corrupt officials. We would also expect the participants of Internet protests to become more mature and less gullible to rumors. With the emergence of Internet opinion leaders alongside the development of microblogging, Internet debate may become more civilized and rational.

However, we should be cautious on the prospect that technological innovation would bring dramatic political change. As we have pointed out in an earlier section, there are limits to Internet protest. The participants are primarily students, not the middle class or middle aged. The interests of young people are short lived. The motivation is solely on moral appeal. Moreover, when people can participate in a protest at home alone, they may not be interested in going out into the street.

Social protest and the prospect of democracy

The unavoidable question about China in the West is the prospect of democracy. Will these social protests help to prepare the coming of a democratic change in China? Before we discuss such a prospect, we need to clarify that democratization and regime collapse are two different things. The collapse of the authoritarian regime may open the door to democratic change, but it is far from certain that this would be the case. Social protests have more relevance to regime stability than to democracy. According to theories of democratization, the likelihood of democracy depends on a variety of factors. The most common ones are divisions within the elite, international influences, and the sustained challenge from a civil society. We will discuss these factors in the context of social protest in the following sections.

Divisions within the elite

Without severe divisions within the elite, a cohesive authoritarian regime with coercive power is likely to last for a long time. The experience of successful democratization has suggested that democracy is likely to be reached either by competing elite factions reaching a pact or the pro-democracy faction winning decisively in the power struggle.[1] We would like to emphasize that elite division may provide political opportunity to opposition, but it does not mean that it is any closer to democracy. For the above scenarios to work there must be at least one elite faction that is committed to democracy.

In China's context, it was the division of reformers and conservatives during the 1989 Tiananmen incident that allowed the student movement to emerge and last for more than a month. However, since 1989, the infamous battle between reformers and conservatives during the 1980s faded away. While we can observe the left and right camps among intellectual circles, such a division is hardly detectable among top leaders. The dubious existence of the so-called Youth League faction and Shanghai faction is either network related or regionally oriented. We do not have a clear sense of the ideological stands of these so-called factions. Without an ideological commitment to democracy by a strong faction, it is very unlikely that we will see a democratic change in China.

The downfall of Bo Xilai in the spring of 2012 revealed some serious divisions among the ruling elite. Yet, it is premature to determine the policy and direction each faction is pushing. Bo is labeled by some as a leftist. However, other than Bo's assault on corrupt officials, it is hard to tell the difference between his policy in Chongqing and that of the central government. The strike on corrupt officials was warmly received by the public, as we have repeatedly argued that corruption violated the informal understanding between the state and society. It is suspected that Bo's downfall might be a counterattack by the falling officials and the powerful interest groups behind them.

In principle, social protests do not produce elite division. Elite division produces political opportunity for social movement, as the 1989 student movement substantiated. However, the social protests we studied in this book are not political protests. In China's context, subsistence expectation protests enjoyed political opportunity due to the tradition of benevolent governance. The sudden bursts of benevolence violation protests—riots—do not need much political opportunity at all. This is why we have observed these many social protests during 2003 to 2010 without any definite knowledge of elite division. Furthermore, as the numerous student political protests in the 1980s exemplified, the then ongoing struggle between the reformers and conservatives, the nonexistence of political protests since 1989 testifies to the absence of elite divisions with different ideological orientations.

The only relevance of social protest to elite division is that it can become a tool in a power struggle. No leaders dare to instigate social protest. Those who did would be ruthlessly punished, as the cases of Hanyuan and Huangshi have demonstrated. However, factions could create a blame game and use social protest to strengthen their respective positions. Again, without a faction that commits to democratization, no matter which faction becomes more powerful by manipulating social protests, China is not going to experience democratic change anytime soon.

International influence

International influence has been considered one of the important factors that may facilitate democratization. Levitsky and Way have specifically broken down international influence into Western leverage and linkage to the West. Leverage creates pressure on regimes that are vulnerable to external influences, such as positive conditionality or punitive sanctions. Leverage usually works for smaller countries that have limited resources and a highly dependent economy, since they are more vulnerable to outside pressure.[2] China, however, is the antithesis: it is large, with enough resources, and the regime is highly insulated from external pressures. Linkage is the density of ties and cross-border flows (political, economic, social, informational and so on) between a particular country with the Western world. Linkage facilitates domestic demands for democratic change. It is a kind of soft power of the West. Its effects on democratization are subtle and diffuse. The domestic demands for democratization in China, in fact, have come from the extensive linkage Chinese society has with the Western world since the opening up of the country.

Except for a couple of ethnic conflicts, we have not observed any international linkages in large-scale social protests. The government is extremely sensitive to any international involvement in social protests. With the highly alert eyes of the government watching its back, it is not easy for INGOs to get involved in domestic social protests. Moreover, the protest organizers are reluctant to connect to international actors. Some may have attempted to contact foreign journalists for protest exposure. However, none want to be accused of having an international "black hand" and reduce their chances of reaching their goals.

Ethnic conflict is the only type of social protest that has external connections. This is because the ethnic groups involved in the conflict usually have their own exiles or groups with similar ethnic origins outside the country. Western governments can exercise influence through these groups. Yet, ethnic conflicts mostly occur in select regions; international influence, if any, would be very limited. A lesser, but possible, candidate of establishing international linkage is the labor protests in the nonstate sector. International labor activists have a small chance to promote workers' rights. However, instigating social protests in China should not be the purpose of international influence. Social protests may or may not subvert the current regime, but they do not contribute to the construction of a functional democratic system.

Civil society

Many pundits believe that social protests symbolize the rise of a civil society in China. This belief is based on two premises. One is the awakening of rights awareness during the protest, which may indicate a breakthrough in the state-society relationship. The other is the possibility that protest organizations may turn into a more durable form of mobilization for the rise of a civil society. These two premises are on somewhat shaky ground.

First, as Perry has eloquently argued, the Chinese conception of "rights" is very different from that of the West, being primarily about economic justice rather than about civil or political rights.[3] Protests do not symbolize a breakthrough in the state-society relationship, but reinforce the moral bondage between the state and society. As we have argued, most of the social protests rose in expectation that the state would address their grievances. As long as protesters consider the state as their savior, they are not going to challenge the it.

Second, with regard to organization, social protests are not social movements. They have short-term goals and are not sustainable. Most social protests are driven by economic grievances. The protest would not last beyond the point at which economic interests are somehow compensated. The conclusion of the social protest would reinforce the regime legitimacy rather than undermining it. Even though riots are not driven by economic interests but by the frustration over social injustice or violation of benevolent governance, nobody would count on riots to overthrow any regime, since participants are not organized and the riot alliance is temporary.

The only hopeful candidate here is the trade unions in FIEs. If the autonomous trade unions could survive in FIEs, they may play a role in the construction of a civil society. Even if this becomes a reality, we need to be aware that the main purpose of the trade unions in FIEs is to represent the interests of the workers vis-à-vis the capitalists, not to challenge the government.

The localized economic interests would prevent protests in different locations from developing a cross-regional alliance and, therefore, pose little threat to the regime. In addition, the purpose of the protest is to gain economic benefit from the state, not to challenge the state. If the state collapsed, where would the protesters demand their economic benefits? The integration of the protest movement is crucial in waging a coordinated challenge to the regime. Unfortunately, there is no such integrating force in China.

Learning capabilities and flexibility of the regime

As we have argued in previous sections, social protests may be related to regime stability, but do not strengthen the factors that would contribute to democratization: elite division, international influence and civil society. We would also like to suggest a factor that would help the survival of the current regime: learning capabilities and flexibility of the regime. Samuel Huntington once argued that adaptability is essential for an institution to survive in the long term.[4] Whether the Chinese regime is going to endure or collapse depends to a large extent on its learning capabilities and flexibility. Many believe that the regime is rigid and refuses to change, and they have long predicted its demise. Yet, the regime has showed an amazing ability to survive in times of crisis. This endurance has to be attributed to the adaptive capabilities of the regime.

The economic reforms introduced since 1978 have demonstrated the flexibility of the communist regime to shift directions. The Communist Party did not have much difficulty in abandoning their policies before and during the Cultural Revolution. The reform strategy of "grasping the stones when crossing the river" characterized the willingness of the regime to experiment and adjust. Overall, the regime primarily adopted a proactive approach to its economic reforms. The government has been willing to experiment with different programs and ideas to move forward, while at the same time adjust its strategies accordingly. So far the economic reform has been quite successful.

With the success of economic development, society gets wealthier and more differentiated. China has moved onto the next stage of transformation—the management of a pluralizing society. In this regard, the regime has been less successful. Its approach to social management is no longer proactive but reactive. The philosophy has been "if it isn't broken, don't fix it." The regime has been busy reacting to various (minor) crises. Local governments are busy firefighting, yet during the process of firefighting, the regime was able to adjust its policies. A typical example was the quick removal of the repatriation system months after the Sun Zhigang incident, which would have taken a couple of years in a democratic system. Another example is the abolition of the agricultural tax.

The government is sometimes oversensitive to public pressure. It never hesitated to discipline corrupt officials exposed on the Internet. For example, only five days after the so-called "most powerful wife of a military commander" incident, in which the wife of a military commander assaulted a staff member of a museum, the husband was sacked. The speed with which this was done makes people wonder whether there is due process for removing officials. This is a typical characteristic of an authoritative government committed to benevolent governance. The benevolent tradition forces the government to address social discontent. However, because of the timely reaction and willingness to change, the Chinese regime has been able to stay in power.

After the explosion of several riots in 2009, the regime enacted a responsibility system for officials above county-level government. It stipulates that if the misconduct of the officials led to the outburst of social protest, they would be held accountable. The central government also organized several training programs for county-level government officials, focusing on ways to deal with "emergency incidents." Under this responsibility system, local governments tried hard to prevent social protest from happening. Although one could argue that these efforts are merely cosmetic and do not address the fundamental flaws of the system, the regime nevertheless has been flexible enough to muddle through. This learning capability is something we have rarely observed in other authoritarian regimes.

The multilevel responsibility structure that was consolidated from the 1990s provides institutional flexibility to the regime. Through such a structure, the central government is able to push the blame level by level down to local governments. With the center staying away from the focus of blame, it is able to maintain its authority and reduce the shock of contentious politics to its claim of legitimacy. The multilevel responsibility structure works well in dealing with contentious politics driven by material demands. However, such a structure may not work well in dealing with politically contentious politics, such as the Xinjiang 7.5 incident and protests over ideological causes.

Some reflections on regime legitimacy

At the beginning of the book we proposed an analytical framework of a responsibility-based regime legitimacy to study social protest in contemporary China. Regime legitimacy is an understanding between the state and society in which society accepts the rule of the state if it fulfills certain promises.

These promises could be accountability to the voters in a democratic system, or social welfare in some other political system, or something else. In this framework, we suggested that social protest, as a challenge to the state, is based on people's understanding of their relationship with the state. People would rise to challenge the state either in the expectation that the state ought to fulfill its responsibilities, or in disgust that the state violated the hidden social contract (regardless of how informal it may be). Examining social protest under the lens of responsibility-based regime legitimacy will present different conclusions than other frameworks, such as the state society dichotomy.

This responsibility-based regime legitimacy in China is composed of three overlapping layers: official morality, benevolent governance and responsibility for the well-being of the people. Throughout the book, we have used these three layers to analyze the large-scale social protests in contemporary China. The overwhelming majority of the protests are subsistence expectation protests, in which people protested in the expectation that the government would be responsible for their economic grievances. There are also social protests that are not based on economic grievances. Large-scale mass disturbances are triggered by the violation of benevolent governance, such as violent law enforcement and unnatural deaths that might be related to corrupt officials. In the conclusion, we would like to discuss some further implications these social protests have on regime legitimacy.

Official morality

No society endorses corruption and every society has moral standards for its officials. Yet, Chinese society has put exceptional emphasis on official morality. The fact that the state serves as the moral preacher has contributed to such a tradition. To be a proper preacher, the government officials and top leaders have to set moral examples for their people. Rule through moral example rather than strict laws has long been accepted as the norm in traditional China. Confucian teaching has always focused on the improvement of the inner self, which is nurturing a moral being. Therefore, society expects government officials to be honest, upright and hardworking. Society has been frustrated by the rampant official corruption since the market reforms that started in the late 1970s. However, because of the secretive nature of corruption, information about it is passed around by rumor. People are gullible and eager to believe every rumor about official corruption. Almost every protest engages in accusations of official corruption. Anticorruption is the most appealing call to mobilize protest participation. This holds true from the Tiananmen incident in 1989 until the most recent protests, and it will be the case for the indefinite future.

There has been a general decline in public morality since the early 1980s. On the one hand, it is the result of market erosion and the seduction of suddenly available wealth. There is widespread cheating, faking and speculation in business deals. On the other hand, official corruption has seriously undermined the bottom line of public morality. The phenomenon of "return what you found on the street and leave the door unlocked at night" is gone. Walking through any residential areas in China today, the most obvious scene is iron bars outside first-floor windows and ever more elaborate and effective security doors. Worst of all, whenever there are legal or moral violations, from murder to plagiarism, people find excuses for such behavior by pointing to official corruption. The underlying message is that the official corruption dwarfs whatever illegal or immoral things people do. The public sentiment is that if the officials do not behave themselves, there is no need for the people to do so.

The government is well aware of such a general decline of public morality. It has tried hard to address the issue by proposing a "spiritual civilization" in the 1980s, "five talks and four beauties [五讲四美]"[5] in the 1990s, and "eight glories and eight shames [八荣八耻],"[6] and "harmonious society" in the last decade. The improvement has been minimal. The government fails to understand that without addressing official corruption, public morality will not improve. It cannot expect the people to be moral while the officials continue to be corrupt. One of the main reasons why public morality was much better under Mao was that the officials in that period were clean and hardworking. A tradition that does not emphasize institutional constraints has to rely on moral constraints, yet these moral constraints are becoming more lax. Historically most of the dynasties fell because of incurable corruption, including the most recent nationalist regime on the mainland. If the communist government does not have the determination to curb official corruption, it may be fatal to regime survival in the foreseeable future.

Benevolent governance

The communist regime has not openly embraced the term of benevolent governance yet. However, embrace it or not, it is the expectation of the people. The term is closely related to the idea of morality. During Mao's time, even though the regime upheld the principle of dictatorship of the proletariat, it also emphasized the ideal of "serving the people." This ideal is not very far from benevolent governance. The tricky part is that one had to fall into the category of people and many fell out during endless political campaigns. At the turn of the twenty-first century, the former Party General Secretary Jiang Zemin once proposed a concept of "rule by virtue," an ancient idea from Confucius and the equivalent of benevolent governance. However, this concept was not followed up later.

Ever since China established Confucianism as the official doctrine, the mandate of heaven has become the basis of regime legitimacy. The stability of the regime depends to a large extent on the moral function of the state and the moral quality of its officials. The frustration over the loss of virtue by the officials and the state will accumulate and wait for an outlet to explode. Even though China was the first country to establish a professional civil service system, it never resolved the issue of effective supervision.

The consequence of the loss of virtue by the government and its officials is the formation of temporary alliances of all social strata, using riots to express disgust at official corruption and sometimes malign governance. Disturbances are not about poverty, but about relative deprivation with regard to both wealth and justice.

Police beating up innocent people is obviously an outrageous violation of benevolence in China's context. That is why this kind of incident incites large-scale riots. This is especially the case where moral justice always takes precedence over legal procedures. In contrast, it was the acquittal of the police officers who were involved in Rodney King's beating, not the beating itself, that triggered the Los Angeles riot in 1992. The American public in general accepts that the police have the right to use violence to enforce laws. The dragging and kicking of protesters during the Occupy Wall Street movement was considered normal procedure of law enforcement and there were no public complaints about it.

The pursuit of substantive justice is symbiotic with benevolent governance. Laws are not sacred and can be ignored if they are considered unreasonable in certain cases. Only benevolent governance would exercise such broad discretion. In other rule-of-law societies, there can also be such exceptions. Yet in China it is the norm rather than the exception. It is true that the Chinese regime stays above the law, but it is the typical reflection of, not the cause of, the lack of respect for procedural justice. The desire for substantive justice will be a stumbling block on China's way to a rule of law society.

There are different degrees of violence in social protests. It seems that the benevolence violation protests are the most violent. Morally motivated protests tend to be emotionally charged. The land dispute protests are also more violent than others in subsistence expectation protests. This is because the farmers lack resources in the dispute confrontations and have to resort to violence to get their message through. The least violent ones are the labor protests in nonstate sectors. As the protests are legal and contractual in nature, it is not very helpful to the course if the protest becomes violent.

When the protests involved the government, either directly or indirectly, moral claims seem to be a major framing strategy. There are two consistent themes in the protests in the state sector. One is the right to subsistence living and the other is anticorruption. Protestors blamed their hardship partially or entirely on official corruption. However, the framing in the protests in the nonstate sector is different, as there are no moral obligations for private or foreign companies. The claims are primarily based on contractual or legal terms.

State responsibility for the well-being of the people

Just as Elizabeth Perry has pointed out, state responsibility for the well-being of the people is a political tradition from Mencius to Mao and beyond. This is the tradition that the post-Mao communist regime has carried through. It is precisely because of this responsibility that the regime has been able to stay in its place through various disruptions.

With the process of transformation continuing, structural displacement will be adjusted. Some of the transitional pains will subside, such as those that are caused by SOE reforms. Other pains will continue, such as the growing pains in the private sector and urbanization. As we pointed out earlier, these are normal pains for any society in transition.

Apparently most of the social protests rose in the expectation that the government should address people's economic grievances. The protests are about subsistence, and they have gone beyond subsistence. In other words, the definition of subsistence has been upgraded together with the rising standard of living. It is not just about state responsibility for disaster relief, it is about state responsibility for affordable education, health care, housing and elderly care. Subsistence expectation protests in the future may be less about subsistence, but the expectation will stay the same. They will be more about comfortable living. Therefore, the protests may be more peaceful and rational when protesters are not as desperate.

Some people argue that without democratic reform, China's traditional way of ruling is unsustainable. It is not about whether democratic reform and rule of law is desirable, it is about the viability of these systems. Procedural justice (election and rule of law) will have a very torturous road to replace substantive justice that is rooted in thousands of years of tradition. No matter what system China eventually adopts, it will always be preoccupied by moral considerations.

Notes

1 Guillermo O'Donnell and Philippe Schmitter, *Transitions from Authoritarian Rule: Tentative Conclusions about Uncertain Democracies* (Baltimore: The Johns Hopkins University Press, 1986); and Michael McFaul, "The Fourth Wave of Democracy and Dictatorship: Noncooperative Transitions in the Postcommunist World," *World Politics* No. 54 (January 2002): 212–44.
2 Steven Levitsky and Lucan Way, "Linkage versus Leverage. Rethinking the International Dimension of Regime Change," *Comparative Politics* Vol. 38, No. 4 (July 2006): 379–400.
3 Elizabeth Perry, "Chinese Conceptions of 'Rights': From Mencius to Mao-and Now," *Perspective on Politics* Vol. 6, No. 1 (2008): 37–50.
4 Samuel Huntington, *Political Order in Changing Societies* (New Haven: Yale University Press, 1968).
5 The "five talks" refer to "civility, courtesy, hygiene, order and morality." The "four beauties" refer to "souls, languages, behaviors and environment."
6 The "eight glories" refer to "loving the mother land, serving the people, respecting science, working diligently, cooperating with others, being honest, observing the law, and fighting hard amid difficulties." The "eight shames" refer to "endangering the mother land, betraying the people, being ignorant, being lazy, being selfish and hurting others' interests, being dishonest, violating the laws, and living extravagantly."

Bibliography

Allport, Gordon W. and Leo Joseph Postman (1947) *The Psychology of Rumor* (New York: H. Holt & Co.).
Arceneaux, Kevin and Robert M. Stein (2006) "Who is Held Responsible When Disaster Strikes? The Attribution of Responsibility for a Natural Disaster in an Urban Election," *Journal of Urban Affairs* Vol. 28, No. 1: 43–53.
Bernstein, Thomas (2004) "Unrest in Rural China: A 2003 Assessment," UC Irvine: Center for the Study of Democracy, www.escholarship.org/uc/item/1318d3rx.
Bernstein, Thomas P. and Lu, Xiaobo (2000) "Taxation without Representation: The Central and Local States in Reform China," *China Quarterly* No. 163 (September): 742–63.
Bi, Jianhai (2001) "The Internet Revolution in China: The Significance for Traditional Forms of Communist Control," *International Journal* Vol. 56, No. 3: 421–41.
Blecher, Marc (2002) "Hegemony and Workers' Politics in China," *China Quarterly* No. 170: 283–303.
Cai, Lily (2008) *Accountability without Democracy* (New York: Cambridge University Press).
Cai, Yongshun (2002) "The Resistance of Chinese Laid-off Workers in the Reform Period," *China Quarterly* No. 170 (June): 327–44.
——(2005) *State and Laid-off Workers in Reform China: The Silence and Collective Action by the Retrenched* (Routledge).
——(2008a) "Local Governments and the Suppression of Popular Resistance in China," *The China Quarterly* No. 193: 24–42.
——(2008b) "Power Structure and Regime Resilience: Contentious Politics in China," *British Journal of Political Science* Vol. 38, No. 03 (July): 411–32.
——(2010) *Collective Resistance in China: Why Popular Protests Succeed or Fail* (Stanford University Press).
Cao, Jinqing, (曹锦清) (2000) 黄河边上的中国（上海文艺出版社）[*China by the Yellow River* (Shanghai Wenyi Press)].
Chan, Anita (2001) *China's Workers Under Assault: The Exploitation of Labor in a Globalizing Economy* (M.E. Sharpe).
Chan, Chris King-Chi and Pun Ngai (2009) "The Making of a New Working Class? A Study of Collective Actions of Migrant Workers in South China," *China Quarterly* No. 198 (June): 287–303.
Chang, Gordon (2001) *The Coming Collapse of China* (Random House).
Chang Jianhua (常建华) (2006), "近代闽台族正制考述",《中国社会经济史研究》2006年第一期. ["Investigation of Mintai Lineage System in Modern Times," *Studies of Chinese Social Economic History* No. 1].

Chase, Michael and James Mulvenon (2002) *You've Got Dissent! Chinese Dissident Use of the Internet and Beijing's Counter-Strategies* (Rand).
Chen, Feng (2000) "Subsistence Crises, Managerial Corruption and Labor Protests in China," *China Journal* No. 44 (July): 41–63.
—— (2003) "Industrial Restructuring and Workers' Resistance in China," *Modern China* Vol. 29, No. 2: 237–62.
Chen, Guidi and Chun,Tao (陈桂棣，春桃) (2004) 中国农民调查 (人民文学出版社) [*Investigation of Chinese Peasants* (People's Literature Press)].
Chen Guying (陈鼓应) (1984) 韩非子今注今释 (中华书局) [*Current Interpretations of Han Feizi* (China Book Bureau)].
Chen, Jie (2004) *Popular Political Support in China* (CA: Stanford University Press).
Chen Jinsheng (陈晋胜) (2004) 群体性事件研究报告（内部发行版）(北京：群众出版社) [*Report on Mass Incidents (internal edition)* (Beijing: Mass Press)].
Chen, Xi (2007) "Between Defiance and Obedience: Protest Opportunism in China," in Elizabeth Perry and Merle Goldman (eds) *Grassroots Political Reform in Contemporary China* (Harvard University Press), 253–81.
Chen Zhiping (陈支平) (2006) "清末民间抗粮与乡族势力"，《厦门大学学报》2006年第1期 ["Resistance to State Grain Procurement and Rural Lineage in the End of Qing Dynasty," *Journal of Xiamen University* No.1].
China Statistics Bureau (1998) 中国灾情报告 1949–1995 [*Report of the Damage Caused by Disaster in China 1949–1995*] (China Statistics Press).
Clinton, Hillary (2010) "Remarks on Internet Freedom," US Department of State official website, www.state.gov/secretary/rm/2010/01/135519.htm.
Cooper, Caroline (2003) "Quietly Sowing the Seeds of Activism," *Far Eastern Economic Review*, April 10: 30.
Deng, Yunte (邓云特) (1998) 中国救荒史 (北京出版社) [*History of Disaster Relief in China* (Beijing Press)].
Diamant, Neil, Stanley Lubman and Kevin O'Brien (eds) (2005) *Engaging the Law in China: State, Society, and Possibilities for Justice* (CA: Stanford University Press).
Diamond, Larry (2010) "Liberation Technology," *Journal of Democracy* Vol. 21, No. 3 (July): 69–83.
Drogus, Carol Ann and Steven Orvis (2008) *Introducing Comparative Politics* (CQ Press).
Duara, Prasenjit (1988) *Culture, Power, and the State, Rural North China, 1900–1942* (CA: Stanford University Press).
Esarey, Ashley and Xiao Qiang (2008) "Political Expression in the Chinese Blogosphere: Below the Radar," *Asian Survey* Vol. 48, No. 5: 752–72.
Fairbank, John King (1983) *The United States and China* (Harvard University Press, 4th edn).
Fairbank, John King and Edwin O. Reischauer (eds) (1979) *China: Tradition and Transformation* (George Allen & Unwin).
Federation of Hong Kong Industries (2007) *Made in PRD: The Challenges and Opportunities for Hong Kong Industry*, research report, www.industryhk.org/english/fp/fp_res/files/made_in_prd_e.pdf (accessed May 17, 2010).
Fewsmith, Joseph (2001) *China since Tiananmen* (Cambridge University Press).
Frazier, Mark W. (2004) "China's Pension Reform and Its Discontents," *The China Journal* No. 51 (January): 97–114.
Freedom, Maurice (1965) *Linage Organization in Southeastern China* (NJ: Athlone Press).
Fu Jiancheng (傅建成) (2006) "新民主主义革命时期中共宗族政策、行为分析"，《安徽史学》2006年期第3期 ["Analysis of the Policies and Behaviors of the

Chinese Communist Party during the New Democratic Revolution," *Anhui Historiography* No.3]
Gallagher, Mary (2007) "Hope for Protection and Hopeless Choices," in Elizabeth Perry and Goldman Merle (eds) *Grassroots Political Reform in Contemporary China* (Mass: Harvard University Press).
Gallagher, Mary Elizabeth (2005) *Contagious Capitalism: Globalization and the Politics of Labor in China* (NJ: Princeton University Press).
Gamson, William and David Meyer (1996) "Framing Political Opportunity," in Doug McAdam *et al.* (eds) *Comparative Perspectives on Social Movements* (Cambridge University Press), 275–90.
Gladney, Dru C. (1991) *Muslim Chinese, Ethnic Nationalism in the People's Republic* (Boston: Harvard University Press).
Goldman, Merle and Elizabeth J. Perry (2002) *Changing Meanings of Citizenship in Modern China* (Boston: Harvard University Press).
Goldstone, Jack and Charles Tilly (2001) 'Threat (and Opportunity): Popular Action and State Response in the Dynamics of Contentious Action', in Ronald R. Aminzade *et al.* (eds) *Silence and Voice in the Study of Contentious Politics* (New York: Cambridge University Press), 179–94.
Gong Qun (龚群) (2002) (ed.) 以德治国论 (辽宁人民出版社). [*On Rule of Virtue* (Liaoning People's Press)]
Gries, Peter Hays and Stanley Rosen (eds) (2004) *State and Society in 21st-Century China* (London: Routledge).
——(2010) *Chinese Politics: State, Society and the Market* (London: Routledge, 2nd edn).
Gu Cheng (顾诚) (2012) 明末农民战争史 (光明日报出版社) [*History of Peasant Wars in the End of Ming Dynasty* (Guangming Daily Press)].
Guo, Xiaolin (2001) "Land Expropriation and Rural Conflicts in China," *China Quarterly* No. 166 (June): 422–39.
Guo, Xuezhi (2002) *The Ideal Chinese Political Leader: A Historical and Cultural Perspective* (Praeger).
Gurr, Ted (2011) *Why Men Rebel* (Paradigm Publishers).
Gustave, Le Bon (2002) *The Crowd: Study of the Popular Mind* (New York: Dover Publications, Inc).
Hachigian, Nina (2002) "The Internet and Power in One-Party East Asian State," *Washington Quarterly* Vol. 25, No. 3 (Summer): 41–58.
Hagaad, Stephan and Robert Kaufman (1995) *The Political Economy of Democratic Transition* (Princeton, NJ: Princeton University Press).
Hall, Stuart (1996) "Ethnicity: Identity and Difference," in Geoff Eley and Ronald G. Suny (eds) *Becoming National: A Reader* (Oxford University Press), 339–49.
Hart, L.A. (1968) *Punishment and Responsibility: Essays in the Philosophy of Law* (Oxford University Press).
Harwit, Eric and Duncan Clark (2001) "Shaping the Internet in China: Evolution of Political Control over Network Infrastructure and Content," *Asian Survey* Vol. 41, No. 3 (May/June): 377–408.
Heimer, Maria and Stig Thogersen (eds) (2006) *Doing Fieldwork in China* (Honolulu: University of Hawaii Press).
Ho, Peter (2000) "Contesting Rural Spaces: Land Disputes, Customary Tenure and the State," in Elizabeth J. Perry and Mark Selden (eds) *Chinese Society: Change, Conflict and Resistance* (London: Routledge Curzon Press), 101–22.

——(2001) "Who Owns China's Land? Policies, Property Rights and Deliberate Institutional Ambiguity," *China Quarterly*: 394–421.
Ho, Ping-ti (1962) *The Ladder of Success in Imperial China: Aspects of Social Mobility, 1368–1911* (Columbia University Press).
Hughes, Christopher R. and Gudrun Wacker (eds) (2003) *China and the Internet: Politics of the Digital Leap Forward* (London: Routledge).
Huntington, Samuel (1968) *Political Order in Changing Societies* (New Haven: Yale University Press).
Hurst, William (2004) "Understanding Contentious Collective Action by Chinese Laid-off Workers," *Studies in Comparative International Development* Vol. 39, No. 2: 94–120.
——(2009) *The Chinese Worker after Socialism* (Cambridge University Press).
Hurst, William and O'Brien, Kevin (2002) "China's Contentious Pensioners," *China Quarterly* No. 170: 345–60.
Inglehart, Ronald (1990) *Cultural Shift in Advanced Industrial Society* (CA: Princeton University Press).
Inglehart, Ronald and Christian Welzel (2005) *Modernization, Cultural Change, and Democracy* (Cambridge University Press).
Jin Jun et al. (晋军、应星、毕向阳、孙立平、郭于华、沈原) (2010) "以利益表达制度化实现社会的长治久安" [Use the Institutionalized Interest Articulation to Maintain Social Stability], A report by the Department of Sociology, Qinghua University, news.qq.com/a/20100419/001123.htm (accessed April 30, 2010).
Jing, Jun (2003) "Environmental Protests in China," in Elizabeth J. Perry and Mark Selden (eds) *Chinese Society: Change, Conflict and Resistance* (London: Routledge Curzon Press, 2nd edn), 204–22.
Kalathil, Shanthi and Taylor C. Boas (2003) *Open Networks Closed Regimes: The Impact of the Internet on Authoritarian Rule*, Carnegie Endowment for International Peace.
Kang Xiaoguang (康晓光) (2008) 仁政：中国政治发展的第三条道路 [*Benevolence: The Third Way of Chinese Political Development*] (Singapore: Bafang Wenhua Press).
Klotz, Robert J. (2003) *The Politics of Internet Communication* (Rowman & Littlefield).
Kornhauser, William (1959) *The Politics of Mass Society* (Illinois: The Free Press of Glencoe).
Ku, Hok Bun (2003) *Moral Politics in a South Chinese Village: Responsibility, Reciprocity, and Resistance* (Roman & Littlefield).
Lampton, David (2008) *Three Faces of Chinese Power: Might, Money, and Minds* (University of California Press), 39–43.
Landry, Pierre (2008) *Decentralized Authoritarianism in China: The Communist Party's Control of Local Elites in the Post-Mao Era* (Cambridge University Press).
——(2009) "Does the Communist Party Help Strengthen China's Legal Reform?" *The China Review* Vol. 9, No. 1 (Spring): 45–71.
Lane, Jan-Erik (2008) *Comparative Politics: The Principal-agent Perspective* (London: Routledge), 23.
Lee, Ching Kwan (1998) "The Labor Politics of Market Socialism: Collective Inaction and Class Experiences among State Workers in Guangzhou," *Modern China* (January): 3–33.
——(2003) "Pathways of Labor Insurgency," in Elizabeth Perry and Mark Selden (eds) *Chinese Society: Change, Conflict and Resistance* (London: Routledge Curzon Press, 2nd edn), 71–92.
——(2007) *Against the Law: Labor Protests in China's Rustbelt and Sunbelt* (CA: University of California Press).

Lee, Kai-fu (李开复) (2011) 微博改变一切 (上海财经大学出版社) [*Microblog Changes Everything* (Shanghai University of Finance and Economics Press)].
Lerner, Daniel (1958) *The Passing of Traditional Society* (New York: The Free Press).
Levitsky, Steven and Lucan Way (2002) "The Rise of Competitive Authoritarianism," *Journal of Democracy* Vol. 13, No. 2 (April): 51–65.
——(2006) "Linkage versus Leverage. Rethinking the International Dimension of Regime Change," *Comparative Politics* Vol. 38, No. 4 (July): 379–400.
Li, Lianjiang, Mingxing Liu and Kevin J. O'Brien (2012) "Petitioning Beijing: The High Tide of 2003–6," *The China Quarterly* No. 210 (June): 313–34.
Li, Zehou (李泽厚) (1986) 中国古代思想史论 (北京: 人民出版社) [*Essays on Classical Chinese Philosophy* (Beijing: Renmin Press)].
Liang, Zai (2010) "Migration and Development in Rural China," *Modern China Studies* Vol. 17, No. 4: 48–74.
——(2012) "Interprovincial Return Migration in Sichuan Province in the 1990s: Individual and Contextual Determinants," manuscript.
Liang, Zhiping (梁治平) (1992) 法辨: 中国法的过去, 现在与未来 (贵州人民出版社) [*Explicating Law: The Past, Present, and Future of Law in China* (Guizhou People's Press)].
Lieberthal, Kenneth (1995) *Governing China: From Revolution Through Reform* (NY: W.W. Norton & Co.), 167–68.
Lieberthal, Kenneth and Michael Oksenberg (1988) *Policy Making in China: Leaders, Structures, and Processes* (Princeton University Press).
Lieberthal, Kenneth G. and David M. Lampton (ed.) (1992) *Bureaucracy, Politics, and Decision Making in Post-Mao China* (Berkeley: University of California Press).
Lipset, Seymour Martin (1981) *Political Man: The Social Bases of Politics* (Johns Hopkins University Press).
Lo, Carlos Wing Hung and Sai Wing Leung (2000) "Environmental Agency and Public Opinion in Guangzhou: The Limits of a Popular Approach to Environmental Governance," *China Quarterly* (September): 677–704.
Lowenthal, Richard (1976) "The Ruling Party in a Mature Society," in Mark Field (ed.) *Social Consequences of Modernization in Communist Societies* (The Johns Hopkins University Press), 81–118.
Lu, Xiaobo (1997) "The Politics of Peasant Burden in Reform China," *Journal of Peasant Studies* Vol. 25, No. 1 (October): 113–38.
Lu, Xiaobo and Elizabeth Perry (1997) *Danwei: The Changing Chinese Workplace in Historical and Comparative Perspective* (NY: M.E. Sharpe).
Lubman, Stanley (2003) *Bird in a Cage: Legal Reform in China after Mao* (Palo Alto: Stanford University Press).
Lynch, Daniel (1999) *After the Propaganda State: Media, Politics, and "Thought Work" in Reformed China* (CA: Stanford University Press).
McAdam, Doug John McCarthy and Mayer Zald (eds) (1996) *Comparative Perspectives on Social Movements: Political Opportunities, Mobilizing Structure, and Cultural Framings* (Cambridge, UK: Cambridge University Press).
McFaul, Michael (2002) "The Fourth Wave of Democracy and Dictatorship: Noncooperative Transitions in the Postcommunist World," *World Politics* No. 54 (January): 212–44.

MacKerras, Colin (2009) "Tibetans, Uyghurs, and Multinational 'China': Han-minority Relations and State Legitimation," in Peter Hays and Stanley Rosen (eds) *Chinese Politics: State, Society and the Market* (Routledge), 222–42.

MacKinnon, Rebecca (2008) "Flatter World and Thicker Walls? Blogs, Censorship and Civic Discourse in China," *Public Choice* No. 134: 31–46.

——(2011) "China's 'Networked Authoritarianism'," *Journal of Democracy* Vol. 22, No. 2 (April): 32–46.

Margolis, Michael (2009) "E-Government and Democracy," in Russell Dalton and Klingemann Hans-Dieter (eds) *The Oxford Handbook of Political Behavior* (Oxford University Press), 765–82.

Martinez-Vazquez, Jorge (2006) "China's Long March to Decentralization," in Paul Smoke *et al.* (ed.) *Decentralization in Asia and Latin America* (UK: Edward Elgar), 88–135.

Mencius (1970) *Mencius*, trans. by D.C. Lau (Penguin).

Mengin, Francoise (2004) *Cyber China: Reshaping National Identities in the Age of Information* (Palgrave Macmillan).

Mertha, Andrew C. (2008) *China's Water Warriors: Citizen Action and Policy Change* (Cornell University Press).

Michelson, Ethan (2008) "Justice from Above or Below? Popular Strategies for Resolving Grievances in Rural China," *The China Quarterly* No. 193: 43–64.

Migdal, Joel Atul Kohli and Vivienne Shue (1994) *State Power and Social Forces: Domination and Transformation in the Third World* (New York: Cambridge University Press).

Montinola, Gabriella Yingyi Qian and Barry Weingast (1996) "Federalism, Chinese Style: The Political Basis for Economic Success," *World Politics* Vol. 48, No. 1: 50–81.

Morozov, Evgeny (2011) *The Net Delusion: The Dark Side of Internet Freedom* (Public Affairs).

Naughton, Barry (1995) *Growing Out of the Plan: Chinese Economic Reform, 1978–1993* (New York: Cambridge University Press).

Norris, Pippa (2001) *Digital Divide: Civic Engagement, Information Poverty, and the Internet Worldwide* (Cambridge: Cambridge University Press).

North, Douglass C., John Joseph Wallis and Barry R. Weingast (2009) *Violence and Social Orders: A Conceptual Framework for Interpreting Recorded Human History* (Cambridge University Press).

Oates, Sarah (2006) *The Internet and Politics: Citizens, Voters and Activists* (London: Routledge).

O'Brien, Kevin and Li Lianjiang (1999) "Selective Policy Implementation in Rural China," *Comparative Politics* Vol. 31, No. 2 (January): 167–86.

——(2005) "Popular Contention and its Impact in Rural China," *Comparative Political Studies* Vol. 38, No. 3 (April): 235–59.

——(2006) *Rightful Resistance in Rural China* (NY: Cambridge University Press).

——(eds) (2008) *Popular Protest in China* (Boston: Harvard University Press).

O'Donnell, Guillermo and Philippe C. Schmitter (1986) *Transitions from Authoritarian Rule. Tentative Conclusions About Uncertain Democracies* (Baltimore: Johns Hopkins University Press).

Oi, Jean (1999) *Rural China Takes Off: Institutional Foundations of Economic Reform* (Berkeley: University of California Press).

Pan Suiming (潘绥铭) (2005) 小姐：劳动的权利 （香港：大道出版社） [*Misses: The Right to Work* (Hong Kong: Dadao Press)].

Peerenboom, Randall (2002) *China's Long March Toward Rule of Law* (Cambridge University Press).
Pei, Minxin (2003) "Rights and Resistance: The Changing Contexts of the Dissident Movement," in Elizabeth Perry and Mark Selden (eds) *Chinese Society: Change, Conflict and Resistance* (London: Routledge Curzon Press, 2nd edn), 31–56.
Perry, Elizabeth J. (1999) "Crime, Corruption, and Contention," in Merle Goldman and Roderick MacFarquhar (eds) *The Paradox of China's Post-Mao Reforms* (Cambridge: Harvard University Press), 308–29.
——(2001) *Challenging the Mandate of Heaven: Social Protest and State Authority in China* (Armonk, NY: M.E. Sharpe).
——(2008) "Chinese Conceptions of 'Rights': From Mencius to Mao-and Now," *Perspective on Politics* Vol. 6, No. 1: 37–50.
Perry, Elizabeth J. and Merle Goldman (eds) (2007) *Grassroots Political Reform in Contemporary China*, Mass: Harvard University Press.
Perry, Elizabeth J. and Mark Selden (eds) (2003) *Chinese Society: Change, Conflict and Resistance* (London: Routledge Curzon Press, 2nd edn).
Przeworski, Adam (1991) *Democracy and the Market* (Cambridge University Press).
——(2000) *Democracy and Development: Political Institutions and Material Well-Being in the World, 1950–1990* (Cambridge: Cambridge University Press).
Putnam, Robert (1993) *Making Democracy Work* (New Jersey: Princeton University Press).
Pye, Lucian (1985) *Asian Power and Politics: The Cultural Dimensions of Authority* (The Harvard University Press).
Qiang Hang and Xie Weiyang (钱杭，谢维扬) (1995) *传统与转型：江西泰和农村宗族形态*（上海社会科学院出版社） [*Tradition and Transition: Rural Lineages in Jiangxi Taihe* (Shanghai Social Science Academy Press)].
Qu Tongzu (瞿同祖) (1981) *中国法律与中国社会*. (中华书局) [*Chinese Law and Chinese Society*] (Chinese Book Bureau).
Rigby, T.H. and Ferenc Feher (1982) *Political Legitimation of Communist States* (Palgrave Macmillan).
Schock, Kurt (2005) *Unarmed Insurrections People Power Movements in Nondemocracies* (Minneapolis: University of Minnesota Press).
Scott, James C. (1976) *The Moral Economy of the Peasant: Rebellion and Subsistence in Southeast Asia* (Yale University Press).
Shambaugh, David (ed.) (2000) *Is China Unstable?: Assessing the Factors* (NY: M.E. Sharpe).
——(2008) *China's Community Party: Atrophy and Adaptation* (University of California Press).
Shirk, Susan (1993) *The Political Logic of Economic Reform in China* (University of California Press).
——(2007) "The Echo Chamber of Nationalism: Media and the Internet," *Fragile Superpower* (Oxford University Press), 79–104.
——(2011) "Changing Media, Changing China," in Susan Shirk (eds) *Changing Media, Changing China* (Oxford University Press), 1–37.
Shue, Vivienne (1988) *The Reach of the State: Sketches of the Chinese Body Politic* (CA: Stanford University Press).
——(2004) "Legitimacy Crisis in China?" in Peter Hays Gries and Stanley Rosen (eds) *State and Society in 21st-Century China* (RoutledgeCurzon), 24–49.

Silver, Beverly J. (2003) *Forces of Labor: Workers' Movement and Globalization since 1870* (Cambridge University Press).
Sinkule, Barbara J. and Leonard Ortolano (1995) *Implementing Environmental Policy in China* (New York: Praeger Press).
Smoke, Paul et al. (2006) *Decentralization in Asia and Latin America* (UK: Edward Elgar).
So, Sherman and Christopher Westland (2010) *Red Wired: China's Internet Revolution* (London: Marshall Cavendish International).
Solinger, Dorothy J. (2009) *States' Gains, Labor's Losses: China, France, and Mexico Choose Global Liaisons, 1980–2000* (Cornell University Press).
Sreberney, Annabella and Gholam Khiabany (2010) *Blogistan: The Internet and Politics in Iran* (London: I.B. Tauris and Co.).
Stockmann, Daniela (2011) "Race to the Bottom: Media Marketization and Increasing Negativity Toward the United States in China," *Political Communication* Vol. 28, No. 3: 268–90.
Strand, David (1990) "Protest in Beijing: Civil Society and Public Sphere in China," *Problems of Communism*: 1–19.
Studwell, Joe (2003) *The China Dream: The Quest for the Last Great Untapped Market on Earth* (Grove Press).
Su, Yang and He, Xin (2010) "Street as Courtroom: State Accommodation of Labor Protest in South China," *Law and Society Review* Vol. 44, No. 1: 157–84.
Sun, Liping [孙立平] (2010) "中国社会正在加速走向溃败" [Chinese Society is Accelerating its Decay], new.21ccom.net/plus/view.php?aid = 7550 (accessed April 30, 2010).
Sunstein, Cass (2007) *Republic.com 2.0* (NJ: Princeton University Press).
Tai, Zixue (2006) *The Internet in China: Cyberspace and Civil Society* (London: Routledge).
Tang Wenfang and Gaochao He (2010) "Separate but Loyal: Ethnicity and Nationalism in China," *Policy Studies* No. 56.
Tang Wenfang and Qing Yang (2008) "The Chinese Urban Caste System in Transition," *China Quarterly* No. 196 (December): 759–79.
Tanner, Murray Scot (2004) "China Rethinks Unrest," *The Washington Quarterly* Vol. 27, No. 3 (Summer): 137–56.
——(2005) "Rethinking Law Enforcement and Society: Changing Police Analysis of Social Unrest," in Neil Diamant et al. (eds) *Engaging the Law in China: State, Society, and Possibilities for Justice* (Stanford University Press), 193–212.
Tarrow, Sidney (1998) *Power in Movement* (Cambridge: Cambridge University Press, 2nd edn).
Taubman, Geoffrey (1998) "A Not-So World Wide Web: The Internet, China, and the Challenges to Nondemocratic Rule," *Political Communication* Vol. 15, No. 2 (April–June): 255–72.
Thornton, Patricia (2002) "Framing Dissent in Contemporary China: Irony, Ambiguity and Metonymy," *China Quarterly* No. 171 (September): 661–81.
——(2003) "The New Cybersects: Resistance and Repression in the Reform Era," Elizabeth J. Perry and Mark Selden (eds) *Chinese Society: Change, Conflict and Resistance* (London: Routledge Curzon Press, 2nd edn), 247–70.
——(2007) *Disciplining the State: Virtue, Violence, and State-Making in Modern China* (Mass: Harvard University Press).
Tilly, Charles and Sidney Tarrow (2006) *Contentious Politics* (Paradigm Publishers).
Tong, James (1991) *Disorder Under Heaven, Collective Violence in the Ming Dynasty* (CA: Stanford University Press).

Tong, Yanqi (1997) *Transition from State Socialism: Economic and Political Change in Hungary and China* (Rowman & Littlefield).

——(2005) "Environmental Movements in Transitional Societies: A Comparative Study of Taiwan and China," *Comparative Politics* Vol. 37, No. 2 (January): 167–88.

——(2009) "Dispute Resolution Strategies in a Hybrid System," *The China Review* Vol. 9, No. 1 (Spring): 17–44.

Tong, Yanqi and Shaohua Lei (2010) "Creating Public Opinion Pressure in China: Large-Scale Internet Protest," *EAI Background Brief* No. 534.

Weaver, Kent (1986) "The Politics of Blame Avoidance," *Journal of Public Policy* Vol. 6, No. 4: 317–98.

Weber, Max (1984) "Legitimacy, Politics and the State," in William Connolly (eds) *Legitimacy and the State* (Oxford: Basil Blackwell).

White, Stephen (1986) "Economic Performance and Communist Legitimacy," *World Politics* Vol. 38, No. 3: 462–82.

Whyte, Martin (2009) *Myth of the Social Volcano: Perceptions of Inequality and Distributive Injustice in Contemporary China* (CA: Stanford University Press).

Wilkinson, Steven I. (2009) "Riots," *Annual Review of Political Science* Vol. 12: 329–43.

Won, Haeyoun (2004) "Withering Away of the Iron Rice Bowl? The Reemployment Project of Post-socialist China," *Studies in Comparative International Development* Vol. 39, No. 2: 71–93.

Wong, R. Bin (1997) *China Transformed: Historical Change and the Limits of European Experience* (Cornell University Press).

World Bank Bureau of East Asian and Pacific Region Poverty Relief and Economic Management (2009) "From Poor Areas to Poor Population: the Evolution of China's Poverty Relief Agenda—An Assessment of Poverty and Inequality in China" (March).

Wright, Teresa (2001) *The Perils of Protest: State Repression and Student Activism in China and Taiwan* (Honolulu: University of Hawai'i Press).

Xiao, Qiang (2007) "The Internet: A Force to Transform Chinese Society?" in Lionel M. Jensen and Timothy B. Weston (eds) *China's Transformation: The Stories beyond the Headlines* (Rowman & Littlefield), 129–43.

——(2011) "The Battle for the Chinese Internet," *Journal of Democracy* Vol. 22, No. 2 (April): 47–61.

Xie, Lei (2009) *Environmental Activism in China* (Routledge).

Xie Luming and Zeng Xiaofeng（谢庐明，曾小锋）(2006) "20世纪二三十年代赣南乡村宗族与苏维埃革命——兼论中国共产党对宗族的认识和政策"，《江西行政学院学报》2006年第1期 ["Rural lineages and the Soviet Revolution in the 1920s and 1930s—The perceptions and policies of the Chinese Communist Party on lineages), *Jiangxi Administration College Journal* No. 1].

Yang, Guobin (2008) "Contention in Cyberspace," in Kevin O'Brien (ed.) *Popular Protest in China* (Cambridge and London: Harvard University Press), 126–43.

——(2009) *The Power of the Internet in China: Citizen Activism Online* (New York: Columbia University Press), 119–20.

Yu, Jianrong [于建嵘] (2007) "中国的骚乱事件与管治危机: 2007年10月30日在美国加州大学伯克利分校的演讲" [Riot Incidents and Crisis of Control: Speech at UC Berkeley, October 10, 2007], China Elections and Governance, www.chinaelections.org./NewsInfo.asp?NewsID=118361 (accessed April 30, 2010).

Zhang Jimin and Zhang Zhuping（张济民，张竹萍）(1991) "对少数民族中的犯罪分子必须实行'两少一宽'"，《青海民族学院学报（社会科学版）》1991年第1期

["We Must Adopt 'Two two lesses and one leniency' to Minority Criminals," *Journal of Qinghai Ethnic College* No.1].

Zhang Nandiyang (2009) "Rumor and Mobilization in Chinese Contentious Politics," PhD dissertation, Chinese University of Hong Kong.

Zhang, Xiaoling and Zheng Yongnian (eds) (2009) *China's Information and Communications Technology Revolution: Social Changes and State Responses* (Routledge).

Zhao, Dingxin (2001) *The Power of Tiananmen: State-society Relations and the 1989 Beijing Student Movement* (Chicago: University of Chicago Press).

Zheng, Chuxuan (1995) *A Comparison between Western and Chinese Political Ideas: the Difference and Complementarity of the Liberal-Democratic and Moral-Despotic Traditions* (Mellen University Press).

Zheng, Yongnian (2007a) *Technological Empowerment: The Internet, State, and Society in China* (CA: Stanford University Press).

——(2007b) *De Facto Federalism in China: Reforms and Dynamics of Central-Local Relations* (Singapore and London: World Scientific Publishing).

——(2009) *The Chinese Communist Party as Organizational Emperor: Culture, Reproduction and Transformation* (London: Routledge).

Zheng, Yongnian and Wu Guoguang (2005) "Information Technology, Public Space, and Collective Action in China," *Comparative Political Studies* Vol. 38, No. 5 (June): 507–36.

Zhou, Yongming (2006) *Historicizing Online Politics: Telegraphy, the Internet, and Political Participation in China* (CA: Stanford University Press).

Zweig, David (2003) "To the Courts or to the Barricades? Can New Political Institutions Manage Rural Conflict?" in Elizabeth Perry and Mark Selden (eds) *Chinese Society: Change, Conflict and Resistance* (London: Routledge Curzon Press, 2nd edn), 123–47.

Index

accountability 8, 68, 171, 214
administrative efficacy 114, 131
anti-Carrefour protest 131–33
anti-dog killing protest 123–24, 186
anti-family planning protest 104
anti-Japanese protest 13, 57, 66, 126–29, 142, 186, 206
anti-pollution protest 6, 13, 56–57, 121–23, 142, 187, 208; (*see also* environmental protest)
anti-taxation protest 57–58

bank employees' protest 51–52, 199
benevolence, benevolent governance 11–12, 27, 31–32, 37, 41, 89, 99–100, 102, 114–16, 119, 179, 187, 208, 210, 212–16
blame avoiding, strategies of: good cop and bad cop 176–79;
responsibility system 55, 99, 116, 140, 177, 179, 213; throwing good money after bad 177, 179–80; blame passing 176–77, 180
buffer zone 11, 24–25, 175, 204

chain gangs 190
Chizhou Incident 113, 117, 108, 118
city management 37, 41, 55, 101, 103–4, 114–15, 118, 208
civil society 9, 167, 170, 209, 211–12
collective action 3, 7, 18–19, 55–56, 68, 82, 159, 202, 214
collectives 1, 10–11, 22–24, 91, 175, 181–82, 203
Confucianism 30–32, 118, 215
Corruption 1, 5, 13, 22, 28–29, 33, 35–37, 40–43, 54–55, 69, 73, 78–79, 90–91, 95, 101–2, 103, 105, 114, 119, 143, 150–52, 168–69, 191, 199, 208, 210, 214–15, 216
credit claiming 174–75

Dazhu Incident 105, 112, 115, 118, 190
decentralization 24, 39
demolition 68, 88, 91, 115, 161, 187, 189
demonstration 7, 13, 47, 57, 62, 66, 76, 82–83, 86, 104, 128–31, 136–37, 161, 184, 206
developmental syndrome 121
dilemmas of concession-repression 20, 203
disturbance 13, 43, 47–48, 50, 55–56, 59–60, 65–66, 98–99, 100, 102, 105, 107, 109, 111, 114, 119, 136, 191, 193, 208, 214; (*see also* riot)

economic grievances 11, 13, 41–42, 55, 57, 99, 211, 214, 217
environmental protest 1, 6, 13, 121, 124, 136
ethnic conflict 13, 50, 55–57 60, 64, 126, 130–31, 133, 139, 142, 180, 189, 208, 211

famine governance 34, 39
fishing law enforcement 150
foreign invested enterprises (FIEs) 5, 22, 41, 62, 67, 79, 206

Gancheng Incident 107, 112
government responses to social protest: concession 5, 7–8, 83, 86, 171, 180, 186–87, 193; discipline 42, 73, 85, 100, 112, 152, 180–83, 190, 194, 198, 179, 213; repression 7–9, 13, 18–19, 27, 40, 49, 63, 113, 180–83, 184–85,

189, 193, 196, 203; tolerance 13, 116, 182–83, 185–86, 193
Guang'an Incident 104

Han-Hui ethnic conflict 130–31, 134, 189
Hanyuan Incident 192
household responsibility system 2, 24, 140
Huangshi Incident 192
human flesh search 164, 170

illegal fund-raising 121, 124, 126, 142
inequality 21, 32–33, 36, 42, 135, 102–3, 208
institutionalization of social protest 66, 181
Internet mass incident 146, 150–51, 154, 159, 166–69, 170–71, 208

Jishou Incident 124–25

labor disputes 1–3, 50, 52, 62, 79, 84, 188, 207
laid-off workers 2–4, 22, 56, 72, 74, 76, 78, 178, 188
land dispute 1, 3, 48, 50, 54–55, 60, 87–89, 90–92, 94–95, 165, 193, 199, 207, 216
land requisition 1–3, 53–54, 68, 88, 91, 164, 187, 189, 191
large-scale social protest 7, 10, 12–13, 41, 47–49, 51–60, 64–67, 83, 99, 121, 142, 176–77, 185, 189, 195–96, 199, 206–7, 211, 214
learning capability 183, 213
legitimacy: responsibility-based 11–12, 27, 36, 39, 41–42, 213–14; performance-based 21, 38–39
Lhasa 3.14 Incident 131–32, 189
lineage conflict 139, 141–42

maintaining stability 175–76, 178, 185
Mandate of Heaven 12, 28–30, 35, 215
market economy 11, 21, 24, 39, 41, 67, 69, 78, 82, 100
marketization 22, 105
Mencius 29, 31, 38, 67, 216
micro revolution 159–60, 171
Microblogging 150, 154–59, 161–62, 166, 198, 209
middle class 56, 123–24, 148–49, 169–71, 209

migrant workers 1, 3, 5, 53, 81–82, 85–86, 162
modernization 14, 22, 91
moral commitment 39
moral economy 12, 33–34, 38, 69, 79
moral responsibility 37, 82, 86, 164, 185, 187
multilevel responsibility structure 12–13, 21, 39–40, 43, 174–78, 181, 183–84, 189–90, 195–96, 199, 201–3, 212–13

netizen 132, 146–48, 151, 153, 155, 157–59, 160–65, 166–69, 170, 197
nonstate sector 14, 41, 50–53, 59–60, 62–63, 65–67, 76, 79–80, 82–84, 87, 94, 186–87, 191, 193, 195, 199, 206–7, 211, 216

parental officials 35–36
Pearl River Delta 49, 62, 82, 86, 184
pension protest 2, 71, 76–78, 182, 187
petition 2, 5–7, 19, 47, 88, 94, 164, 177–78, 191
planned economy 2, 11, 21, 24, 41, 52, 68, 76, 95
political opportunity structure 7, 18–19, 41
privatization 50–51, 66, 71–73, 75, 78–79, 95, 206–7

relocation compensation 53, 88, 189
relocation protest 13, 55, 68, 88, 187, 189
right to subsistence 4, 33, 56, 76, 95, 123, 216
rightful resistance 3–4, 6
riots 1, 13, 19, 33, 37, 43, 55, 57, 98, 100, 102–3, 109, 111, 113, 116–18, 119, 167, 183–84, 189, 203, 208, 210, 212–13, 216
Rui'an Incident 109
rule by man 32
rule by virtue 30–31, 215
rule of law 4, 8, 36, 101, 128, 136, 153, 216–17
rumor 75, 93, 103, 105–9, 116–19, 125, 127, 132, 158–59, 164, 166, 170, 209, 214

Shishou Incident 104, 102, 114, 116, 177, 181, 190, 192
soccer fans riot 47, 57
social movement 2–3, 6, 12, 18–19, 98, 117, 157, 170, 183, 210

socioeconomic transformation 1, 9, 11, 13, 21–22, 41, 119, 206
state owned enterprises (SOEs) 2, 5, 14, 51, 67, 71, 78, 92, 207
state-society relations 11–12, 18–20, 22, 24–26, 35, 41, 139, 211
subsistence 4–5, 8, 12–13, 19, 32–35, 38, 40, 42, 56, 67–69, 73, 77–78, 90, 93–95, 99–100, 122–23, 138, 146, 169, 206–7, 210, 214, 216–17
substitute teachers 94–95
Sun Zhigang Incident 150, 154, 158, 168, 194, 197, 213
"surround and watch" 159, 161–62, 167, 169–70

tax reform 24, 179
taxi drivers' protest 51, 59, 183
teachers' protest 51, 92, 94–95
Tianwang Incident 74, 78
Tieshu Incident 73, 78
Tonggang Incident 75, 78, 170

transitional pains 11, 13–14, 21–22, 41, 49, 66, 92, 94, 142, 217

unemployment 21, 39, 51, 53, 71, 75–76, 82, 101, 187
urbanization 14, 67, 22, 87, 95, 207, 217

Wanzhou Incident 108, 113
Weibo 151
Weng'an Incident 105, 113–14, 118, 183
work unit 1, 10–11, 22–25, 100–101, 175, 179, 181–82, 203
Wukan Incident 199, 201–3

Xinjiang 7.5 Incident 133–34, 136, 204, 213

Yangzi River Delta 62, 82, 86, 184

Zhengzhou Incident 103, 118, 190